Writing Pirates

Writing Pirates

Vernacular Fiction and Oceans in Late Ming China

Yuanfei Wang

UNIVERSITY OF MICHIGAN PRESS

Ann Arbor

Published in the United States of America by the
University of Michigan Press
Manufactured in the United States of America
Printed on acid-free paper
First published June 2021

A CIP catalog record for this book is available from the British Library.

Library of Congress Cataloging-in-Publication data has been applied for.

ISBN 978-0-472-13254-6 (hardcover : alk. paper)
ISBN 978-0-472-03851-0 (paper : alk. paper)
ISBN 978-0-472-90248-4 (OA)

DOI: https://doi.org/10.3998/mpub.11564671

GEISS HSU
FOUNDATION

This publication was made possible in part by an award from the James P. Geiss and Margaret Y. Hsu Foundation.

Cover: Cover image from Qiu Ying's *Wokou tujuan*, stored at the Institute for Advanced Studies on Asia, Tokyo University. Reproduced with permission.

Acknowledgments

This book could not have come into being without the generosity and help of many individuals and institutions over the past ten years. The SSRC short-term residency grant enabled me to be affiliated with the University of Southern California as a visiting scholar during the Covid-19 pandemic. I thank Brian Bernards for being my host at USC. I finished all the final revisions at home in Los Angeles. I was relieved of teaching duty to complete the manuscript, thanks to a Chiang Ching-kuo Foundation for International Scholarly Exchange Grant, a UGA Willson Center Research Fellowship, and a UGA Faculty Research Grant. A SSRC Postdoctoral Fellowship for Transregional Research at Columbia University helped with the early stages of this project. I thank the Nalanda-Sriwijaya Centre at the Institute of Southeast Asian Studies in Singapore for a Junior Fellowship. My fieldwork in Singapore, Cambodia, and Indonesia was crucial for this book and for expanding my scholarly purview. I thank the warm hospitality and tremendous help of Shen Lei, Shen Yang, and Zhao Shibin during my fieldwork in the Taizhou region of Zhejiang province. I am grateful to an AAS dissertation workshop, a Harvard-Yenching library travel grant, a UGA first-book subvention award, and a James P. Geiss and Margaret Y. Hsu Foundation Publication Subvention Award.

I thank these people who have read and commented on my manuscript at various stages: Hang Xing, David Rolston, Chris Baker, Peter Shapinsky, Ann Walter, Tansen Sen, Geoff Wade, Robert Von Glahn, Ania Loomba, Tina Lu, Jessica Moyer, and Kaijun Chen. The work in progress benefited from conversations with Robert Batchelor, Antony Reid, John Miksic, Xiaojue Wang, Engseng Ho, Prasenjit Duara, Nianshen Song, Guojun Wang, Siyen Fei, and Shang Wei. I am indebted to my doctoral dissertation advisor Victor Mair, who enlightened me with his unusual insights into world history, Chinese language, and China's literature. Discussions with Shu-mei Shih were highly valuable and constructive. Robert Hegel always sends in unwavering support and offers good advice. Haun Saussy continues to be a source of inspiration with his brilliant scholarship in comparative literature, kindness, and incisive suggestions on the manuscript.

I thank the anonymous readers of the University of Michigan Press who provided solid suggestions for revisions. It has been my fortune to work with the editor Christopher Dreyer, who advocated for my project from the very beginning. Melissa Scholke thoroughly page proofed the manuscript and communicated well with the typesetter. My gratitude goes to Qian Jiang for generously sending along a few important images. Jamyung Choi and Chen Yiyuan lent their time to find images for me.

A slightly different version of chapter 2 was published as: "Java in Discord: Unofficial History, Vernacular Fiction, and the Discourse of Imperial Identity in Late Ming China (1570–1620)," in *positions: asia critique*, (2019) 27 (4), 623–52. A section in chapter 1, in a revised form, was published as "Siam as Chinese Utopia: Overseas Chinese, Colonialism, and Race in the Seventeenth-Century Chinese Novel *The Sequel to the Water Margin*" in *Journal of the Siam Society*, vol. 108: 2 (October 2020), 1–16.

This book is dedicated to my family—my parents Yixian Wang and Rongyin Feng, my husband Kai Zhu, and my daughter Olivia Zhu—whose love is as deep as the ocean.

Contents

Digital materials related to this title can be found on
the Fulcrum platform via the following citable URL:
https://doi.org/10.3998/mpub.11564671

Introduction

Chinese Discourse of Pirates and the Early Modern Global World

Between 1405 and 1433, the Ming dynasty emperor Yongle 永樂 (1402–1424) sponsored Admiral Zheng He 鄭和 (1371–1433) to make seven voyages to the Indian Ocean.[1] The Strait of Malacca, connecting the South China Sea with the Indian Ocean, became strategically important to the Ming empire and rose as the prominent seaborne marketplace. After the Ming state withdrew from the Indian Ocean, Christopher Columbus crossed the Atlantic seeking those same waters. His 1492 landing on a Caribbean island introduced Europeans to the Americas. The Age of Discovery thus began. The rapid growth of maritime trade connected East Asia and Southeast Asia with Europe and the Americas.[2] In 1602, the Dutch founded the East Indian Company in Jayakarta on Java. In 1641, the Dutch captured Malacca from the Portuguese and came to dominate the eastern Indonesian archipelago trade. This period was also the age of Asian expansion. People from East Asia and Southeast Asia traded local products for foreign commodities such as porcelain, silk, spices, gold, silver, and animals. When the Ming sea ban policy restricted maritime trade, these seafaring merchants became pirates and continued to seek fortune without official sanction. Unlike its European counterparts, the Ming state did not sponsor overseas colonialism, but diasporic communities emerged nonetheless, as thousands of Chinese people migrated to such countries as

1. Edward Dreyer, *Zheng He: China and the Oceans in the Early Ming Dynasty 1405–1433* (New York: Pearson, 2007); Wang Gungwu, "The First Three Rulers of Malacca," *Journal of the Malaysian Branch of the Royal Asiatic Society* 41, no. 1 (213; July 1968), 11–22; Geoff Wade, "Melaka in Ming Dynasty Texts," *Journal of the Malaysian Branch of the Royal Asiatic Society* 70, no. 1 (272; 1997), 31–69.

2. Anthony Reid, *Southeast Asia in the Age of Commerce 1450–1680: Expansion and Crisis* (New Haven: Yale University Press, 1993), 19.

Ryukyu, Japan, Java, Manila, and Batavia.[3] On the turbulent and fortune-bearing seas, the East and the West competed and collaborated. The Japanese daimyo Toyotomi Hideyoshi 豐臣秀吉 (1537–1598), launched the Japanese invasions of Korea in 1592 with an aim to eventually conquer China. The powerful Zheng 鄭 family operated a multicultural and transnational maritime trade enterprise. They vied with the Dutch East India Company and seized the island of Taiwan from the Dutch in 1662.[4]

Economic historians have explored the connections, similarities, and differences between China and the West in the early modern world economy. Immanuel Wallerstein, firmly rooted in a Eurocentric view, notes that capitalism came into existence when a European division of labor emerged after 1450.[5] Completely dismissing China's interaction with the premodern world, Wallerstein assumes that China as the static and archaic Orient would not emerge as a modern state until the West first evolved from a premodern "world-empire" into the modern "world economies" of capitalism.[6] Janet Abu-Lughod proposes to view Europe in the context of the world trade system to allow for multiple centers and heterogeneous spaces. Believing that China could develop a parallel modern economy, in the European model, based upon overseas colonization, Abu-Lughod hypothesizes that the Ming empire's maritime withdrawal by terminating Admiral Zheng He's maritime expeditions came from an anxious desire to distinguish its imperial identity from that of the Mongol Yuan dynasty (1271–1368).[7] Attributing the Ming state's sea ban as originating in Ming cultural identity and acknowledging the Ming tributary trade was only the

---

3. Wang Gungwu, *China and the Chinese Overseas* (Singapore: Eastern Universities Press, 2003), 84–99; Kenneth R. Hall, "Multi-Dimensional Networking: Fifteenth-Century Indian Ocean Maritime Diaspora in Southeast Asian Perspective," in "Maritime Diasporas in the Indian Ocean and East and Southeast Asia (960–1775)," ed. Norman Yoffee, special issue, *Journal of the Economic and Social History of the Orient* 49, no. 4 (2006): 454–81; Anthony Reid, "Hybrid Identities in the 15th-Century Straits," in *Southeast Asia in the Fifteenth Century,* eds. Geoff Wade and Sun Laichen (Hong Kong: Hong Kong University Press, 2010), 307–32.

4. Xing Hang, *Conflict and Commerce in Maritime East Asia: The Zheng Family and the Shaping of the Modern World, c. 1620–1720* (New York: Columbia University Press, 2015).

5. Immanuel Wallerstein, "The Rise and Future Demise of the World Capitalist System: Concepts for Comparative Analysis" *Comparative Studies in Society and History* 16, no. 4 (1974): 387–415.

6. Immanuel Wallerstein, "The Rise and Future Demise," 390.

7. Janet Abu-Lughod, *Before European Hegemony: The World System A.D. 1250–1350* (New York: Oxford University Press, 1989), 347.

tip of the iceberg of private maritime trade, she nonetheless does not look further into the salient piracy problems along China's coast.[8] Kenneth Pomeranz compares Chinese merchant immigrants in Southeast Asia to New World settlers in the Americas. In the eighteenth century, the absence of the Chinese state's direct "military and political backing," he argues, enabled "Dutch and Spanish colonial authorities to prevent large Chinese merchant communities of Manila and Batavia from buying lands."[9] Zheng Chenggong's 鄭成功 (1624–1662) maritime empire in Taiwan elucidates that China had an overseas empire parallel to Europe's armed trading and colonization abroad. But the Zheng family's short-lived example highlights only how colonization was an anomaly of the Chinese state system in comparison to Europe's colonial norm.

The fields of comparative literature and world literature used to consider non-Western literature as on "the other" shore. When Goethe invented the term "world literature" in 1827, he envisioned that foreign literatures in translation could enable their European, especially German, readers to venture abroad through reading. The adventure, naturally, departed from European ports, not from Indian, Chinese, African or Malayan ones. Franco Moretti notes the profound inequality of a "literary world system." Literature from the core (German and French literatures) forms the "foreign debt" and interrupts the structure of literatures from the periphery (the Third World).[10] This contrasts with Edward Said's contrapuntal perspective in *Culture and Imperialism*, which reads "the forgotten other" back into the European novel. Said discerns that Jane Austen's novel *Mansfield Park* as a cultural form represents the mutual dependence of the longer and more openly colonial movement of the British empire and the domestic movements of the characters at a small-scale estate.[11] Yet these prominent scholars have not considered that the Orient could be the colonizing subject and that Chinese literature could have similar cultural forms expressive of Chinese maritime expeditions.[12]

----

8. Janet Abu-Lughod, *Before European Hegemony*, 344.

9. Kenneth Pomeranz, *Great Divergence: Europe, China, and the Making of the World Economy* (Princeton: Princeton University Press, 2000), 202.

10. Franco Moretti, *Distant Reading* (London: Verso, 2013), 46.

11. Edward W. Said, "Jane Austen and Empire," in *Raymond Williams: Critical Perspectives*, ed. Terry Eagleton (Boston: Northeastern University Press, 1989), 150–64.

12. Emma Teng notes that the premise that the West as "the colonizer" and the Orient as "the colonized" is deeply entrenched inside and outside the academy. See Emma Teng, *Taiwan's Imagined Geography: Chinese Colonial Travel Writing and Pictures, 1683–1895* (Cambridge, MA: Harvard University Asia Center, 2004), 7.

G. W. F. Hegel links the sea exclusively to European experience: "The European state is truly European only in so far as it has links with the sea."[13] Homer's Odysseus configures the *homo economicus* and exemplifies, according to Theodor Adorno and Max Horkheimer, the Enlightenment rationality in the Frankfurt School of thought.[14] In *The Novel and the Sea*, Margaret Cohen contends that Odysseus can be seen as the prototype of the seafaring captains and pirates in Western sea adventure fiction that could alter the dominant narrative about the rise of the novel on land. Indeed, from Daniel Defoe's *Robinson Crusoe* to Samuel Taylor Coleridge's *The Rime of the Ancient Mariner*, from Robert Louis Stevenson's *Treasure Island* to J. M. Barrie's *Peter Pan*, from legends of the pirate Blackbeard to the Hollywood film series *Pirates of the Caribbean*, the omnipresent saltwater tides drive disenchanted seafarers to worlds of adventures. Fearsome and daring, they exude a powerful human agency. They strive against all odds to seize fortune-making opportunities even in the face of a shipwrecked destiny.

Can high seas offer an alternative interpretation of late Ming vernacular fiction? This book argues that the turbulent oceans of the sixteenth and seventeenth centuries brought forth radical insights and perspectives on empire, race, and authenticity for Chinese culture and literature. Through the seafaring activity of pirate merchants and pirates, an early Chinese discourse of the sea came into being. This period saw the pinnacle of a tempestuous maritime world as raids by *wokou* 倭寇 piracy raids spread across the Jiangnan region (South of the Yangzi River) between the 1540s and 1560s, Hideyoshi invaded Korea (1592–1598), and Fujian- and Taiwan-based pirates terrorized the seventeenth-century seas. In such a time of terror, a flourishing publishing industry produced a large body of vernacular literature about pirates, oceans, and exotic islands, along with a proliferation of unofficial histories and geographical accounts of naval combats and cultures offshore. Corresponding to the frequent but irregular piracy raids and maritime battles, this volatile cultural discourse of the sea lasted for around one hundred years.

The Chinese term *wokou* is a multivalent term. With its two individual scripts—*wo* (Japanese) and *kou* (bandits)—the word signifies seven types of people linked to the sea: the Japanese of the archipelago's western rim;

---

13. Georg Wilhelm Friedrich Hegel, *Lectures on the Philosophy of World History*, trans. T. H. B. Nisbet (Cambridge: Cambridge University Press, 1980), 196.

14. Theodor Adorno and Max Horkheimer, *Dialectic of Enlightenment*, trans. John Cumming (New York: Continuum Books, 1972), 4.

unlicensed merchants; seafaring bands composed of Japanese, Chinese, Korean, European, South and Southeast Asian, and African seamen who raided and traded across East Asia; Chinese smuggler lords; residents of the western Japanese littoral from Tsushima Island to the Kii Peninsula; all Japanese; and sea people and water demons.[15] This Chinese idiom is not equivalent to the English words "pirate," "corsair," "buccaneer," or "Barbary pirate." However, studying late Ming Chinese literature and the history of *wokou* sheds much light upon common images, themes, and phenomena across cultures and literatures.

In *The Philosophy of History*, Hegel summarizes that "the sea gives us the idea of the indefinite, the unlimited, and the infinite, and in feeling his own infinite in that Infinite, man is stimulated and emboldened to stretch beyond the limited: the sea invites man to conquer, and to piratical plunder, but also to honest gain and to commerce."[16] The bountiful and cruel ocean treats everyone equally, however. The sea does not care where you are from. Seamen rely on their own craftsmanship, adroitness, and cunningness to survive. Nautical charts are sailors' craft. Chinese sailing charts such as the maps of Zheng He's voyages and the Selden Map employ a Chinese vertical and horizontal perspective.[17] Dutch cartographers used triangulation to chart sea maps.[18] Pirates speak pidgin languages. Pirates terrorized land-based authorities, as the weak against the strong. In the golden age of piracy from 1650 to 1730, piracy flouted the colonial programs of the trans-Atlantic and transoceanic British empire to form a critical form of engagement with nationalism and imperialism.[19] In the piracy raids that plagued coastal China during the Jiajing 嘉靖 reign (1521-1567), the freebooters menaced the Ming empire's official tributary

15. Peter D. Shapinsky, "Envoys and Escorts: Representation and Performance among Koxinga's Japanese Pirate Ancestors" in *Sea Rovers, Silver, and Samurai: Maritime East Asia in Global History 1550-1700*, eds. Tonio Andrade and Xing Hang (Honolulu: University of Hawai'i Press, 2016), 40.

16. Georg Wilhelm Friedrich Hegel, *The Philosophy of History*, with prefaces by Charles Hegel and the translator, J. Sibree, M.A. (New York: Willey, 1944), 90.

17. For the sea charts of Zheng He maps, see Mei-lin Hsu, "Chinese Marine Cartography: Sea Charts of Premodern China," *Imago Mundi* 40 (1988): 96-112. For the Selden Map, see Robert Batchelor, *London: The Selden Map and the Making of a Global City, 1549-1689* (Chicago: University of Chicago, 2014).

18. Thomas Suarez, *Early Mapping of the Pacific: The Epic Story of Seafarers, Adventurers and Cartographers Who Mapped the Earth's Greatest Ocean* (Singapore: Periplus Editions, 2004).

19. Marcus Rediker, *Villains of All Nations: Atlantic Pirates in the Golden Age* (Boston: Beacon Press, 2004).

world system. Pirates collude to persevere. Japanese sea lords established autonomy by developing maritime networks and collaborating with land-based authorities.[20] Living in the cruelly uncontrollable environment at sea, vulnerable seamen put their faith in luck, superstition, and religion.[21] Barbary pirates converted their Christian captives into Islam.[22] East Asian pirates prayed to the Empress of Heaven to protect them on the sea.[23] These similarities attest to historian Victor Lieberman's notion of "strange parallels" between East Asia and the Atlantic world in the seventeenth century.[24] In the same spirit, this book hopes to delineate late Ming Chinese sea fiction as a parallel of Western sea fiction. As comparativist Haun Saussy points out, pursuing similarity is the starting point of a comparative project that not only brings meaning to a common theme or image by illuminating its cultural and historical context but also illuminates "why this similarity matters, what causes it, what the effects are, and what we might learn from it for future observations."[25]

Writing Pirates: Concepts and Methods

This book offers a historicist and diachronic study of Chinese sea literature and its relations with historiography and languages and literatures in early modern maritime Asia. It discerns the Chinese discourse of the sea through Chinese fictional and historical writings on pirates, piracy, and maritime Asian countries (Japan, Siam, and Java).

The concept of "discourse" derives from Foucault's seminal work *The History of Sexuality* in which he describes how cultural conventions and mechanisms of power shaped modern scientific and psychoanalytic discourses on sexuality:

---

20. Peter D. Shapinsky, *Lords of the Sea: Pirates, Violence, and Commerce in Late Medieval Japan, Michigan Monograph Series in Japanese Studies 76* (Ann Arbor: Center for Japanese Studies, University of Michigan, 2014), 14.

21. Marcus Rediker, *Villains of All Nations*, 186.

22. Adrian Tinniswood, *Pirates of Barbary: Corsairs, Conquests, and Captivity in the Seventeenth-Century Mediterranean* (New York: Penguin, 2010).

23. Robert Antony, *Like Froth Floating on the Sea: The World of Pirates and Seafarers in Late Imperial China* (Berkeley: Institute of East Asian Studies, University of California, Berkeley, 2003), 152–63.

24. Victor Lieberman, *Strange Parallels: Southeast Asia in Global Context, ca. 800–1830* (Cambridge: Cambridge University Press, 2003).

25. César Domínguez, Haun Saussy, and Darío Villanueva, *Introducing Comparative Literature: New Trends and Applications* (London: Routledge, 2015), 74–75.

The central issue, then, is not to determine whether one says yes or no to sex, whether one formulates prohibitions or permissions, whether one asserts its importance or denies its effects, or whether one refines the words one uses to designate it; but to account for the fact that it is spoken about, to discover who does the speaking, the positions and viewpoints from which they speak, the institutions which prompt people to speak about it and which store and distribute the things that are said.[26]

Since the multitude of discourses and their formation are spread throughout society, from the state to local and marginal institutions and individuals, we need to look at the power relations of these discourses. In *Culture and Imperialism*, Edward Said closely associates discourse with authorial voices and the West's "dominating act."[27] Borrowing from Foucault and Said, I suggest that late Ming sea fiction resulted from an emerging discourse that sought to link authorial voices, the subjectivity of marginalized individuals, and cultural fantasies about exotic islands and tropical archipelagos.

The late Ming discourse of pirates is complicatedly comprised of both the imperialistic narratives and the public and personal narratives constituted by unofficial histories and vernacular fiction. These two types of polarizing narratives coexist, codepend, compete with, fuse with each other, and contradict with each other. The discourse of pirates covers fragmented but connected maritime regions: Siam, Java, Japan, southeast coastal China, and Vietnam. This discourse also intersects with various traditions. Chapter 1 shows how the discourse of pirates connects to the fictional prototype of outlaws in the novel *The Water Margin* and intersects with the history of the Chinese diaspora in Siam. While the land-based novel delimits the discourse of pirates, its sequel establishes the discourse of the sea through portraying Chinese diaspora's seaborne colonialism in Siam. Chapter 2 studies the cultural memory of Sino-Java relations and its important role in constituting the discourses of pirates in which four authors appropriate the verbal authority of the emperors to construct their own versions of "imagined empires," imbued with their own personal sentiments. In chapter 3, the discourse of Japanese language and literature continues the philological and phonological Confucian tra-

---

26. Foucault particularly examines how modern psychological and scientific discourses consider "sexual liberation" as "truth." Michel Foucault, *The History of Sexuality* (New York: Pantheon Books, 1978), vol. 1, 11.

27. Edward Said, *Culture and Imperialism* (New York: Vintage Books, 1993), 51, 273.

dition and incorporates a significant dimension of dialects and vernacular speech. Chapter 4 examines how the discourse of Japanese pirates (*wokou*) focuses on racial, sartorial, and linguistic differences, complicated by the late Ming problem of personal identity and authenticity. Chapters 5 and 6 analyze history and fiction writings on Chinese pirate kings published in Jiangnan and Vietnam. The concept of "authenticity" became pivotal in this discourse, which increasingly shifted toward the public sphere, generating intracultural and cross-cultural literary and generic adaptation.

The title of my book, *Writing Pirates*, has double meaning. The "pirates" refer both to the fictional and historical figures who appear in the works this book examines and the authors who wrote about them. Some disenfranchised authors compared themselves to their heroic pirate characters who bravely challenged the Chinese empire's "dominating discourse." The double voices of "pirates" recall Bakhtin's term "heteroglossia." The characters' speech in the genre of the novel only "refracts" authorial intentions: "It serves two speakers at the same time and expresses simultaneously two different intentions."[28] The word "writing" also connotes the prestige of writing in the formation of late Ming discourse of the sea. "Writing" emphasizes the process of transcribing and translating all kinds of verbal acts, including pronunciations, hearsay, observations, witnesses, speeches, and discourses, into written forms.

In this book, "writing" specifically means written narratives—history writing and fiction writing. Edward Said considers that narrative, like discourse, represents power, and that narrative's teleology relates to the "global role of the West."[29] Hayden White further equalizes historiography with literary writing and distinguishes narrative from discourse: "A discourse that openly adopts a perspective that looks out on the world and reports it and a discourse that feigns to make the world speak itself and speak itself as a story."[30] In this sense, I broaden the concept of "fiction" to include both unofficial histories and novels and short stories. Besides such narrative works, chapter 3 also studies Sino-Japanese bilingual glossaries and Chinese translations of *waka*, or Japanese court poetry. Based upon Edward Said's notion that humanistic disciplines such as philology and lexicology channel Orientalism's "imperialistic view of the world," I

---

28. Mikhail Bakhtin, "Discourse in the Novel," in *The Dialogic Imagination* (Austin: University of Texas Press, 1982), 324.

29. Edward Said, *Orientalism* (New York: Vintage Books, 1978), 15.

30. Hayden White, "The Value of Narrativity in the Representation of Reality," in "On Narrative," ed. W. J. T. Mitchell, special issue, *Critical Inquiry* 7, no. 1 (Autumn 1980): 5–27.

equally treat these trans-linguistic practices as types of imperialistic narratives.[31]

The "pirates" in "writing pirates" underlines the agency of pirates and authors in the writing process to form discourses. Pirates speak vernacular and vulgar languages, which symbolize the subversive power these lowly bandits possess against high-minded imperial authority. Pirates are always written about. They rarely write. But pirates who do write indicate the pirate's authorial and dialogic position in the discourse. In this regard, the image of "pirates" alludes to Bakhtinian dialogism, which allows every word to encounter an alien word within the word itself. In contrast to linguist Ferdinand de Saussure's concept that "language is a well-defined object in the heterogeneous mass of speech facts,"[32] language for Bakhtin is internally dialogic. The vitality of language lies in its heterogeneousness, as manifested by the elastic dynamics between the signifier and the signified, between the word, its addresser, and addressee.[33]

The word "pirates" also stands for authors and compilers of "low genres," which in traditional China included unofficial histories, travel writings, vernacular fiction, folk songs, foreign languages, glossaries, and even pirated editions. Bakhtin emphasizes that low verbal arts can ridicule and overthrow the centralized authority. Alluding to Bakhtin, the meaning of "pirates" keeps shifting and drifting, as does the Chinese term *wokou*. Specific context determines the word's specific meaning. But even within a defined context, the meaning of "pirates" remains highly fluid; its signification is amorphous and indeterminate. In this book, the term signifies bandits, smugglers, outlaws, sea marauders, maritime merchants, emigrants, and sea people of different races and ethnicities. Notably, the term "pirates" also signifies disenfranchised scholars and officials. Unable to succeed in the increasingly competitive civil examination, they were demoted because their honest remonstrations offended authorities. They became vernacular fiction writers, compilers, and publishers to make a living, and they were dissatisfied with the state and the society. "Pirates" also connotes overseas adventurers and spies who compiled ethnographic accounts and collected foreign languages and literature; the term also connotes non-Chinese cultures that sought to appropriate or defy the "dominating" Chinese imperial culture. All of these pirates are adrift in a seman-

---

31. Edward Said, *Orientalism*, 15

32. Ferdinand de Saussure, Wade Baskin trans., Charles Bally and Albert Sechehaye eds., *Course in General Linguistics* (New York: McGraw-Hill Book Company, 1915), 14.

33. Mikhail Bakhtin, "Discourse in the Novel," 259–423.

tic ocean of uncertainty and adaptability. The subversive energy of these writings ebbs and flows, but their undercurrents continuously roil from the mid-sixteenth to mid-seventeenth century.

The polarity of authenticity and falsehood is prominent in the discourse of pirates. The Jiajing-era raids often created chaotic situations that provoked apprehension and suspicion. Ming officials, the locals, and even the pirates themselves struggled to discern truth from duplicity in the discord. Jiang Wu observes that all East Asian countries in the seventeenth century struggled to search for their own sense of authenticity.[34] The late Ming Chinese discourse of pirates particularly manifests this seventeenth-century authenticity crisis. Focused on the images of pirates as deceivers, traitors, profiteers, and barbarians, the discourse thus concerns the authenticity of Chinese sovereignty, Chinese race, Chinese scripts and culture, sincerity and loyalty, and personal identity. Whereas imperial narratives often condemn pirates as traitors and villains, public narratives on pirates, especially embodied in the vernacular novels and short stories published from the 1560s to the 1660s, display the rhetoric of oxymoron. The pirates are sincere, romantic, loyal, and noble.

Further, the late Ming discourse of "pirates" intertwines with the entangled concepts of empire, imperialism, colonialism, race and ethnicity, and protonationalism. This complicated knot of concepts is inextricably linked to the discourse of nationalism and colonialism during the Qing dynasty (1644–1912) and beyond and to modern diaspora studies. Benedict Anderson considers that the genre of the novel transmitted through print capitalism embodies the "sociological landscape" of the "imagined community" of the nation-state.[35] The "sociological landscape" of Chinese premodern literature taps into China's cultural memory to construct an "imagined empire." Egyptologist Jan Assmann defines cultural memory as an institutionalized external cultural coding, storage, and retrieval that is best channeled through the invention of the act of writing.[36] It "exists in the forms of narratives, songs, rituals, masks, and symbols."[37] The cultural memory that influenced the late Ming discourse

---

34. Jiang Wu, *Leaving for the Rising Sun: Chinese Zen Master Yinyuan and the Authenticity Crisis in Early Modern East Asia* (New York: Oxford University Press, 2015), 19.

35. Benedict Anderson, *Imagined Communities: Reflections on the Origin and Spread of Nationalism* (London: Verso, 2006), 30.

36. Jan Assmann, *Cultural Memory and Early Civilization: Writing, Remembrance, and Political Imagination* (Cambridge: Cambridge University Press, 2011), 8.

37. Jan Assmann, Astrid Erll, and Ansgar Nünning (Hg.), "Communicative and Cultural Memory," in *Cultural Memory Studies: An International and Interdisciplinary Hand-*

of pirates includes the historic Song–Jurchen wars (1125–1129; 1132–1142) and China's foreign relations in the Indian Ocean, East China Sea, and the Silk Road.

This book also argues that late Ming sea fiction simultaneously evinces an oceanic mode of Chinese diasporic expansion and Ming Chinese "imperialism." In her study of Qing expansionism through the case of Taiwan, Emma Teng questions the scholar's restricted use of the word "imperialism" for Qing dynasty. She calls for placing Qing expansionism within the broader framework of colonial studies rather than limiting the scholarly discussion within the silo of area studies.[38] The same problem applies to Ming studies. Although the cases studied in this book do not concern Ming imperial expansionism—in fact, the sea ban policy restricted both official and unofficial maritime expansion—the late Ming discourse of pirates indicates that the Ming empire's authority was conceived as the sovereignty of authenticity. This imperial authenticity is associated with the sacred authority of the Han Chinese emperors, the cultural superiority of Han Chinese language and civilization, and the prestige of the Han Chinese bloodline. The sea fiction studied in this book constructs cultural fantasies of military conquest, imperial dominance, and colonialism that evidence such "imperialism."

Imperialism closely connects to concepts of race and ethnicity. In this book, I argue that the concept of race does exist in premodern China. Racial discourse was intimately yoked with imperialism, protonationalism, the Chinese diaspora, and Chinese cultural imagination of the "other" in maritime Asia. Robert Bartlett argues that we need to acknowledge the existence of "race" as a biological group since medieval times. The medieval Latin words *gens* and *natio* imply the idea of race as descent groups. *Gens* specifically connotes breeding and pedigree as signified in words such as "blood," "stock," and "family."[39] By contrast, Qing historian Pamela Crossley distinguishes race from ethnicity from a modern point of view, emphasizing "race" as articulation of fixity in some groups in terms of "moral or cultural character," "ancestral affiliations," untransformability, or unassimilability.[40] She also notes that the Ming worldview encompassed

book, eds. Astrid Erll and Ansgar Nünning (Berlin and New York: Walter de Gruyter, 2008), 109–18, 112; Jan Assmann, *Cultural Memory and Early Civilization*, 111.

38. Emma Teng, *Taiwan's Imagined Geography*, 10.

39. Robert Bartlett, "Medieval and Early Modern Concepts of Race and Ethnicity," *Journal of Medieval and Early Modern Studies* 31, no. 1 (Winter 2001): 39–56.

40. Pamela Kyle Crossley, *A Translucent Mirror: History and Identity in Qing Imperial Ideology* (Berkeley: University of California Press, 2002), 14.

a concept of racial descent, roughly consonant with the descent group construct of early modern Europe, and that the formation of the Manchu Qing dynasty was clearly marked with racial consciousness.[41] Emma Teng further distinguishes racial discourse from ethnic discourse in Qing cartographical representations, the former focusing on fundamental distinctions such as the biological distinction between humans and animals and the latter concentrating on cultural differences as a matter of degree.[42] In my discussion, I conflate "race" and "ethnicity" because I note the difficulty of distinguishing the two concepts clearly. In the first four chapters on Siam, Java, and Japan, I discuss how race is linked to somatic features, bloodline, social hierarchy, morality, sexuality, customs, and language. Race and ethnicity are a category innate to late Ming discourse of pirates and the sea.

The late Ming discourse of pirates is the harbinger of the vigorous rhetoric of early twentieth-century nationalism and colonialism. In his "Biographies of Eight Great Men in Chinese Colonialism" *Bada Zhongguo zhimin weiren zhuan* 八大中國殖民偉人傳, the influential Chinese thinker and reformer Liang Qichao 梁啟超 (1873–1926) defines the Chinese diaspora in Southeast Asia as consisting of adventurous "pirates" (*haidao* 海盜 or *haizei* 海賊).[43] Observing that Western countries sponsored overseas colonization and that China never had such a tradition, Liang Qichao notes that "the Chinese race has an in-born expansionist nature" 我民族之天然膨脹力. He praises a few Chinese "pirates" who later became kings of Southeast Asian countries as exemplary national subjects of China. These "pirates" are Liang Daoming 梁道明 and Zhang Lian 張璉—kings of Sanfoqi, an anonymous king of the country of Poluo 婆羅, an anonymous king of the country of Shunta 順塔 in Java, the Siamese king Zheng Zhao 鄭昭, Wu Yuansheng 吳元盛 of the Daiyan 戴燕 kingdom, Luo Da 羅大 of the Kundian 昆甸 kingdom, Ye Lai 業來 of Singapore, and Pan Hewu 潘和五 of the Philippines. Lamenting that these Chinese maritime merchants and pirates are buried in "dusty and worm-eaten books" (沈沈蠹簡), hardly known to posterity, Liang Qichao glorifies the overseas achievements (*shiye* 事業) of these "pirates": "They should be compared to Moses, Columbus, Livingston, and William Dampier" (非摩西則哥倫布立溫斯敦也否則亦克雷武威廉賓也).[44]

---

41. Pamela Kyle Crossley, "Thinking About Ethnicity in Early Modern China," *Late Imperial China* 11, no. 1 (June 1990): 1–35.

42. Emma Teng, *Taiwan's Imagined Geography*, 14.

43. Liang Qichao 梁啟超, "Zhongguo zhimin bada weiren zhuan" 中國殖民八大偉人傳, in *Yin Binshi heji* 飲冰室合集 (Shanghai: Zhonghua shuju), 1.

44. Liang Qichao, "Zhongguo zhimin," 4.

Liang Qichao proudly advocates for Chinese settlers to engage in the violence of piracy and pillaging. (The character *dao* 盜, meaning to rob or bandits, in the Chinese binome *haidao* already signifies violence against property rights.) In "Sinophone Studies," Shu-mei Shih points out the settlers' violence toward native and minority peoples, and the related violence of forgetting such history and disavowing ethnic diversity and minority in the present.[45] But Liang takes this as an expression of national pride during a time when China faced national crisis. For instance, in the section on Siam, he writes, "since ancient times, Siam has been the colony of China" 暹羅自古為中國殖民地. What is most striking in Liang Qichao's narrative is that he terms the Chinese pirates *haidao* or *haizei* rather than *wokou*. His disassociation of the Chinese pirates from their Japanese collaborators may well signify his anti-Japanese nationalistic sentiments. For instance, he states that the Siamese king and the Chinese emigrant Zheng Zhao is much more accomplished than the Japanese emigrant in Siam named Yamada Nagamasa 山田長政 (1590–1630):

Japan has a man named Yamada Nagamasa. He was just a minister of Siam. However, the Japanese make sacrifice to him and glorify him by singing and dancing. They record his behaviors and connections in Siam and make paintings of his military achievements. He is remembered in poetry and theater. Numerous works are written about him. The Japanese think that one man is enough to make their national history shine. How can he be compared to our Zheng Zhao?

日本有一山田長政不過曾為暹羅相耳。而日人屍祝之歌舞之，記其行誼，繪其戰績，被以詩歌，演以說部，不可勝述。謂得一人足以光國史也。以之比我鄭昭何如?[46]

The Chinese translation of European sea adventure novels in the early twentieth century might also have influenced Liang Qichao's concept of pirates as colonizers and overseas adventurers. Working with former navy official Zen Zonggong 曾宗巩, Lin Shu 林紓 (1852–1924) published his cotranslation of Defoe's *Robinson Crusoe* in 1906. In the preface, he highlights that his goal in translation is to "strengthen the spirit of adventure

---

45. Shu-mei Shih, "Introduction: What is Sinophone Studies?" in *Sinophone Studies: A Critical Reader*, eds. Shu-mei Shih, Chien-hsin Tsai, and Brian Bernards (New York: Columbia University Press, 2013), 5–6.

46. Liang Qichao, "Zhongguo zhimin," 4.

and remove the habit of dependency" 振冒險之精神，怯依賴之習慣。[47] Late Ming discourse of pirates anticipated early twentieth-century intellectuals' advocacy of maritime adventure and overseas colonialism, which in turn took European experiences as models to follow.

A native Chinese worldview shaped the late Ming experience of pirates. The view still placed China as the center of the world. Japan, Korea, and Southeast Asia were China's "Orient." In his influential work *Orientalism*, Edward Said analyzes European attitudes toward the East. The East as "the other" is excluded as inferior to the superior European "self." Said calls attention to how various humanistic disciplines such as philology, lexicography, history, biology, political and economic theory, novel writing, and lyric poetry serve Orientalism's "imperialistic view of the world."[48] Similarly, in the sixteenth and seventeenth centuries, Chinese fiction, poetry, history, travel writing, and philology served China's own Orientalistic and imperialistic view of the world.

Late Ming discourse of pirates channels voices of disenfranchised and marginal individuals—outlaws, pirates, maritime merchants, captives, the "other" of China, the Chinese diaspora, and the authors who wrote about them. Citing Fanon and Foucault, Homi Bhabha proposes the difficulty of writing the history of the people at an empire's margins and in a transnational era, raising the question of how to address the "differential temporalities of cultural histories" that are written away in the "fixed and reified" form of official history.[49] The tension between cultural belonging and statelessness and homelessness is central to the late Ming discourse of pirates. The maritime renegades are stretched between their cultural aspirations and the persecution of land-based authorities, between the excitement of overseas adventures and disenchantment with their homeland.

Outline

The book is divided into six chapters and three parts, each with two chapters. Each part, focusing on one maritime region, shows how Chinese cul-

---

47. For a study of Lin Shu's translation, see Michael Hill, *Lin Shu Inc: Translation and the Making of Modern Chinese Literature* (Oxford: Oxford University Press, 2012).

48. Edward Said, *Orientalism*, 15.

49. Homi Bhabha, "Dissemination: Time, Narrative, and the Margins of the Modern Nation," in *Nation and Narration*, ed. Homi Bhabha (London: Routledge, 1990), 302–3.

tural and racial imagination of that seaborne space constitutes the Chinese discourse of pirates. Each chapter examines a facet of this discourse. Part I focuses on Siam and Java, the major maritime kingdoms in Southeast Asia. Chapter 1 looks at how late Ming fictional narratives of pirates underrepresent and are superimposed on the history of Chinese emigration to Siam. The chapter offers a historicist and revisionist analysis of one of the four great Ming novels—*The Water Margin* (*Shuihu zhuan* 水滸傳, late sixteenth century)—and its most important sequel—Chen Chen's 陳忱 (1615–1670) *The Sequel to The Water Margin* (*Shuihu houzhuan* 水滸後傳, 1664). The novel's bandit heroes are the literary prototypes of Chinese pirates, yet the work maintains a terrestrial orientation and circumscribes the Chinese discourse of the sea. *The Sequel* fully channels the author's and the pirates' subjectivity and develops the discourse of Chinese pirates as a diaspora in Southeast Asia. Their free trade, pillage, and colonization in Siam correspond to a Chinese racial and sexual fantasy about this foreign land. The chapter emphasizes the importance of the sequel as the "weapon of the weak" in representing transnational encounters in the early modern global world.

Chapter 2 discusses how Chinese cultural memory of the history of Sino-Java relations informed both unofficial historical and fictional narratives of pirates in Java. In the face of "Japanese" pirates and Hideyoshi's invasion of Korea, Yan Congjian 嚴從簡 (*jinshi* 1559), He Qiaoyuan 何喬遠 (1558–1632), Luo Yuejiong 羅曰褧 (*juren* 1585), and Luo Maodeng 羅懋登 compare imminent maritime realities with China's diplomatic history with Java. Java's important geopolitical position in the Indian Ocean and Zheng He's multiple visits to Java during his voyages nearly two centuries before made Sino-Java relations a focused point of comparison. Channeling personal anxieties and nationalistic sentiments, they tapped into the verbal authority of the Hongwu 洪武 (1368–1399) and Yongle emperors to narrate an invincible "imagined empire." While the historical narratives *Shuyu zhouzi lu* 殊域周咨錄 (*Records of Surrounding Strange Realms*, 1574), *Wang Xiangji* 王享記 (*Records of the Emperors' Tributes*, ca. 1597–1620), and *Xianbin lu* 咸賓錄 (*Records of All Guests*, ca. 1591), written in classical language, tend to moralize and idealize China's tributary world order, the vernacular fiction *Sanbao taijian xiyang ji* 三寶太監西洋記 (*Eunuch Sanbao's Voyages on the Western Ocean*, ca. 1598) paints a more realistic picture of the late Ming state in the early modern global world by involving heterogeneous voices of the "other." Altogether, the four narratives reveal the late Ming literati's deep apprehension of Ming imperial identity, their political criticism of the state, and their divergent and even self-conflicting views toward maritime commerce, the tributary system, immigrants, and foreign peoples.

Part II focuses on the late Ming discourse of Japan and Japanese pirates. Chapter 3 considers the compilations of military geographical treatises, Japanese-Chinese glossaries, and the translation and transcription of *waka* as significant practices of the discourse of Japan. Such discursive practices constituted an early phase of the eighteenth-century Neo-Confucian tradition of philology, phonology, and evidential scholarship and continued the long history of Chinese translation of foreign languages. Importantly, these discursive practices also incorporate the significant dimension of dialects and vernacular speech. Representing an imperialistic narrative, such practices heralded twentieth-century modern language movements and debates on Chinese national language and dialects on the global stage.

Chapter 4 discusses Feng Menglong's 馮夢龍 (1574–1646) vernacular story "Old Eight Yang's Strange Encounter in the Country of Yue" (*Yang Balao Yueguo qifeng* 楊八老越國奇逢) included in his short story collection *Tales Old and New* (*Gujin xiaoshuo* 古今小說, 1620) to illuminate the late Ming discourse of Japanese race and ethnicity and Chinese cultural belonging. The story of a Chinese maritime merchant "turned Japanese pirate" caters to the late Ming popular racial and ethnic perception that associated Japanese with pirates and pirates with Japanese. Its depiction of Japanese race and ethnicity incorporates substantial knowledge of Japanese language, somatic features, and cultural customs. The Chinese trader's transformation into a captive, a pirate, and then back to a Chinese subject recapitulates the social groups who mingled in the maritime world. The multilinguistic registers within written vernacular Chinese indicate a meaning-oriented Chinese empire that keeps assimilating and translating foreign languages and dialects into early modern Mandarin Chinese.

Part III considers historical and fictional narratives of the pirate kings Wang Zhi 王直 (d. 1559) and Xu Hai 徐海 (d. 1556). Chapter 5 discusses four historical narratives: Cai Jiude's 采九德 *A Survey of the Japanese Pirate Raids* (*Wobian shilüe* 倭變事略, 1558), Yan Congjian's *Records of Surrounding Strange Realms*, He Qiaoyuan's (1558–1632) *The Emperors' Tributes*, Xu Xueju's 徐學聚 (*jinshi* 1583) *Thorough Records of the Quelling of Japanese Pirates in Southeast China in the Jiajing Reign* (*Jiajing dongnan pingwo tonglu* 嘉靖東南平倭通錄, ca. 1583), and Zhang Nai's 張鼐 (1572–1630) *Records of Pirate Raids in Wusong 1554–1555* (*Wusong Jia Yi Wobian zhi* 吳淞甲乙倭變志, 1615). These authors create different "imagined empires" through various portrayals of the piracy raids, the renegades, and the Ming army commander Hu Zongxian's strategies to quell the pirates. The history writings show a paradigm shift from a focus on the state and public authorities to local and common people.

Chapter 6 continues to analyze the emergence of the public sphere from the 1620s to the 1640s in Jiangnan's booming commercial publication industry. The chapter examines three *huaben* vernacular stories: Zhou Qingyuan's 周清源 (fl. 1619–1654) "Quelling Pirates," collected in *The Second Collection from the West Lake* (*Xihu erji* 西湖二集, 1623) Lu Renlong's 陸人龍 publication of *Model Words to Shape the World* (*Xingshi yan* 型世言, 1632), an anthology that was pirated at least twice; and Qingxin Cairen's 青心才人 scholar-beauty novel *The Romance of Jin, Yun, and Qiao* (*Jin Yun Qiao zhuan* 金雲翹傳), published in the 1640s and later transmitted to Vietnam and adapted into the Vietnamese epic *The Tale of Kieu* (1820) by Nguyễn Du. In this highly moldable literary space, the authors all discuss aspects of "authenticity," which cultivated both intracultural and transcultural literary innovation.

In conclusion, this book lays out the structure and development of the Chinese discourse of pirates in late sixteenth and early seventeenth centuries. I argue that this Chinese discourse of the sea brought forth radical insights and perspectives on empire, race, and authenticity to Chinese culture and literature. It formed a complicated, ambivalent, and hybrid discourse of pirates, maritime merchants, diaspora, and foreign cultures and people, which heralded the modern discourse of nationalism and colonialism in the twentieth century.

I
Southeast Asia

CHAPTER ONE

The Sea and the Sequel

The Water Margin (late sixteenth century) is a controversial book. Its heroes are 108 bandits occupying an antigovernment camp at Liangshan Marsh during the Southern Song dynasty (1127–1279). Depicted as Daoist figures, the outlaws are "demonic kings" (*mojun* 魔君) and "thirty-six heavenly and seventy-two earthly killers" (三十六員天罡星，七十二座地煞星),[1] who are rewarded with divine rank among the stars in the novel's denouement. David Rolston has examined the seventeenth-century critic Jin Shengtan's 金聖嘆 (1608–1661) commentary and redaction of the novel and discusses Jin's opposition to the amnesty granted to the bandits and the author-like role Jin played in creating the novel's seventy-chapter edition.[2] Disturbed by the darker side of the bandits' world, C. T. Hsia and Sun Shuyu 孫述宇, among other critics, point out the novel's violence, gang morality, and misogyny.[3] C. T. Hsia notes the heroes' impassioned retaliation against their friends' enemies shows a "distinctive aura of human truth."[4] Andrew Plaks observes that the pervasive and perfunctory violence in *The Water Margin* is ironically "a manifestation of a basic uncertainty."[5]

---

1. Shi Nai'an 施耐庵 and Luo Guanzhong 羅貫中, *Outlaws of the Marsh*, trans. Sidney Shapiro (Bloomington and Beijing: Indiana University Press and Foreign Languages Press, 1999), vol.1, 1; Luo Guanzhong 羅貫中 and Shi Nai'an 施耐庵, *Shuihu zhuan* 水滸傳 (Beijing: Renmin wenxue chuban she, 1990), 1.

2. See David Rolston's "Chin Sheng-t'an on How to Read the *Shui-hu chuan* (*The Water Margin*)," in *Traditional Chinese Fiction and Fiction Commentary: How to Read Between the Lines* (Stanford: Stanford University Press, 1997), 19–50.

3. See Wai-yee Li, "Full-Length Vernacular Fiction" in *Columbia Anthology of Traditional Chinese Literature*, ed. Victor H. Mair (New York: Columbia University, 1994), 620–58.

4. C. T. Hsia, *The Classical Chinese Novel: A Critical Introduction* (New York: Columbia University, 1968), 85.

5. Andrew Plaks, *The Four Masterworks of the Ming Novel* (Princeton: Princeton University Press, 1987), 320.

Contrary to such critics who view *The Water Margin* as an abstract narrative of "human truth" or a "basic" human condition, I historicize the novel. I embed it in sixteenth-century maritime trade networks that connected China to the East China Seas and the Indian Ocean. The novel's radical experimentation in representations of male-male friendship and an antigovernment brotherhood is accompanied by an enthusiasm for connecting this internal microcosm with a macrocosmic externality—the hydraulic and maritime space at large. Keith McMahon states that the internal world of a traditional Chinese fiction can be made to "transition to" (*rusun* 入榫) or be "mirrored by" (*zhaoying* 照應) the external world.[6] *The Water Margin*'s advocacy of the inland hydraulic network and shipboard fraternity demonstrates a remarkable intellectual and cognitive shift connecting the late Ming fiction to the oceanic sphere.

This fluid space of water routes also signifies *jianghu* 江湖 (literally, rivers and lakes)—the underworld, the outlaw network that operates independently from and in resistance to the land-based empire. Henri Lefebvre perceives the indispensable role inland water routes play in connecting the ever-evolving markets at local, regional, and national levels. The water routes form an "abstract and contractual network which bound together the 'exchangers' of products and money."[7] *The Water Margin*'s floating space demarcates a commercial and spiritual field that seeks to subvert and replace the orthodox land-rooted polity and ideology.

This inland hydraulic network connects China to the Indian Ocean. First, the Chinese loanword "Java" (*Zhaowa* 爪哇) is inserted into the narrative in a vernacular idiom. When the merchant Ximen Qing 西門慶 is accidentally hit by the falling curtain pole of Pan Jinlian 潘金蓮, he is angry at first, but upon seeing the beautiful lady, he becomes enchanted. The narrator says, "His anger had drilled straight into the country of Java and his facial expression transformed into a smile" 那怒氣直鑽過爪洼國去了變作笑吟吟的臉. This idiom shows narrative awareness of the island of Java, in the Indian Ocean. (Chapter 2 continues to discuss how this comedic pun involving Java was related to the thriving private maritime trade, pirate raids, and Toyotomi Hideyoshi's invasion of Korea.)

Second, *The Water Margin*'s literary mapping of an inland hydraulic network and descriptions of certain bandit heroes as traders, smugglers, and sailors are invested with an implicit interest in links between local markets

---

6. Keith McMahon, *Causality and Containment in Seventeenth-Century Chinese Fiction* (Leiden: E. J. Brill, 1988), 18.

7. Henri Lefebvre, *The Production of Space*, trans. Donald Nicholson-Smith (Oxford: Blackwell, 1991), 266.

and national and international markets. The commodities that the pirates Guo Sheng 郭盛, the Tong 童 brothers, and Lü Fang 呂方 smuggle—mercury, salt, and herbal medicine—were all highly sought-after in Ming-era East Asia and Southeast Asia. Before Guo Sheng joins the bandits, he sells mercury from his junk on the Yellow River; the sinking of his vessel ultimately leads him to banditry. The Italian Jesuit who lived in Ming China, Matteo Ricci, once noted that mercury was a commodity that Portuguese merchants purchased from Guangdong and transported to Japan and India to trade for silver.[8] In the early seventeenth century, thirty to forty Chinese junks shipped mercury, together with other Chinese commodities like iron and porcelain, to Manila every spring.[9] In the late seventeenth century, a European trader noted that selling Chinese mercury to New Spain (Mexico) earned a three hundred percent profit.[10] The Tong brothers, one nicknamed Dragon from the Cave and the other called River-Churning Clam, smuggle salt on the Yangzi River.[11] Salt was a commonly smuggled commodity in China and beyond because the Ming state attempted to control its system of licenses for the wholesale salt trade. A Ming record indicates that a Chenghua-era 成化 (1465–1487) Chinese salt merchant named Xie Wenbin 謝文彬 smuggled salt on the seas and then emigrated to Siam where he was appointed a minister. Finally, the bandit Lü Fang, who names himself after the famous *Romance of Three Kingdoms* hero Lü Fang 呂布, sells herbal medicines in Shandong. The Grand Canal that passes by Shandong ends at the Qiantang River in Zhejiang, connecting to the East China Sea and the Japanese market for Chinese herbal medicines. Hou Jigao's 候繼高 *The Geography and Customs of Japan* (*Riben fengtu ji* 日本風土記, 1592) records that "Japanese doctors regarded Chinese herbal medicine as superior" and every time the Japanese traded in China, they would obtain bezoar stones and musk as "supreme treasures" (*zhibao* 至寶). One hundred *jin*[12] of licorice was valued at three hundred *liang* of gold.[13]

Third, the geography of *The Water Margin*'s setting accurately maps to

---

8. Jonathan Spence, *The Memory Palace of Matteo Ricci* (New York: Penguin Books, 1984), 186.

9. Timothy Brook, *Vermeer's Hat: The Seventeenth Century and the Dawn of the Global World* (New York: Bloomsbury Press, 2008), 170.

10. Jonathan Spence, *The Memory Palace of Matteo Ricci*, 304; Fernand Braudel, *Wheels of Commerce* (London: Phoenix, 2002), 169, 406.

11. *Outlaws of the Marsh*, 1: 572; *Shuihu zhuan*, 476.

12. The *jin* or catty historically equated to about 604 g, but is now equal to 500 g in China. One *liang* historically was equal to 37.8 g, and now equals to 50 g.

13. Hou Jigao 候繼高, *Zensetsu heisei ko Nihon fudoki* 全浙兵制考日本風土記 (Kyoto: Kyoto Daigaku Kokubun Gakkai, 1961), 35.

various real-life interconnected rivers and ports. The famous tiger-killing hero Wu Song 武松 kills four officials at Flying Cloud Pond 飛雲浦 in Qinghe 清河 county, Shandong province. The Flying Cloud Pond is "linked by streams and rivers" 四面都是野港闊河.[14] The robber Wang Ying 王英 comes from the Huai 淮 River Valley. The bandits Song Jiang 宋江, Dai Zong 戴宗, and Li Kui 李逵 drink wine and eat fish together on the Xunyang River 潯陽江, a branch of the Yangzi River in Jiangxi Province. They have a chance encounter with Li Jun 李俊, a helmsman on Yangzi River ships, and Li Li 李立, a wine wholesaler. The Li brothers collaborate to smuggle goods (*sishang* 私商) on the Yangzi River.[15]

The bandits at the center of the novel are depicted as having mastery over the waters. A brilliant example is Zhang Shun 張順, the White Streak in the Wave (*langli baitiao* 浪裡白條). No other work of premodern Chinese fiction surpasses *The Water Margin* in its admiring portrayal of a bandit—as adroit swimmer, courageous sailor, and capable smuggler. He can "swim forty to fifty *li* on the surface of the water" and "stay underwater for seven days and seven nights"[16] 水底下伏得七日七夜. This hyperbolic rhetoric resembles the language used to depict Southeast Asian Kunlun slaves 昆侖奴 and Japanese pirates in accounts published at the time, suggesting *The Water Margin*'s implicit connections to such maritime traffic. Like such real-life pirates, Zhang Shun, with his brother Zhang Heng 張橫, "dominated all the smuggling along the Xunyang River"[17] 潯陽江邊做私商. A poem praises the glamorous rebel and sailor:

東去長江萬裡，　　　　　　Eastward on the Yangzi River,
內中一個雄夫，　　　　　　lives a hero.
面如傅粉體如酥，　　　　　His face is as white as flour; his
　　　　　　　　　　　　　　body as slender as pastry.
履水如同平土。　　　　　　He steps on the water like
　　　　　　　　　　　　　　stepping on earth.
心雄欲摘驪珠。　　　　　　Driven by his ambition, he wants
　　　　　　　　　　　　　　to gather pearls on Mount Li.
翻波跳浪性如魚，　　　　　Like a fish, he jumps on waves
　　　　　　　　　　　　　　and tides.

14. *Outlaws of the Marsh*, 1: 474; *Shuihu zhuan*, 396.
15. *Outlaws of the Marsh*, 1:572; *Shuihu zhuan*, 475–76.
16. *Outlaws of the Marsh*, 1:585; *Shuihu zhuan*, 487.
17. *Outlaws of the Marsh*, 1:587; *Shuihu zhuan*, 489.

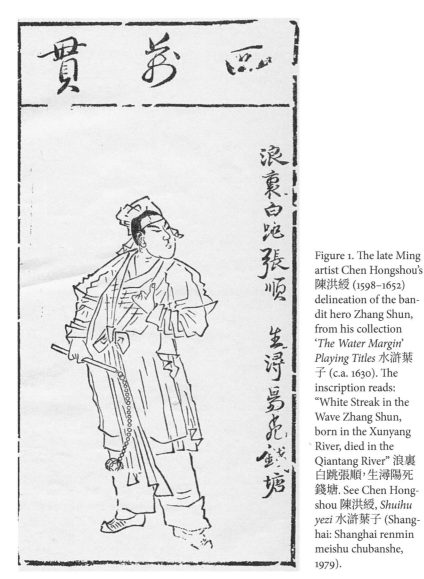

Figure 1. The late Ming artist Chen Hongshou's 陳洪綬 (1598–1652) delineation of the bandit hero Zhang Shun, from his collection *'The Water Margin' Playing Titles* 水滸葉子 (c.a. 1630). The inscription reads: "White Streak in the Wave Zhang Shun, born in the Xunyang River, died in the Qiantang River" 浪裏白跳張順，生潯陽死錢塘. See Chen Hongshou 陳洪綬, *Shuihu yezi* 水滸葉子 (Shanghai: Shanghai renmin meishu chubanshe, 1979).

膽大能探禹穴，　　　　　　　He is so courageous that he can
　　　　　　　　　　　　　　　venture into the cave of the
　　　　　　　　　　　　　　　Great Yu.

張順名傳千古。　　　　　　　Zhang Shun's name will be
　　　　　　　　　　　　　　　known for one thousand
　　　　　　　　　　　　　　　years.[18]

At their base in Liangshan Marsh, the bandits create a fraternity on the water and aboard their thousands of ships.[19] The geographical location is "full of waterways" 深港水汊[20] and "creeks and inlets and twisting paths, and ponds, and pools of unknown depth" 港汊又多，路徑甚雜，抑且水蕩坡塘，不知深淺。[21] The bandits' acts of bravery and heroism take place on these waters: "Thousands of boats fore and aft sailed into battle on the lakes, a hundred and more heroes arrayed themselves in ranks left and right in the stronghold in the marsh" 蓼兒窪内，前后摆数千只战舰艨艟。水浒寨中，左右列百十个英雄好汉。[22] The waterways in Mount Liang embody the bandits' subversive energy.

Yet empire, loyalism, and cultural belonging circumscribe this hydraulic arena. Song Jiang's uncertainty of his sovereign legitimacy over China and his reverence of the imperial throne eventually lead to his submission to the state. Although his crew defeat the hundreds of "sea loach boats" (*haiqiu chuan* 海鰍船) led by the evil minister Gao Qiu 高俅 three times, the bandit leader releases the minister, wishing for the imperial decree of pacification (*zhao'an* 招安). After Song's surrender, on imperial order, the sworn brothers embark on a military campaign against the Khitan Liao kingdom at Shanzhou 檀州 (near Beijing). They navigate northward, from the Cai River to the Yellow River, then all the way to the Lu River 潞水, which in turn connects to the Wei River 渭河. These watercourses limn the veins of the Chinese empire to which the outlaws are bound.

These captains and sailors who submit to imperial rule never reach the sea. After they defeat the peasant army uprising led by Fang La 方腊, they shipwreck at the estuary of the Qiantang River 錢塘江:

18. Shapiro's translation seems to be based upon Jin Shengtan's edition, which does not include this verse in the fuller versions.

19. Margaret Cohen uses this concept of "shipboard fraternity soldered by craft" to describe the nation of the United States. See Margaret Cohen, *The Novel and the Sea* (Princeton: Princeton University Press, 2010), 153.

20. *Outlaws of the Marsh*, 284; *Shuihu zhuan*, 235.

21. *Outlaws of the Marsh*, 286; *Shuihu zhuan*, 236.

22. *Outlaws of the Marsh*, 169; *Shuihu zhuan*, 142.

Zhang Heng, Hou Jian, Duan Jingzhu, and I led sailors to find a ship by the sea. When we sailed to Haiyan, we expected to reach the Qiantang River. However, because of our bad luck with "wind and water," we drifted into the ocean. When we hurriedly sailed back to the shore, the wind greatly damaged the ship. Everybody fell into water. Hou Jian and Duan Jingzhu did not know how to swim, so they were both drowned. The rest of us fled. When I swam to the estuary, I entered into Zheshan Harbor. There, tides carried me to Banshan from where I swam back home.

小弟和張橫並侯健、段景住帶領水手，海邊覓得船只，行至海鹽等處，指望便使入錢塘江來。不期風水不順，打出大洋裡去了。急使得回來，又被風打破了船，眾人都落在水裡。侯健、段景住不識水性，落下去淹死海中，眾多水手各自逃生四散去了。小弟赴水到海口，進得赭山門，被潮直漾到半山，赴水回來。[23]

Their bad luck with winds and tides (*fengshui bushun* 風水不順) portends their cultural and geographical constraint. In the "Preface to the Loyal and Righteous Outlaws of the Marsh," the philosopher Li Zhi 李贄 (1527–1602) praises Song Jiang's "intense sense of loyalty and justice" 忠義之烈.[24] He urges administrators and rulers to read the book:

> That's why the one who runs the country can't afford not to read it. If only he'd read it once, then the loyal and righteous wouldn't be out at the water margin anymore—instead they'd be right back beside the ruler. The wise prime ministers can't afford not to read it. If only they'd read it, then the loyal and righteous wouldn't be out at the water margin anymore—instead they'd be right back at court. The chiefs of staff and the field commanders, they can't afford not to read it either. If only they'd read it someday, then the loyal and righteous wouldn't be out at the water margin anymore—instead they'd be back in the cities to serve and protect the homeland. However, if it isn't read, then the loyal and righteous won't

---

23. The translation is mine. So far, I have not been able to find any translation of the last forty chapters of the *fanben* recension. For the original text, see *Shuihu zhuan*, 722.

24. Li Zhi, *A Book to Burn and a Book to Keep (Hidden): Selected Readings,* eds. Rivi Handler-Spitz, Pauline Lee, Haun Saussy (New York: Columbia University Press, 2016), 126. For the original Chinese, see Li Zhi 李贄, Zhang Jianye 張建業 ed., *Fenshu* 焚書 (Beijing: Shehui kexue wenxian chubanshe, 2000), 102.

be beside the ruler, or at court, or in our cities. Where will they be? At the water margin. This is the indignation expressed by *The Water Margin*.[25]

故有國者不可以不讀，壹讀此傳，則忠義不在水滸而皆在於君側矣。賢宰相不可以不讀，壹讀此傳，則忠義不在水滸，而皆在於朝廷矣。而部掌軍國之樞，督府專閫外之寄，是又不可以不讀也，苟壹日而讀此傳，則忠義不在水滸，而皆為幹城心腹之矣。否則不在朝廷，不在君側，不在於城腹心，烏在乎？在水滸。此傳之所為發憤矣。若夫好事者資其談柄，用兵者藉其謀畫，要以各見所長，烏睹所謂忠義者哉！[26]

Li Zhi esteems the bandits who wreak violence to seek justice as patriotic citizens in the World Upside Down—a world where authority has lost its legitimacy. This is radical departure from Confucian teachings, which never condone, much less advocate, banditry. Even Grand Historian Sima Qian 司馬遷, who praises swordsmen as trustworthy in the "Biographies of Wandering Swordsmen" (*Youxia liezhuan* 遊俠列傳), does not endorse their misconduct and villainy.[27] The orthodox Confucian ideology in the plain-tale narrative *Proclaiming Harmony* (*Xuanhe yishi* 宣和遺事), upon which *The Water Margin* was based, subjects the bandits to elimination. For the radical thinker Li Zhi, however, the warriors' violent and conscientious resistance to political corruption and social repression proves their patriotism and loyalism.

---

25. Li Zhi, *A Book to Burn*, 127.

26. Li Zhi, *Fenshu*, 102.

27. Sima Qian in *Shi ji* writes, "The wandering swordsmen today, although their behaviors are not in accord with moral standards, their words are trustworthy, and their conduct is reliable. They keep their promises. They sacrifice their own lives to save gentlemen in danger. In the face of the matter of life and death, they are not afraid of putting their skills to use and do not brag about their virtues. They are indeed worthy of praises" 今遊俠，其行雖不軌於正義，然其言必信，其行必果，已諾必誠，不愛其軀，赴士之阨困，既已存亡死生矣，而不矜其能，羞伐其德，蓋亦有足多者焉. Sima Qian further stresses that although Household Zhu 朱家, Tian Zhong 田仲, Duke Wang 王公, Ju Meng 劇孟, and Guojie 郭解 in the Han dynasty often violate laws, nonetheless, they are righteous, honest, and modest people. They are much better than those competing factions who extract money from the poor and bully the weak. Scholars interpret Sima Qian's narrative of wandering swordsmen as compensating for his grievance about his own experience. See Sima Qian 司馬遷, *Shi ji* 史記 (Beijing: Zhonghua shuju, 1959), vol. 10, 3181.

These fair-minded and honest outlaws are the arbiters of the correct course of the Chinese empire.

Eric Hobsbawm points out the impossibility of capturing "popular proto-nationalism" in premodern societies, in which rulers and the literate exclusively held the instrument of language.[28] He also argues that underworld robbers are "one of the most universal social phenomena known to history" and reflect similar situations in peasant societies, whether in China, Peru, Sicily, Ukraine, or Indonesia.[29] Popular culture's need for heroes like noble bandits creates these images. The noble robber is "the champion, the righter of wrongs, the bringer of justice and social equity." His relation with the peasants is that of total solidarity and identity. When oppressors cannot be overthrown, the oppressed seek alleviation in the figure of the noble bandit; even when they half accept the law that condemns him, the brigand yet represents divine justice and a higher form of society that is powerless to be born.[30] Prasenjit Duara notes that the Ming imperial superscription of Guandi 關帝, the god of war, enabled elites "to demonstrate their allegiance to the official image, and thus the changes succeeded in considerably reshaping the interpretive arena of the Guandi myth." Popular culture also developed the ability to accommodate itself to "the prestigious official image."[31] From the Daoist point of view, the outlaws' submission and their assimilation into imperial mechanisms are based upon the Daoist ritual of sublimation that continually integrates outsiders into an ever-expanding pantheon.[32] This continuity of the imperial state through the act of subscription or sublimation cannot be disrupted without substantial institutional change.

Thus, although the bandits seek to subvert the existing social order, they reinforce it in the end. Keith McMahon notes that late Ming fiction reflects the Neo-Confucian philosophy of the mind. The beginning and the end represent *weifa* 未發, which is contained by the orthodox ideology, while the conflict-ridden middle is *yifa* 已發, which exceeds ideological containment.[33] For Fredric Jameson, the antagonism between the ban-

---

28. Eric J. Hobsbawm, *Nations and Nationalism since 1780: Programme, Myth, Reality* (Cambridge: Cambridge University Press, 1992).

29. Eric J. Hobsbawm, *Bandits* (Middlesex, England: Penguin Books, 1985), 18.

30. Eric J. Hobsbawm, *Bandits*, 56.

31. Prasenjit Duara, "Superscribing Symbols: The Myth of Guandi, Chinese God of War," *The Journal of Asian Studies* 47, no. 4 (November 1988): 785.

32. Mark Meulenbeld, *Demonic Warfare: Daoism, Territorial Networks, and the History of a Ming Novel* (Honolulu: University of Hawai'i Press, 2015).

33. Keith McMahon, *Causality and Containment*, 29.

dits and the officials, between the good and the evil, suggests the genre of romance. In romance, the knight's quest—the genre's basic narrative structure—brings the world one step closer to its ideal form.[34] In *The Water Margin*, the ending can be seen as the romance's symbolic act. Yet here, after the narrative paints an idealized picture of society, that social reality is sustained, not transformed. The generic structure of the romance contains the bandits' subversion within their enchantment with China. The Chinese empire is the ideal form.

Seafaring Adventures: Disenchanted Pirates, Free Trade, and Island Colonialism in *The Sequel to The Water Margin*

If *The Water Margin* represents the sixteenth century as a utopian golden age populated by heroes, then *The Sequel to The Water Margin* (*Shuihu houzhuan* 水滸後傳, hereafter *The Sequel*, 1664) symbolizes a seventeenth century that is "the poorest in utopian thought."[35] In 1644 the Ming dynasty fell, and the Manchus took over China to establish the Qing 清 dynasty (1644–1912). The Ming–Qing transition, like China's earlier dynastic transitions, was an era of great uncertainty for the Chinese. During the conquest, numerous Chinese women and men were killed, committed suicide, and surrendered in shame.[36] Some loyalists chose to abandon officialdom to live as independent scholars and monks in resistance to the foreign regime. Literati such as Gu Yanwu 顧炎武 (1613–1683), Gui Zhuang 歸莊 (1613–1673), and Chen Chen 陳忱 (1615–1670) established the Poetry Club of Astonishment and Recluse (*Jinyin shishe* 驚隱詩社) to resist the Qing dynasty. Gu Yanwu further became an official of the Southern Ming (1644–1683) which later retreated to Burma (Myanmar) and Taiwan.[37] The former pirate and smuggler Zheng Zhilong 鄭芝龍 (d. 1661), the founding

34. Fredric Jameson, "Magical Narratives: Romance as Genre," in "Critical Challenges: The Bellagio Symposium," special issue *New Literary History* 7, no. 1 (Autumn 1975): 135–63.

35. Jose Antonio Maravall observes a broad baroque disenchantment in seventeenth-century Spain. See Jose Antonio Maravall, *Culture of the Baroque: Analysis of a Historical Discourse*, trans. Terry Cochran (Minneapolis: University of Minnesota Press, 1986), 92.

36. On the catastrophic impact of the Qing invasion and the downfall of the Ming on the Chinese people, see, for example, Lynn A. Struve, "Confucian PTSD: Reading Trauma in a Chinese Youngster's Memoir of 1653," in *History & Memory*, 16, no. 2 (fall/winter 2004), 14–31.

37. Lynn A. Struve, *The Southern Ming, 1644–1662* (New Haven: Yale University Press, 1984).

father of the Zheng family maritime enterprise who submitted to the Ming and became an official, was executed by the Manchus in Beijing. Zheng Zhilong's half-Japanese son, Zheng Chenggong, proclaimed Ming loyalism and led the Han Chinese army to fight vehemently against the Manchus in mainland China.[38]

The Sequel symbolically captures the activities of overseas Chinese in Southeast Asia. The Ming–Qing transition witnessed numerous Chinese migrating into Southeast Asia and forming Chinese diasporic communities. Immigration offered overseas Chinese opportunities to reinvent their lives and identities. Lin Er, also known as Ta Khun Lok, a native of Putian in Fujian province, for example, migrated to Siam in the late 1640s and soon became a vassal appointed to rule the city of Nakhon Si Thammarat.[39] Wang Gungwu insightfully notes that the two decades from the 1620s to the 1640s marked the peak of Chinese commercial activities in Southeast Asia. After the fall of the Ming, thousands of Chinese lived on the mainland in the empires of Vietnam and Siam, in the Malay Archipelago, Moluccas, Makassar, Bali, and West Borneo.[40]

The Sequel rewrites the ending of its parent novel *The Water Margin*. A native of Nanxun 南潯 in Zhejiang, Chen Chen grew up in the late Ming and lived through the Ming–Qing transition. In his preface to *The Sequel* he expresses his despair over the Ming's fall and his reclusion for over twenty years afterwards. To his mind, the Wanli 萬曆 reign (1573–1620) was a golden age. To honor this flourishing era, he predated the preface to 1608. Chinese literati who survived the fall of the Ming tended to have cultural nostalgia for the late Ming period. Wai-yee Li points out how late Ming courtesans epitomize the early Qing male literati's cultural ideal: "self-conscious passion, dramatic gestures, and deep concern with the

---

38. Hang Xing, *Conflicts and Commerce in Maritime East Asia: The Zheng Family and the Shaping of the Modern World, c. 1620–1720*, Studies of the Weatherhead East Asian Institute, Columbia University (New York: Cambridge University Press, 2016).

39. For a study of Chinese diaspora during Ming–Qing transition, see Xing Hang, "Soaring Dragon amid Dynastic Transition: Dates and Legitimacy Among the Post-Ming Chinese Diaspora," in *The Ming World*, ed. Kenneth Swope (London: Routledge, 2019), 279–303.

40. For Chinese settlements in Indonesia in the fifteenth century, see Anthony Reid, "Hybrid Identities in the 15th-Century Straits," 307–32. For a study on the Chinese diaspora in Southeast Asia during the Ming–Qing transition, see, for example, Hang Xing, "Soaring dragon amid dynastic transition: dates and legitimacy among the post-Ming Chinese diaspora," in *The Ming World*, 279–303.

meaning of creating a self or a persona."[41] By dating his book to the late Ming period, Chen Chen intends to revalorize passion, heroism, and self-invention.

The Water Margin has several sequels—Chen Chen's *The Sequel* and Yu Wanchun's 余萬春 (1794–1849) *Records of Quelling Bandits* (*Dangkou zhi* 蕩寇志, 1847) are the two most popular. *The Water Margin* has been translated into Thai several times. The first translation was initiated by Somdet Chao Phraya Chuang Bunnak (1808–1883) during the reign of King Rama V (1868–1910). A few famous scenes from *The Water Margin* are among the most well–loved Chinese operas performed in Thailand.[42] Existing English-language scholarship on *The Sequel* reads the Siam in the narrative as a symbolic place: a utopia that restores the bygone Ming dynasty or a metaphor for Taiwan, where Zheng Chenggong retreated and resisted Qing.[43] David Der-wei Wang sees *The Sequel* as "not a rupture but an overseas re-establishment of Chinese orthodoxy."[44] But this chapter aims to consider Siam as a regime of alternative possibility to the "Chinese orthodoxy." I propose a different approach, reading Siam in *The Sequel* as the Siam of the historic Ayutthaya Empire (1351–1767). Siam is configured as a multiethnic military and commercial kingdom and a haven for outlaws and refugees. Disenchanted with a Chinese empire dominated by evil ministers, Chinese pirates, merchants, and other diasporic Chinese envision Siam as a regime of alternative possibility.

The Sequel opens on a world of despair. The Song imperial court is not only searching for the escaping bandits of Mount Liang, who yearn for freedom on the seas, but it has also prohibited maritime trade. Pirate Hu

---

41. Wai-yee Li, "The Late Ming Courtesan: Invention of a Chinese Ideal," in Ellen Widmer and Kang-I Sun Chang, eds., *Writing Women in Late Imperial China* (Stanford: Stanford University Press, 1997), 46–73.

42. I thank one anonymous reviewer for this information. For a preliminary study of the Thai translation of Chinese stories, see Prapin Manomaivibool, "Thai Translations of Chinese Literary Works," in Claudine Salmon, ed., *Literary Migrations: Traditional Chinese Fiction in Asia (17th–20th Century)* (Singapore: Institute of Southeast Asia Studies, 2013), 196–98.

43. Ellen Widmer, *Margins of Utopia: Shui-hu hou-chuan and the Literature of Ming Loyalism* (Cambridge, MA: Harvard University Asia Center, 1987); Martin W. Huang, *Snakes' Legs: Sequels, Continuations, Rewritings, and Chinese Fiction* (Honolulu: University of Hawai'i Press, 2004), 32–33.

44. David Der-wei Wang, *Fin-de-siecle Splendor: Repressed Modernities of Late Qing Fiction, 1849–1911* (Stanford: Stanford University Press, 1997), 289.

Cheng 昌成 is captured, his exotic goods unjustly confiscated. Obtained from the tropical islands near Siam, the goods include agarwood, amber, rhinoceros horns, and corals. Disappointed by the political persecutions in China, Li Jun, the Yangzi River pirate and smuggler, decides to move overseas:

> "I, Li Jun, am young and strong. My ambition has not dwindled. Wherever I go, I can establish myself. It is just that things will always come to an end. I am happier while I am drinking liquor with my buddies. I heard that Song Jiang and Scholar Lu both died of poison. Their loyalty was cast away like flowing water. Had I not escaped, I could have been like them." After speaking, he drank again.

> "若論我李俊，年力正壯，意氣未衰，哪裏不再做些事業？只是古今都有盡頭，不如與兄弟們吃些酒，圖些快活罷。聞說宋公明盧員外俱被鴆死，往日忠心付之流水。我若不見機，也在數內了。" 說罷，又吃。[45]

After receiving a heavenly prophecy, he comes to believe that he is destined to "develop his career overseas" 到海外去別尋事業. He does "not want to deal with these petty-minded people here anymore" 不要在這裏與那班小人計較了。[46]

Li Jun is not alone in his disenchantment; the feeling is omnipresent. The bandit Dai Zong, who submitted to the Song, is exhausted by his service for the rapacious Song minister Tong Guan and the feckless government, which signs a disgraceful alliance treaty with the Khitan Liao and the Jurchen Jin. In a dream, the long-deceased Li Kui appears to Dai Zong and leads him across the "vast and boundless waters" 大水漫漫一望無際 to a foreign kingdom. Li Kui requests him to enter the golden palace and sit by the foreign king. Dai Zong hesitates. Li Kui chides him for not heeding the order of Song Jiang, who in *The Sequel* clearly advocates for the outlaws' overseas settlement in Siam: "How loyal are you? You do not respect our elderly brother's [Song Jiang's] commands, and you want to

45. Chen Chen 陳忱, *Shuihu houzhuan* 水滸後傳, in *Zhongguo tongsu xiaoshuo minzhu diyi ji, disan ce* 中國通俗小說名著第一集第三冊, ed. Yang Jialuo 楊家駱 (Taibei: Shijie shuju, 1968), 80.

46. Chen Chen, *Shuihu houzhuan*, 94.

Figure 2. Chen Hong-shou's portrayal of the Chinese pirate Li Jun. The inscription reads: "River-Stirring Dragon Li Jun, living by the sea, followed by his people" 混江龍李俊，居海濱，有民人. See Chen Hongshou, *Shuihu yezi*.

deliver documents for the traitor Tong Guan!" 你這廝好不忠義！哥哥的將令倒不遵，卻與童貫這奸賊遞文書麼！[47]

Having decided to leave China, Li Jun disguises himself as a pirate. Followed by an entourage comprising his family and two hundred some fishermen leading ten fishing boats, he departs from the Wusong 吳淞 River

---

47. Chen Chen, *Shuihu houzhuan*, 138.

Figure 3. A Portuguese trading ship in Nagasaki in the late sixteenth and early seventeenth century. Artist: Kano Naizen. Source: Kobe City Museum. Image courtesy of Wikimedia Commons.

and sails toward the dark blue ocean.[48] Concerned that their fishing boats will be unable to withstand the fierce oceanic voyage, Li Jun and his gang plunder a Japan-bound European naval vessel (*haibo* 海舶) operated by two "Western merchants" (*xishang* 西商). On their way, they capture a giant whale: "Its erected dorsal fin resembles a large red flag. With flowing whiskers, emitting foamy water, the creature swims forth" 豎起脊翅如大紅旗一般，揚須噴沫而來.[49] Capturing the whale signals the pirates' entry into the maritime world of freedom and autonomy where they can "launch their ambitious careers" (*kai baye* 開霸業).

Siam is an assemblage of islands. Li Jun quickly conquers Golden Turtle Island 金龜島 by defeating its corrupt and lustful ruler, Sha Long 沙龍

---

48. Martin W. Huang, *Snakes' Legs*, 27.
49. Chen Chen, *Shuihu houzhuan*, 110.

(Sand Dragon). The Golden Turtle Island is the strongest among the twenty-four islands ruled by the Siamese king Ma Saizhen 馬賽真 residing in the Siamese capital. Each island has a chieftain. Chen Chen compares such geopolitical ties between the islands and the Siamese court to the feudalist terrorization (*fanzhen geju* 藩鎮割據) in the Tang empire after the An Lushan 安祿山 rebellion (775–763). There are 300 *li*[50] between Golden Turtle Island and the Siamese capital. Surrounded with mountains and city walls, Golden Turtle Island is accessible by only one entrance from the sea.

Sand Dragon is a "caved barbarian" (*dongman* 洞蛮). Strong, tall, and muscular, yellow hair all over his body, he can lift objects weighing thousands of *jin*. He shoots arrows with accuracy, easily wields a heavy ax of fifty *jin*, and rides and navigates the seas with ease. He is "murderous by nature" (*xing jihao sha* 性極好殺) and loves to drink "snake-infused coconut wine" (*bashe yejiu* 巴蛇椰酒). Knowing the lustful Sand Dragon rapes the captured women at night, Li Jun sneaks into the city after nightfall, kills him, and burns the city to the ground with gunpowder. Before long, the Chinese pirates also defeat the Siamese army. Such conquest leads to not only colonization of the entire Siamese kingdom but also acculturation, as Hua Fengchun 花逢春 forms an alliance marriage with the Siamese princess Yuzhi 玉芝.

Under Li Jun's rule, Siam becomes a kingdom of military defense and maritime commerce, a shelter for refugees and outlaws, and a utopia of freedom: "[Li Jun] summoned outcasts and opened markets to trade. Siam gradually became richer and stronger" 招徠流亡，與客商互市，日漸富強.[51] Characters from *The Water Margin* then begin to appear on Siam's shores. The Chinese doctor An Daoquan 安道全 is shipwrecked on his way back from Korea. The waves float him to Siam, where Li Jun rescues him. Numerous bandits from Mount Liang are forced to seek refuge in Siam: Dai Zong, Huyan Zhuo 呼延灼, Zhu Tong 朱仝, Chai Jin 柴進, Yan Qing 燕青, Lin Zhen 淩振, and Guan Sheng 關勝. Siamese people view the outlaws as representatives of the Song dynasty. But Li Jun believes that "the Chinese are all evil, crooked, and jealous. They are hard to live with. The people beyond the seas are honest and straightforward. Therefore, they can be easily educated and civilized" 中國人都是奸邪忌妒，是最難處的。海外人還有些坦直，所以教化易行.[52] Li Jun's disillusion with

---

50. The *Li*, also known as Chinese mile, was historically about one-third of a mile.
51. Chen Chen, *Shuihu houzhuan*, 114.
52. Chen Chen, *Shuihu houzhuan*, 115.

China corresponds to the ethnographic depiction of Siam as a place whose "geography and cultural customs are no different from those of China" 山川風土與中華無異. This generates the possibility for the bandits to escape from China and settle in Siam.

Li Jun's colonization of the fictive Siam alludes to the Chinese diasporic communities in the actual Siam. The pirates in *The Sequel* may refer to the historical Chinese salt merchant Xie Wenbin 謝文彬 during the Chenghua reign. Xie smuggled salt across the seas and then emigrated to Siam where he was appointed as a minister. Later, he became an ambassador in Siam's tributary mission to China, where he traded Southeast Asian textiles.[53] Another famous pirate in history is Lin Daoqian 林道潛. *Veritable Records of the Ming* (*Ming shilu* 明實錄) shows that "In the fourth month of the eighth year of the Wanli reign, maritime pirate Lin Daoqian secretively occupied some islands and made maritime troubles. Generals could not pursue him. He then escaped to Pattani and made Siam his den" 萬曆八年閏四月，海賊林道乾者，竊據海島中，出沒為患。將士不能窮追，而大泥，暹羅為之窟穴。[54] In an essay titled "Yinji wangshi" 因記往事, Li Zhi, a native of the port of Quanzhou and a contemporary of Lin Daoqian, answers someone who mocks him for being a lawless Fujianese, comparing him to the renegade Lin Daoqian. Li Zhi then glorifies the great pirate for his talent and courage. He notes that the pirate far exceeds the government in terms of moral character, since "when the whole world was turned upside down, a sense of injustice filled the hearts of brave men, but heroes saw no opportunity to perform their tasks [of service to the state]: thus they were pushed into piracy" 唯舉世顛倒，故使豪傑抱不平之恨，英雄懷罔措之戚，直驅之使為盜也。[55]

In history, under King Narai (1656–1688), the Ayutthaya Empire's capital was firmly oriented toward international maritime trade. Foreigners were accommodated in emigrant quarters around the city, and they were hired as court officials and corvées. The Chinese paid poll taxes and were treated as clients and exempted from corvée labor. Strategically positioned on the Chaophraya River and other connected regional riverine systems,

---

53. Yan Congjian 嚴從簡, *Shuyu zhouzi lu* 殊域周咨錄 (Beijing: Zhonghua shuju, 1993), 278–86.

54. *Shenzong Wanli shilu* 神宗萬曆實錄 99/4, in *Ming Shilu* 明實錄 (Taipei: Zhongyang yanjiu yuan lishi yuyan yanjiusuo, 1961–7), 1977.

55. See Li Zhi, "Yinji wangshi" 因記往事, in *Fenshu*, 146. Also see Tang Lixing, *Merchants and Society in Modern China: From Guild to Chamber of Commerce* (London: Routledge, 2017), 9–20, and Xing Hang's conference paper "The Enigma of Lin Daoqian: The Pirate and Historical Memory in Maritime East Asia," presented at 2018 AAS.

Ayutthaya was both protected from pirate raids downstream from the Gulf of Siam and accessible by boats and ships.[56] Further, *The Sequel* reflects the social spectrum of Siam, ranging from upstream agricultural zones to downstream deltas and littorals. The plot of Chinese pirates conquering and colonizing the Siamese islands corresponds to the fact that Chinese settlers residing in riverine downstream areas and coastlines acted as intermediaries with China-based sojourners who rarely went beyond the South China Sea.[57]

The Japanese also went to Siam in considerable numbers in the seventeenth century. By 1605, the new shogun Tokugawa Ieyasu德川家康 (1543–1616) had issued eleven licenses to merchants to undertake trade voyages to Southeast Asia. Four were for Siam, four for Pattani, two for Shinichu, and one for Kachan.[58] Japanese migrants settled outside the city of Ayutthaya in a place known today as "the Japanese quarter" and competed with the Chinese diasporic merchants. Both communities traded in Cambodia, in the Champa, along the southern and central Vietnam coastlines, and in Taiwan. The Thai traded deer hides, ray skins, sappanwood, and black lac with Japan in exchange for silver and copper currency.[59] Another factor spurring Japanese migration to Siam was the persecution of Christians in Japan. Japanese Christian converts enjoyed greater religious freedom in Ayutthaya than in their homeland, much as the Mount Liang bandit heroes found political freedom.[60] Doctor An Daoquan notes

---

56. Ilicia J. Sprey, "International Maritime-Based Trade in the Thai Realm of Ayutthaya in the Sixteenth through Eighteenth Centuries: Deer Hide Trade Asian Access Point for Re-Evaluation," in *Subversive Sovereigns Across the Seas: Indian Ocean Ports-of-Trade from Early Historic Times to Late Colonialism*, eds. Kenneth R. Hall, Rila Mukherjee, and Suchandra Ghosh (Kolkata: The Asiatic Society, 2017), 109–45.

57. Kenneth R. Hall, "Identity and Spatiality in Indian Ocean Ports-of-Trade C. 1400–1800," in *Subversive Sovereigns Across the Seas*, 49.

58. Iwamoto Yoshiteru and Simon James Bytheway, "Japan's Official Relations with Shamuro (Siam), 1599–1745: As Revealed in the Diplomatic Records of the Tokugawa Shogunate," *Journal of the Siam Society* 99 (2011): 81–103.

59. Ryuto Shimada, "Economic Links with Ayutthaya: Changes in Networks between Japan, China, and Siam in the Early Modern Period," *Itinerario* 37, no. 3 (2013): 92–104; Iwao Seiichi, "Reopening of the Diplomatic and Commercial Relations Between Japan and Siam During the Tokugawa Period," *Acta Asiatica* 4 (1963): 1–31; and Iwao Seiichi, "Japanese Foreign Trade in the 16th and 17th Centuries," *Acta Asiatica* 30 (1976): 1–18.

60. Charnvit Kasetsiri and Michael Wright, *Discovering Ayutthaya* (Bangkok: Social Sciences and Humanities Textbooks Foundation, 2019), 152.

how he feared speaking the truth in Song China and that this fear was a major motivation for seeking refuge in Siam.

The competition between the Chinese and the Japanese diasporas in Southeast Asia is fictionalized in *The Sequel* as Hideyoshi's battles with Li Jun. After Li Jun comes to rule Siam, the unruly king of Qingni 青霓 Island—Iron Monk 鐵羅漢—devises with Tu Kong 屠崆 of White Stone Island 白石島, Yu Loutian 余漏天 of Fishing Island 釣魚島, and Ge Peng 革鵬 of Yellow Weed Island 黃茅島 to seek military assistance from Japan to vanquish Li Jun and his allies. In response, the fictional anonymous shogun whom the narrator calls "king of Japan" (*wowang* 倭王) declares Siam to be Japan's territory: "Siam is our kingdom on the seas. How can we let it be occupied by Chinese? Summon Hideyoshi to lead ten thousand soldiers to kill Li Jun and snatch back our territory of Siam" 我海外之邦，豈容中國人所占！就差關白領一萬兵隨你去，必要殺那李俊，取暹羅國土.[61] Hideyoshi's invasion in Siam may allude to Japanese immigration in 1612–1630.[62] The celebrated emigrant Yamada Nagamasa is one noteworthy example. The Nagamasa of history was a leader of the Siamese Japanese community who excelled at military exploits and services and promoted commercial trade and diplomatic relations between Siam and Japan after the King of Siam's death in 1621. He was involved in the royal succession from the dying days of King Songtham in 1628 to the consolidation of King Prasat Thong in 1629–1630, but was killed in 1630 when his growing power came be seen as a threat to the royal monarchy.[63] (In the nationalistic imagination of early twentieth-century Japan, Yamada Nagamasa becomes the glorious representative of the Japanese empire in Kobayashi Shizuo's eponymous noh drama. When Japan's Imperial Army captures Yangoon, Nagamasa expresses his delight in seeing the light of the Land of the Gods' shining "to all directions."[64])

61. Chen Chen, *Shuihu houzhuan*, 318.

62. Yoneo Ishii, "Seventeenth Century Japanese Documents about Siam," *Journal of the Siam Society* 59 (2), 161–74; Cesare Polenghi, *Samurai of Ayutthaya: Yamada Nagamasa, Japanese Warrior and Merchant in Early Seventeenth-Century Siam* (Bangkok: White Lotus Press, 2009).

63. Yoshiteru Iwamoto, "Yamada Nagamasa and His Relations with Siam," *Journal of the Siam Society* 97 (2007): 73–84.

64. See Yoshiteru Iwamoto, "Yamada Nagamasa and His Relations with Siam," 73–84; Donald Keene, "Japanese Writers and the Greater East Asia War," *The Journal of Asian Studies* 23, no. 2 (February 1964): 214–15. For premodern narratives of him, see Saitō Masakato, "A Short Narrative of Foreign Travel of Modern Japanese Adventurers," trans. Capt. J. M. James, *Transactions of the Asiatic Society of Japan* 7 (1879): 191–204.

Hideyoshi's invasion of Siam particularly shows Chinese cultural memory and anxieties about a threatening foreign invasion. The Imjin war in Korea, that happened seventy years before the publication of *The Sequel*, was a strong source of anxiety that was displaced onto the exotic and politically safe land of Siam. Standing in as a typical foreign invader, Hideyoshi may also represent the Manchu conquest of China.

The Sequel embellishes the account of the Japanese with a story from the Patola Shahi dynasty (AD 600–800) in the western Himalayas. Hideyoshi sends five hundred "black demons" (*heigui* 黑鬼) to drill holes in the bottoms of Li Jun's ships. This invokes the scene in *The Water Margin* in which pirate Zhang Shun sinks the Song army's ships with the same hull-drilling strategy. To defeat the Japanese, Li Jun requests Daoist Gongsun Sheng 公孫勝 to conjure a snowstorm in the tropics. The heavy snow falls continuously for one day and one night. The ocean freezes into solid ice. Hideyoshi and his soldiers are all "frozen to death, made into crystal figurines" 如水晶人一般，僵僵凍死了.[65] Chen Chen notes that he has adapted the fantastic episode from He Qiaoyuan's 何喬遠 account *The Mountain of Fame* (*Mingshan cang* 名山藏):

> In the Tianbao reign (742–756) of the Tang emperor Xuanzong (r. 685–762), the Patola Shahi [who ruled the country of Bolor in today's Northern Pakistan during the sixth through eighth centuries] did not submit five-colored jades as tribute. Li Linpu advised the emperor to conquer the country. The emperor summoned forty thousand soldiers together with various barbarian armies to conquer it. When they were close to the country of the Patola Shahis, a Daoist among them claimed that the Tang army was not righteous and therefore the conquest would be doomed. The troops marched several hundred *li*. Suddenly, a strong wind arose. Snowflakes fell as if they had wings. The wind blew up a small sea whose water was all frozen into icy pillars. The forty thousand people were all frozen to death. The corpses of the soldiers were either standing or sitting, as transparent as crystals. Only one Chinese and one barbarian were able to return. I read about this event from *The Mountain of Fame*. So I appropriated this story here.

> 唐玄宗天寶中，小勃律不貢五色玉，李林甫讚上伐之。敕四萬人
> 兼統諸番兵征之。及逼勃律，中有術者，言無義不祥，天將大風

矣。行數百裏，忽驚風四起，雪花如翼。風激小海，水成冰柱，四萬人皆凍死。兵士屍立者、坐者、瑩徹可數。唯番漢各一人得還。事見名山藏文。借用此。[66]

The Sequel inventively imagines Hideyoshi as a Siamese king yet in a manner that clearly fictionalizes the Siamese and Japanese monarchies. The fictive Hideyoshi rides a white elephant and wears a king's crown "inlaid with eight types of gems and jewels" (*babao qiancheng* 八寶嵌成). *The Records of Four Barbarian Embassies* (*Siyi guankao* 四夷館考) similarly describes a certain Siamese king who wore "a gold crown decorated with gems" 冠金嵌寶石帽.[67] Nonetheless, a Siamese king would not have ridden a white elephant, which were royal palladia, symbols of power and prosperity. Moreover, he would never have given away a white elephant, which would cede his power. *The Phra Vessantara Jataka*, the best-known story in Siam, tells what happens to a king who gives away his white elephant—he is deposed and driven into the forest. Thus, *The Sequel* fabricates both Siamese and Japanese royal customs.

Siam establishes an ideal sovereign model for overseas Chinese. At the end of *The Sequel*, Li Jun civilizes Siam. He applies the Song dynasty's sacrificial and ritual customs and orders the Siamese commoners to "completely correct their barbarian customs" 盡改暹羅蠻俗. He builds Confucian temples and orders Chancellor Wen 聞 to acculturate the ministers' children and Siam's social elite. He trains soldiers, sets up military camps on the water, builds warships, and purchases weapons. He also builds a Chinese embassy (*huayi guan* 華驛館) to accommodate envoys and ambassadors from China and neighboring countries.[68] He dispatches ambassadors to establish diplomatic relations with Korea, Ryukyu, Champa, and Vietnam, and further to rule the twenty-four islands of Siam, including Golden Turtle Island, Green Dragon Island, Fishing Island, and White Stone Island. But Li Jun does not expand Siam's tributary system to mirror the extent of China's realm encompassing "all under heaven," or *tianxia* 天下. Siam remains an isolated island: "A jade palace of seashell roofs, a caved mansion of purity and void" 貝闕瑤宮，清虛洞府.[69]

---

66. Chen Chen, *Moling Cai Yuanfang piping Chongding shuihu houzhuan* 秣陵蔡元放批評重訂水滸後傳 (Taibei: Tianyi chuban she, 1975), vol. 9, 46.

67. Wang Zongzai 王宗載, *Siyi guankao* 四夷館考 (Beijing: Dongfang xuehui, 1924), vol. 2, 19–24.

68. Chen Chen, *Shuihu houzhuan*, 353.

69. Chen Chen, *Shuihu houzhuan*, 312.

The Multi-Racial Empire: Han Chinese Racism, Inter-Racial Marriage, and Sexuality

Based on the model of the historical Ayutthaya Empire, regionally inter-connected through diplomacy and trade, Siam in *The Sequel* is a multiethnic cosmopolitan society where indigenous Siamese, Japanese, and Chinese collaborate in maritime trade and national defense. The central concerns of race and ethnicity in this diverse polity are evinced in the deployment of "hybridity" and "pure blood," concepts that often appear in the context of marriage discussions and sartorial descriptions. In his book *Asia as Method: Toward Deimperialization*, Kuan-Hsing Chen uses the term "Han Chinese racism" to point out that "racism existed long before China's encounter with the West" and that a shared racial consciousness based on kinship and blood ties supported both mainland and overseas Chinese to claim "an alternative modernity" in order to contest Western dominance in the global arena.[70] My analysis of the Chinese pirates' racial consciousness in *The Sequel* hopes to further bring out such ambivalent racial underpinnings in early modern Southeast Asia and China before the advent of Western colonialization in these regions.

The soldiers on Golden Turtle Island are hybrid images of Japanese and indigenous Siamese people. Dress is a marker of ethnic difference: "The barbarian soldiers all used variegated cloth to cover their hair, tied in the shape of a river snail. They wore cotton jackets, with six-foot-long Japanese katana swords hanging on the two sides" 那蠻兵都是斑布盤頭，結著螺螄頂，穿綿花軟甲，掛兩把倭刀，有六尺多長。[71] The sartorial portrayal roughly corresponds to historical records describing Siamese ethnic clothing. *Overall Survey of the Star Raft* (*Xingcha shenglan* 星槎勝覽) records that in Siam, "Men and women tied up their hair in a cone, used white cloth to cover their hair. They wore long garments, a blue-colored cloth wrapping around the waist" 男女椎髻，白布纏頭，穿長衫，腰束青花色布手巾。[72] The katana swords indicate the presence of Japanese warriors. In the Ayutthaya period, numerous Japanese mercenaries joined the Siamese army to enhance Ayutthaya's military defense.

---

70. Kuan-Hsing Chen, *Asia as Method: Toward Deimperialization* (Durham: Duke University Press, 2010), 4. Also see Fiona Lee, "Han Chinese racism and Malaysian contexts: cosmopolitan racial formations in Tan Twan Eng's 'The Garden of Evening Mists,'" in *Inter-Asia Cultural Studies*, 20 (2), 220–37.

71. Chen Chen, *Shuihu houzhuan*, 101.

72. Feng Chengjun 馮承鈞, *Xingcha shenglan* 星槎勝覽 (Beijing: Zhonghua shuju, 1954), 11–12.

Figure 4. Bald-headed Japanese mercenaries, carrying Japanese swords and dressed in Japanese-style robes, in a Siamese army in the seventeenth century. See Charnvit Kasetsiri and Michael Wright, *Discovering Ayutthaya* (Bangkok: Social Science and Humanities Textbooks Foundation, 2019), 152. Reproduced with permission.

Whereas differing dress reinforces ethnic boundaries rather than racial integration, adopting a national costume also transforms outsiders into insiders. The Chinese women abducted by Sand Dragon from Xiangshan 香山 of Guangdong all dress as Siamese women who wear exotic hairstyles, jewelry, fabrics, wild flowers, and dancing skirts. One cross-dressing woman is alluringly described:

缽盂頭高堆黑髮，	Black hair on top of her head piles up into a vase's shape.
銀盆臉小點朱唇	Her silvery round face is small, so are her red lips.
西洋布袄到腰肢，	The jacket made of western-ocean fabric reaches her waist.
紅絹舞裙拖腳面。	Her red-silk dancing skirt drags onto the ground.

胸前掛瓔珞叮當，	Her necklace rings ding-dong on her chest.
身上插野花香艷。	Aromatic and dazzling wild flowers decorate her body.
眼波溜處會勾人，	Her eyes, like a whirlpool, draw men in.
眉黛描來多入畫。	Her black eyebrows can enter into a painting.
謾言吳國能亡滅，	Rumors have it that she can topple down the Wu kingdom.
眼見金鰲亦蕩傾。[73]	Now we see that the Golden Turtle is also vanquished.

Although the Chinese woman is a captive, she is turned into a Siamese seductress, demonstrating the transborder social mobility on the seventeenth-century ocean. Sense of self is fluid, like the fluidity of ethnicity and culture. Siamese people, *The Sequel* tells us, are not much different from the Chinese.

The Siamese man's possession of Chinese women at once evokes Chinese fears of being assimilated into a foreign culture and, further, sparks fantasies of colonial conquest through sexual contact. Early modern European writing analogizes sexual and colonial conquest.[74] Similarly, the erotic and sexual otherness embodied by Siamese woman evokes the male Chinese self's desire to conquer and dominate fertile foreign lands. The Chinese men's alliance marriages with Siamese princesses further denotes Chinese desire for colonial expansion. The Siamese king Ma Saizhen is "gentle and weak" (*yourou shaoduan* 優柔少斷). Li Jun thus proposes his sworn brother Hua Fengchun to engage in an alliance marriage with Ma Saizhen's daughter, the princess. Their ultimate goal of the union is to dominate Siam and secure their political power in the foreign land.

Li Jun and his fellow Chinese emphasize the otherness of the Siamese, but the Siamese king and the queen are both of Chinese lineage. The queen is herself Chinese, hailing from the Eastern Capital of China. The king descends from the legendary Han general Ma Yuan 馬援 (14 BC–49 AD),

---

73. Chen Chen, *Shuihu houzhuan*, 115.

74. Ania Loomba, *Shakespeare, Race, and Colonialism* (Oxford: Oxford University Press, 2002), 29.

known as the Wave-Quelling General (Fubo jiangjun 伏波將軍), so he too has a Chinese bloodline. This means that the princess herself is also most likely pure Chinese. In emphasizing the Siamese monarchy's Chinese heredity, *The Sequel* reveals the fears of miscegenation among diasporic Chinese and assumes a hierarchy of different bloodlines. In their marriages, diasporic Chinese must maintain "pure Chinese blood."

In the narrative, cultural and linguistic superiority is central to maintaining "pure" Chinese blood among the ruling elite through legal marriage. The princess "dresses as a Chinese" (*zhonghua zhuangshu* 中華裝束). She is "virtuous and liberal, skilled at Chinese literature and calligraphy. Learning from her mother, she speaks fluent Mandarin without any barbarian accent" 公主更兼賢達，精通文墨，隨著母後一口京話，並無半句蠻音。[75] The Siamese ruler Li Jun also marries the daughter of Chancellor Wen for her inheritance of Confucian ritual and ethic ideals. Li Jun's close allies also form alliance marriages among themselves to secure both their Chinese identity and political power. Huyan Zhuo 呼延灼 marries his daughter to the son of Xu Sheng 徐晟. Insisting that his son must marry a woman from a "Confucian scholarly family" (*shuli zhijia* 書禮之家), Song Qing 宋清 arranges the marriage of his son with the daughter of Xiao Zhongmi 蕭中秘. To secure the Chinese ruling elite's power in Siam, Li Jun promotes marriage between lesser Chinese officials and the daughters of local Siamese families: "It is not inconvenient for the Chinese to marry Siamese people. Soldiers and commoners will feel peace; guests and hosts will forget about their identities. People will think of themselves as natives. Soldiers will not desert" 不妨與暹羅國民家互相婚配，將見兵民相安，主客相忘，人懷土著之思，軍無逃伍之慮。[76]

Historically, diasporic Chinese were acculturated into Southeast Asia. For instance, Ma Huan's 馬歡 *Survey of Oceanic Shores* (*Yingya shenglan* 瀛涯勝覽, 1451) records how Chinese immigrants in Siam were able to have sexual relationships with the wives of local men:

> They all follow the decisions of their wives, [for] the mental capacity of the wives certainly exceeds that of the men. If a married woman is very intimate with one of our men from the Central Country, wine and food are provided, and they drink and sit and

---

75. Chen Chen, *Shuihu houzhuan* 水滸後傳 in *Guben xiaoshuo jicheng* 古本小說集成 (Shanghai: Shanghai guji chubanshe, 1994) vol. 1: 358.

76. Chen Chen, *Shuihu houzhuan in Guben xiaoshuo jicheng*, vol. 2: 1182.

sleep together. The husband is quite calm and takes no exception to it; indeed he says "My wife is beautiful, and the man from the Central Country is delighted with her."[77]

皆從決於妻。其婦人誌量果勝男子。若有妻與中國人通美，則置酒飲以待，同飲共寢，其夫恬不為怪，乃曰："我妻色美，中國人喜愛。"[78]

It has been suggested that Chinese diasporic marriages with local Southeast Asian women produced "creole" or Peranakan communities: "descendants of mobile men and local women." Such communities were created not only by the Chinese diaspora but also the Arab and Indian diasporas. Their hybrid descendants became leading merchants and rulers of local polities.[79] One of the earliest examples of mixed marriage is a South Asian sojourner who married a princess in southern Vietnam. In another case, an early sixteenth-century northeast coast Java Demak ruler married an east Java Majapahit court princess.[80]

Nonetheless, the hierarchy of bloodlines in *The Sequel* suggests that hybridity is strictly prohibited among the elite class. Racial prejudice overlaps with class and cultural hierarchy. Étienne Balibar observes a kind of "neo-racism" in his study of early modern history and reflects on racism toward Muslim immigrants in modern-day Europe. He points out that anti-Semitism in early modern Europe informed a perception of Islamic cultural difference as an inflexible barrier between Muslims and white Christians.[81] *The Sequel* similarly features a Chinese cultural and linguistic superiority that shows Chinese immigrants' anxieties over their identity in overseas contexts. Such seventeenth-century diasporic sentiments permeate Chen Chen's novel of disillusioned pirates and immigrants outside of China.

At the same time, Sand Dragon symbolizes the Chinese perception of

77. Ma Huan, *Ying-yai sheng-lan: "The Overall Survey of the Ocean's Shores,"* trans. J. V. G. Mills (London: Cambridge University Press, 1970), 104.

78. Ma Huan 馬歡, Feng Chengjun 馮承鈞 ed., *Yingya shenglan jiaozhu* 瀛涯勝覽校注 (Beijing: Zhonghua shuju, 1955), 19.

79. Engseng Ho, "Inter-Asian Concepts for Mobile Societies," *Journal of Asian Studies* 76, no. 4 (November 2017): 907–28.

80. Kenneth R. Hall, "Commodity Flow, Diaspora Networking, and Contested Agency in the Eastern Indian Ocean, c. 1000–1500," *TraNS: Trans-Regional and National Studies of Southeast Asia* 4, no. 2 (July) 2016: 387–417.

81. Étienne Balibar, "Is There a Neo-Racism?," *Race, Nation, Class: Ambiguous Identities*, by Étienne Balibar and Immanuel Wallerstein (London, 1991), 17–28.

Southeast Asians and South Asians as overly sexual and lustful. The strangeness of the exotic geography is represented through the Siamese men's enhanced sexual practice. Ma Huan records that Siamese men in their twenties

> take the skin that surrounds the *membrum virile,* and with a fine knife shaped like [the leaf of] an onion, they open it up and insert a dozen tin beads inside the skin; [then they close it up] and protect it with medicinal herbs. The man waits till the opening of the wound is healed; then he goes out and walks about. The [beads] look like a cluster of grapes. . . .
>
> If it is the king of the country or a great chief or a wealthy man [who has the operation], then they use gold to make hollow beads, inside of which a grain of sand is placed, and they are inserted [in the *membrum virile*]; [when the man] walks about, they make a tinkling sound, and this is regarded as beautiful. The men who have no beads inserted are people of the lower classes. This is a most curious thing.[82]

> 則將陽物周圍之皮，用如韭菜葉樣細刀挑開，嵌入錫珠十數顆，皮肉用藥封護，待瘡口好時才出行走，如葡萄壹般。……　如國王或大頭目或富人，則以金為空珠，內安砂子壹粒嵌之，行動扱扱有聲為美。不嵌珠之男子，則為下等人也。最為可笑也。[83]

The tropical climate of Southeast Asia and South Asia contributed to the heated fascination with love and passion in late Ming China. The Neo-Confucian philosopher Wang Yangming 王陽明 (1472–1529) asserted that human mind can lead to "self-conscience and knowledge" (*liangzhi* 良知), revising the orthodox Confucian master Zhu Xi's 朱熹 (1130–1200) view that human reason or nature (*xing* 性) is a corrective to the human mind.[84] To promote the agency of love and passion, the playwright Tang Xianzu

---

82. Ma Huan, *Ying-yai sheng-lan,* 104.

83. Ma Huan, *Yingya shenglan jiaozhu,* 20.

84. See Wang Yangming 王陽明, *Chuanxi lu* 傳習錄, ed. Ye Shaojun 業紹鈞 (Taibei: Taiwan shangwu yinshu guan, 1967), 257. Also see Peter Bol's "Confucian Learning in Late Ming Thought" in *The Cambridge History of China, vol. 8, The Ming Dynasty, Part 2, 1368–1644,* eds. Denis C. Twitchett and Frederick W. Mote (Cambridge: Cambridge University Press, 1998), 708–88; and See Martin W. Huang, *Desire and Fictional Narrative in Late Imperial China* (Cambridge: Harvard University Asia Center, distributed by Harvard University Press, 2001) Harvard East Asian Monographs 202: 5–85.

湯顯祖 (1550–1616) composed the famous romantic play *The Peony Pavilion* (*Mudan ting* 牡丹亭, 1617), which represents the dream world of the heroine Du Liniang 杜麗娘. She dies, lovelorn, after dreaming of making love to a man named Liu Mengmei 柳夢梅, whose love also resurrects her from death. The dream lover hails from Liuzhou 柳州 in Guangxi 廣西, geographically associated with the subtropical region of China's southwestern borders. The Ming novel *Jin Ping Mei cihua* 金瓶梅詞話 (*The Plum in the Golden Vase*) details the merchant Ximen Qing's use of a sex toy called a Burmese bell (*mianling* 緬鈴), a small hollow metal ball containing a drop of mercury. Rolling inside the vagina, the ball enhances the woman's pleasure. In an account by Venetian traveler Niccolò de' Conti (1395–1469), during his visit to the Ava Kingdom (1364–1555) that ruled upper Burma, the "Burmese bells" described by de' Conti resemble closely the penis inserts of Siamese men: "This they do to satisfy the wantonness of the women: because of these swellings, or tumours, of the member, the women have great pleasure in coitus."[85] The Chinese later adopted vaginal metal balls for women as an alternative to penis inserts for men. Historian Sun Laichen has concluded that penis bells came to Chinese attention during the Ming frontier war in the 1570s when Burmese and Thai soldiers were captured. This coincided with the occurrence of the Late Ming cult of love.[86] More symbolically represented in *Jin Ping Mei cihua* is an Indian monk who bestows Ximen Qing with an aphrodisiac. The medicine's overdose directly incurs the libertine's excessive ejaculation, which leads to his abhorrent death. The Indian monk is described vividly as a phallus, reflecting the merchant's libido.[87] In summary, the tropical geography and exotic customs in Siam, Burma, and India—kingdoms in South and Southeast Asia—became the locus of erotic imagination in the late Ming cult of love with which Chen Chen was familiar.

---

85. Sun Laichen, "Burmese Bells and Chinese Eroticism: Southeast Asia's Cultural Influence on China," *Journal of Southeast Asian Studies* 38, no. 2 (2007): 259.

86. Sun Laichen, "Burmese Bells," 271.

87. See Martin W. Huang, *Desire and Fictional Narrative in Late Imperial China*, 101; and Shang Wei, "The Making of the Everyday World: *Jin Ping Mei cihua* and Encyclopedias for Daily Use," in *Dynastic Crisis and Cultural Innovation: From the Late Ming to the Late Qing and Beyond*, eds. David Der-wei Wang and Shang Wei (Cambridge: Harvard University Press, 2005), 89.

The Suppressed Author, the Empty Space, and the Omitted Early Modernity

Authorship is a question variously discussed in studies of early modern literature. Martin W. Huang's "Boundaries and Interpretations" invokes Michel Foucault's "What Is an Author?" to argue that "*xushu* 續書 was [. . .] an act of *shu* 述 (transmission) designed to '*police' or control the readings of another work by others*" (italics mine). The ancient concept of "initiating" or "creating" (*zuo* 作) that was attributed to the Sages was transferred, over time, to "authors" (*zuozhe* 作者); and commentators' work of interpretation seeks to maintain, in some degree, the force of the authors' initiatory acts.[88] There is a certain parallel with Foucault's distinction between "the author-function," which exists to control interpretation, and the role of "initiators of discourse," whose works can always be returned to for renewal and rediscovery. This parallelism marks the seventeenth-century need for interpretation and its specific type of modernity: Ming–Qing transition, transoceanic wars, and migration. Within such discourses, commentators (and writers of sequels) must "return to the origin" and rediscover "the empty spaces that have been masked by omission or concealed in a false and misleading plenitude" and the opportunities "left by the author's disappearance."[89] But repetition does not necessarily mean submission. (Foucault was thinking of, among other examples, Lacan's "return to Freud," which certainly brought innovations.) In claiming that Chinese sequels are "testimony to the prestige of its parent work" and that Chen Chen's *The Sequel* is a "continuity" of the "old" nation, Huang inevitably undermines the agency of sequels and the possibility of delineating a kaleidoscopic early modern Chinese literature.

In "The Diachronics of Early Qing Visual and Material Culture," Jonathan Hay proposes to engage Ming–Qing China within the framework of global early modernity. He warns that the Sinological methods typical of Ming–Qing historiography tend to regard modernity as an imported concept.[90] David Der-wei Wang's famous phrase "repressed modernity" has also had the effect of deemphasizing the relevance of the concept of

88. Martin W. Huang, *Snakes' Legs*, 26.

89. Michel Foucault, "What Is an Author," *Language, Counter-Memory, Practice: Selected Essays and Interviews by Michel Foucault*, trans. Donald Bouchard and Sherry Simon, ed. Donald Bouchard (Ithaca, NY: Cornell University Press, 1977), 135.

90. Jonathan Hay, "The Diachronics of Early Qing Visual and Material Culture," in *The Qing Formation in World-Historical Time*, ed. Lynn A. Struve (Cambridge, MA: Harvard University Asia Center, 2004), 303–44.

modernity for the late imperial period. But Hay points out that modernity "offers a way both of taking China out of that isolation and of acknowledging the multiethnic, and multicultural character of Ming and especially Qing society."[91] Deeply aware of the teleological risk of reading modernity into the past, he proposes a multidimensional and multinarrative diachronics of Qing history.[92] For example, loyalist paintings by "remnant subjects" (*yimin* 遺民) in the early Qing dynasty show an "iconoclastic relationship to the past," locating these loyalists in an "interdynastic temporality," offering a "poetics of power constructed around the authority of the past."[93]

Importantly, *The Water Margin*'s pseudonymous author Shi Nai'an 施 耐庵 remains anonymous, although the literary work became canonized over time. There is no doubt, however, that Chen Chen is the author of *The Sequel*. As the prefacer of his own work, he genuinely considers his pirates as the "remnant subjects" who have utmost subjectivity and who possess integrity, standards, and insight:

> Alas! I know the hearts of the ancient remnant subjects of the Song dynasties. They were poor, miserable, and downtrodden, complaints filled up their bellies. I did not have enough alcohol to pour upon and melt such sorrow obstructed in my chest. Therefore, I borrowed the ending of [*The Water Margin*] to compose this book. My heroes are righteous, honest, loyal, insubmissive, proud, and humble. They censure with gentleness and admonish with propriety. Their words become mottos. Their adventures turn into marvels. They differ from Xu Bo who wailed over the chaotic world and Liu Si who arraigned people for wrongdoings.

> 嗟乎！我知古宋遺民之心矣。窮愁潦倒，滿腹牢騷，胸中塊磊，無酒可澆，故借此殘局而著成之也。然肝腸如雪，意氣如雲，秉誌忠貞，不甘阿附，傲慢寓謙和，隱諷兼規正，名言成串，觸處為奇，又非漫然如許伯哭世、劉四罵人而已。[94]

This idea that great suffering makes a great author originated with Sima Qian, who elected to suffer the shameful punishment of castration in

---

91. Jonathan Hay, "The Diachronics," 304.

92. Jonathan Hay, "The Diachronics," 308.

93. Jonathan Hay, "The Diachronics," 309.

94. Chen Chen, *Shuihu houzhuan in Guben xiaoshuo jicheng* 古本小說集成 (Shanghai: Shanghai guji chubanshe, 2017), 2.

order to finish writing *Shi ji* 史記, which became *the* canon of early Chinese history. Li Zhi, the first person to equalize the lowly genre of vernacular fiction with the highbrow genre of historiography elicits the agency of suffering in the creation of great works:

> Sima Qian once said: "'Shuinan' [The difficulty of persuasion] and 'Gufen' [A loner's anger] were works authored (*zuo*) by a virtuous man who wanted to express his anger." Thus we may say that the men of virtue in ancient times could not have authored those wonderful works had they not experienced great sufferings and frustrations (*bufen ze buzuo*). Had they authored them without sufferings, hardship, and frustrations at first, they would have acted like someone who trembled when he was not cold or who groaned when he was not sick. Even if he did author something, what would be the value? *The Water Margin* is a work written as a result of great anger.[95]

> 太史公曰："《說難》、《孤憤》,賢聖發憤之所作也。"由此觀之,古之賢聖,不憤則不作矣。不憤而作,譬如不寒而顫,不病而呻吟也,雖作,何觀乎?[96]

The Water Margin represents "great anger" caused by profound anguish and misfortune through bandits who aspire to great achievements and to fulfill their ambitions but are denied of such opportunities because of social injustice. These sincere bandits' vernacular speech and male-male friendship release their suppressed anger and thoughts. Bandit Ruan Xiaowu 阮小五 says, "We're not less capable than others. But who recognizes our worth" 我弟兄三個的本事,又不是不如別人,誰是識我們的?[97] He recognizes his friend's talent. Ruan Xiaowu confesses, "Although they haven't had any education, they're very loyal to their friends, and are good bold fellows, so we became quite close" 與他相交時,他雖是個不通文墨之人,為見他與人結交真是義氣,是個好男子,因此和他來往。[98] The bandit heroes' heartfelt recounting of their experiences to their friends and sworn brothers becomes central to *The Water Margin*'s vernacular storytelling. For example, in chapter 38, "Song Jiang told [his friend Dai Zong] about the many warrior-heroes he encountered on the road and the matter of the gathering. Dai Zong also confessed from his heart. He

---

95. This translation is from Martin W. Huang, *Snakes' Legs*, 27.
96. Li Zhi, *Fenshu*, 101.
97. *Outlaws of the Marsh*, 107; *Shuihu zhuan*, 228.
98. *Outlaws of the Marsh*, 106; *Shuihu zhuan*, 220.

recounted the event of him communicating with Scholar Wu" 宋江訴說
一路上遇見許多好漢，眾人相會的事務，戴宗也傾心吐膽，把和這吳
學究相交來往的事，告訴了一遍.[99] The terms *sushuo* 訴說 (to express)
and *qingxin tudan* 傾心吐膽 (to confess from his heart) show that self-
expression is the *sine qua non* of *The Water Margin*'s storytelling and the
bandits' loquacious verbal communication. Conversations deepen the
heroes' friendship: "They talked intimately and without reserve" 兩個正
說到心腹相愛之處. Self-expression is spontaneous, ceaseless, and insuppressible. Just when Song Jiang, Dai Zong, Zhang Shun, and Li Kui are
"talking freely while drinking" 各敘胸中之事，正說得入耳,[100] a sing-
song girl comes in to sing. "His speech interrupted" (打斷了他的話頭),
while he is about to "boast of his bold exploits" (要賣弄胸中許多豪傑的
事務), Li Kui jumps up and knocks her down by pressing his two fingers
against her forehead![101]

Self-expression in Chen Chen's *The Sequel* is channeled more with
authorial intention, which unprecedentedly emphasizes the subjectivity of
the author and overseas Chinese.

> People in the past said *The Scripture of Southern Florescence* is a
> book of anger. *The Story of the Western Wing* is a book of longing.
> *The Śūraṅgama Sūtra* is a book of enlightenment. *Encountering
> Sorrow* is a book of lament. Now I observe that the heroes in *The
> Sequel* rise during turbulent social transition, thus the novel con-
> tains the anger of *Southern Florescence*. Its sorrow and resentment
> reflect the lovelorn of *The Western Wing*. The hermits from the cen-
> tral plain exiling on the seas show laments of *Encountering Sorrow*.
> The metaphor of the Oyster Beach and the Palace of Elixir and Dew
> shows the enlightenment in *The Śūraṅgama Sūtra*. Isn't that this
> book combines the strengths of the Four Masterpieces? However, I
> regret even more for the remnant subjects in the ancient Song
> dynasties. In such a murky world, why did [the author] have to use
> the rhetoric of fabrication to manifest and illuminate on things, so
> much so that they cannot be hidden away? Did not [the author] fear
> that he broke the Creator's taboo? It must be that this author was
> imminent on death, poor, sick, lonely, and childless. His ragged
> clothes torn and coarse meals deficient, he frequently resented peo-

99. *Outlaws of the Marsh*, 284; *Shuihu zhuan*, 594.
100. *Outlaws of the Marsh*, 290; *Shuihu zhuan*, 599.
101. *Outlaws of the Marsh*, 291; *Shuihu zhuan*, 607–8.

ple. He considered drowning himself in rivers and oceans. This author is certainly not a person who wears luxurious garments in blue and purple, rides vehicles pulled by strong horses, accompanied with beautiful women, or showered with money. Can those big-belly rowdies say even a useful word? Can I find somebody [like this author] to prove my hypothesis?

昔人雲：《南華》是一部怒書，《西廂》是一部想書，《楞嚴》是一部悟書，《離騷》是一部哀書。今觀《後傳》之群雄之激變而起，是得《南華》之怒；婦女之含愁斂怨，是得《西廂》之想；中原陸沈，海外流放，是得《離騷》之哀；牡牻灘、丹露宮之警喻，是得《楞嚴》之悟。不謂是傳而兼四大奇書之長也！雖然，更為古宋遺民惜。渾沌世界，何用穿鑿，使物無遁形，寧不畏為造化小兒所忌？必其垂老，窮顛連痼，孤煢絕後，而短褐不完，藜藿不繼，屢憎於人，思沈湘蹈海而死，必非紆青拖紫，策堅乘肥，左娥右綠，阿者堆塞，飽饜酒肉之徒，能措一辭也！安得一識其人以驗予言之不謬哉？[102]

Emotional suppression and social subjection as the great author's *sine qua non* demonstrates what Walter Benjamin observes—it is when the ability to give counsel or tell a story about one's experience declines that the novel emerges. According to Benjamin, "The uncounseled novelist who also cannot counsel others writes the novel to carry the incommensurable to extremes in the representation of human life."[103] The sincere bandits and pirates in both *The Water Margin* and *The Sequel* occupy what Mikhail Bakhtin describes as the "ritual location of uninhibited speech," where there is no servility, false pretense, or obsequiousness. The bandits' profanities and curses are James Scott's "undominated discourse" and Jürgen Habermas's "ideal speech situation."[104] In "On Miscellaneous Matters" 雜說 (1592), Li Zhi discusses the essential role of self-expression for an author. He claims that a truly superior work is written by a talented author who, when seeing a scene "that arouses his feelings" 見景生情, then "pours out the grievances in his heart" 訴心中之不平, after drinking a cup of wine: "After spewing out jade, spitting pearls, illuminating the

102. Chen Chen, *Shuihu houzhuan in Guben xiaoshuo jicheng*, 2.

103. Walter Benjamin, "Storyteller: Reflection on the Work of Nikolai Leskov [1936]," *Illuminations* (New York: Harcourt Brace Jovanovich, 1968), 83–109.

104. James Scott, *Domination and the Arts of Resistance* (New Haven: Yale University Press, 2008), 176.

Milky Way, and creating the most heavenly writings, he listens to no one but himself, goes crazy and howls loudly, sheds tears and moans with sorrow, and is unable to stop" 既已吞玉唾珠，昭回雲漢，為章於天矣，遂亦自負，發狂大叫，流涕慟哭，不能自已.[105]

This chapter argues for the subjectivity of *The Sequel*'s author, who channels the voices of overseas Chinese "remnant subjects." The publications of *The Water Margin* and *The Sequel* were closely related to an early modernity in which China was connected with globality. However, in the face of maritime perils and opportunities during the Ming, *The Water Margin* contains the outlaws with sentiments of empire, loyalism, and cultural belonging. Taking place after the Ming–Qing transition, *The Sequel*, however, makes explicit an alternative seaborne path for disenfranchised Chinese maritime merchants, pirates, and migrants to seek subjectivity and establish themselves. In its "interdynastic" temporality, the sequel successfully constructs the subjectivity and independence of a maritime utopia. This is because vernacular fiction is a minor and lowly literary genre, especially so for sequels. Unlike their parent work, sequels are never considered masterpieces. But it is precisely through such a minor and decanonized genre that we see its iconoclastic capability to reenvision history and China, to represent the indissoluble historical reality of transnational migration and early modern modernity. In this sense, *The Sequel* becomes "the weapon of the weak" and their "hidden transcripts," in James Scott's terms.[106]

---

105. Li Zhi, *A Book to Burn*, 104. Li Zhi, *Fenshu*, 91.

106. On the idea of "minor transnationalism," see Françoise Lionnet and Shu-mei Shih, eds., "Introduction," in *Minor Transnationalism* (Durham, NC: Duke University Press, 2005), 7.

CHAPTER TWO

Java in Discord

"His anger had drilled straight into the country of Java, and his facial expression transformed into a smile" 那怒氣直鑽過爪洼國去了變作笑吟吟的臉.[1] So the narrator of *The Water Margin* describes the merchant Ximen Qing's reaction as he is first struck by Pan Jinlian's curtain pole and then enchanted by her striking beauty.

This episode from chapter 24 of *The Water Margin* summarizes the subject of this chapter: in what ways does inclusion of the "other" (Java) affect language of the self (Chinese)? The vernacular idiom inserted into this fictional episode involves the exotic word "Java." The merchant's personified emotion is imagined to travel to a foreign land, Java. That emotion is anger, which, together with drunkenness, lust, and avarice, manifests the late Ming notion of desire.[2] Although this Chinese world of desire plunges all the way to Java, the Chinese loanword for Java (Zhaowa or Zhuawa) is written as a pun. In the more common transcription of 爪哇, the character for *wa* uses the mouth radical 哇. The author's pun replaces this *wa* with the homonym using the water radical 洼. The result is a word meaning puddle, and Java, according to the joke, is just a puddle. The ambiguous idea of Java, whether construed as a foreign land or an ordinary puddle, bespeaks the question of how representation of the "other" transforms language of the self.

The comedic pun is a synecdoche of the polyphonic character of sixteenth-century vernacular fiction. As Bakhtin has observed, the vernacular novel, like a pun, transgresses grammatical and semantic rules to

---

1. Shi Nai'an 施耐庵, *Shuihu quanzhuan* 水滸全傳 (Shanghai: Shanghai guji chuban she, 1988), 290; Lanling Xiaoxiaosheng 蘭陵笑笑生, *Jin Ping Mei cihua* 金瓶梅詞話 (Hong Kong: Xianggang taiping shuju, 1993), vol. 1, 96.

2. Martin W. Huang, *Desire and Fictional Narrative*, 104–5.

Figure 5. Illustration of the accidental encounter between Pan Jinlian and Ximen Qing in *Jin Ping Mei cihua*. When Ximen Qing catches sight of a beautiful young lady, the narrator says, "His anger had drilled straight into the country of Java and his facial expression transformed into a smile." See Lanling Xiaoxiaosheng 蘭陵笑笑生, *Jin Ping Mei cihua* (Hong Kong: Xianggang taiping shuju, 1993), vol. 1, 93.

subvert the "serious and oppressive languages of official culture."[3] The pun in the episode above plays with the homonym of the scripts to emphasize the exotic sound of "Java" and thus provokes laughter. Its vernacular idiom heightens the accidental experience of an enchanted encounter with a strange woman, violating the official language of self-containment and a hierarchical world order. The narrative patterning in late Ming Chinese vernacular fiction similarly configures containment and transgression of the Heavenly Principle and emphasizes the moral consequences caused thereby.[4]

The official language of dynastic China was a classical idiom based on the lexicon of archivists and historians. By contrast, vernacular fiction, or the "small talk of low-ranking officials" (*baiguan xiaoshuo* 稗官小說), has been seen as expressing the voices of common people usually excluded from official discourse. But in late Ming China, a flourishing industry of vernacular novels arose together with a proliferation of unofficial histories and geographical accounts of *siyi* 四夷, or non-Chinese peoples. In the sixteenth century, the Ming's official tributary relations with Southeast Asia, South Asia, and countries on the Indian Ocean were suspended.[5] Why and how to narrate China's history of foreign relations when the classical ideal of official tributary order is suspended? How does inclusion of the history of foreign peoples affect the discourse on China's imperial identity at presence? To answer these questions, this chapter focuses on late Ming narratives of Javanese peoples and Yuan/Ming-Javanese diplomatic history in three unofficial histories and one vernacular novel: Yan Congjian's *Shuyu zhouzi lu* (*Records of Surrounding Strange Realms*, 1574, hereafter *Strange Realms*); He Qiaoyuan's *Wang Xiangji* (*Records of Emperors' Tributes*, hereafter *Emperors' Tributes*) included in his unofficial biographical history *Mingshan cang* 名山藏 (*Hidden under the Mountain*, ca. 1597–1620); Luo Yuejiong's *Xianbin lu* (*Records of All Guests*, ca. 1591, hereafter *All Guests*); and Luo Maodeng's vernacular novel *Sanbao taijian xiyang ji* (*Eunuch Sanbao's Voyages on the Western Ocean*, ca. 1598, hereafter *Voyages*).

The thriving private maritime trade brought forth maritime trouble to the late Ming state. *Wokou* raided coastal China and Hideyoshi invaded

---

3. Peter Stallybrass and Allen White, *The Poetics and Politics of Transgression* (Ithaca: Cornell University Press, 1986), 10.

4. Keith McMahon, *Causality and Containment*, 15–16.

5. Li Kangying, *Ming Maritime Trade Policy, 1368–1567* (Wiesbaden: Harrassowitz Verlag, 2010), 10.

and ravaged Korea. In the face of such instability, Yan Congjian, He Qiaoyuan, Luo Yuejiong, and Luo Maodeng looked to China's history for an illuminating counterpoint to their dire present. Java had held an important geopolitical position in the Indian Ocean during the zenith of Ming maritime exploration, and Zheng He had visited it repeatedly on his voyages sponsored by the Yongle emperor.[6] Sino–Java relations was thus their point of comparison.

Three incidents in the history of Sino–Java relations proved memorable and hence became the content of narration. Each of these incidents was noteworthy because it involved of an act of transgression by Javanese individuals or by Chinese immigrants against the Chinese official tributary order, followed by an unexpected response by a Chinese emperor. First, a Chinese envoy was assassinated on his mission to Sanfoqi 三佛齊 to recognize its independence from the Javanese Majapahit empire in 1377.[7] The Hongwu emperor accepted 300 "black slaves" (Kunlun slaves) and one gold-leaf memorial as compensation from the Javanese king Hayam Wuruk. Second, 170 members of the Chinese embassy were murdered in Java during the battles between the Eastern Javanese King and the Western Javanese King in 1406. The Yongle emperor lightened the penalty by accepting only 10,000 ounces of gold as compensation, a mere sixth of the amount demanded. Third, Zheng He destroyed Chinese pirate leader Chen Zuyi's 陳祖義 fleets at Sanfoqi in 1406–1407. Chen Zuyi was a seafaring lord who had occupied Palembang following the Javanese invasion of Southern Sumatra to protest its dependency of Java in 1377.[8]

To represent China's history of foreign relations, the three unofficial histories and one vernacular novel discussed here not only include official histories and canonical Confucian texts but also tap into a wide range of lesser-known textual sources. Ge Zhaoguang argues that cultural memory, as preserved in everyday encyclopedias, travelogues, and mythologies, showed inaccurate representations of the world, leading to epistemological conservatism and ignorance among late Ming literati.[9] Leo Shin

6. Edward Dreyer, *Zheng He.*

7. Sanfoqi later is also called Jiugang or Old Port, a center of the Indonesian maritime empire of Śrīvijaya. Here I only render Sanfoqi as it is in its Chinese transcription. Dreyer's rendition of Sanfoqi is Palembang, See Edward Dreyer, *Zheng He,* 53. Southeast Asian historian O. W. Wolters renders Sanfoqi at this time as Malayu-Jambi. See O. W. Wolters, *The Fall of Śrīvijaya in Malay History* (London: Lund Humphries, 1970), 57.

8. Edward Dreyer, *Zheng He,* 40–41, 55.

9. Ge Zhaoguang 葛兆光, "Shanhai jing, Zhigong tu, he Luxing ji zhong de yiyu jiyi" 山海經，職貢圖和旅行記中的異域記憶, in *Mingqing wenxue yu sixiang zhong zhi*

further points out that late Ming literati displayed great interest in categorizing non-Chinese peoples. But their shared passion for "broad learning" (*bowu* 博物) only reinforced the authority of classical texts rather than leading to a critical reflection on China's superiority or a scientific attitude toward learning about foreign peoples and cultures.[10] This chapter argues instead that the literati's liberal inclusion of various textual sources and subjective representations of historical events resulted from a deep uncertainty regarding China's imperial identity and an astute awareness of historical reality in their own times. Their rewriting of China's imperial history strengthens their political and emotional affinity with the Ming empire, with which their social and cultural identities are also associated. In the following sections, I first dissect how the three unofficial histories represent the historical events in a manner suffused by the authors' personal and subjective sentiments. I then analyze how the vernacular novel challenges official discourse through a literary embodiment of historical reality and political criticism.

The Empire of Edicts: The Virtual Diplomat and the Naked Savages

Yan Congjian, a scholar from Jiaxing of Zhejiang Province, held office in the Bureau of Envoys in the Department of Rites. In 1563, he was demoted to district governor of Wuyuan 婺源 in Jiangxi Province and associate minister of Yangzhou. Before long, he was dismissed from office and returned to his hometown at Jiaxing. Despite his frustrated advancement in officialdom, Yan Congjian published a few works on the history of Chinese foreign relations, including *Strange Realms, Annan's Tribute Missions to China* (*Annan laiwei jilue* 安南來威輯略), and *Compendium of Documents and History* (*Shizhi wenxian tongbian* 史職文獻通編).

Yan Congjian attaches importance to the power of imperial edicts that embody imperial tributary order based upon the diplomatic policy of "cherishing men from afar" (*huairou yuanren* 懷柔遠人). In the preface, his uncle Yan Qing 嚴清 points out that Japanese and Mongols emerged as

zhuti yishi yu shehui—xueshu sixiang pian 明清文學與思想中之主體意識與社會——學術思想篇 (Taibei: Zhongyang yanjiu yuan zhongguo wenzhe yanjiu suo, 2004), 345–67.

10. Leo Shin, "Thinking about Non-Chinese in Ming China," in *Antiquarianism and Intellectual Life in Europe and China, 1500–1800,* eds. Peter N. Miller and François Louis, The Bard Graduate Center Cultural Histories of the Material World (Ann Arbor: University of Michigan Press, 2012), 8.

"minor ailments" (*xianjie zhiyang* 纖介之恙) of the Ming empire. In order to cure these "diseases," one had to appropriate effective diplomatic strategies historically employed by China. In his opinion, Zheng He's annihilation of traitors like Chen Zuyi at Sanfoqi demonstrates the effectiveness of a syncretic approach that combines "proclamations" (*wengao* 文告) with "military intervention" (*weirang* 威攘). Unlike his uncle, Yan Congjian emphasizes diplomacy.[11] Deeming it urgent to communicate with non-Chinese peoples to maintain the Sinocentric order, he considers envoyship an ideal profession for a literatus who wants to actualize his ambition "in the world" (*sifang* 四方, literally, in the four directions). It is the rhetorical eloquence and political wisdom that literati gain by perusing the Confucian canon in preparation for the civil examination that accounts for a successful diplomat.

Yan Congjian's urgent desire to rewrite China's history of foreign relations implies anxiety, both over the Ming empire's border troubles and over his own authority as a writer of imperial history. Claiming his version of imperial history is by no means proper history, he notes that several comments interspersed in the texts are his *zashuo* 雜說, or trivial opinions. *Shuo* 說 in this context means "discourse," as distinguished from a narrative or a story.[12] Aside from his *zashuo*, Yan Congjian would surely not admit that his historical narratives are his discourse. But intriguingly, while defending his profuse inclusion of early and mid-Ming materials, he notes the fragmentary nature of the documents stored in secluded libraries. As soon as he encounters some of these pages, he will "transcribe them all" (*bijin zhuzhi* 必盡著之). *Zhu* means to make known, to write, and even to authorize. To *zhu* the fragmented materials was to establish himself as an author and thereby redeem his failed official career. Although making materials known does not mean imposing upon them a form of story, Yan Congjian makes it clear that his greatest fear is "being incapable of articulating meaning" (*zhiju qi yuyanbuxiang* 恗懼其語焉不詳) rather than "poorly selecting the materials for his narrative" (*weilun qi ze yan bujing* 未論其擇焉不精).

Yan Congjian regards it a great honor to "utter heavenly words" (*kouxian tianyu* 口銜天語). It is likely that his transcription of edicts enables him to be a virtual envoy traveling into the past to witness and to intervene in diplomatic events from history. The imperial edicts delivered and

---

11. Yan Congjian 嚴從簡, *Shuyu zhouzi lu* 殊域周咨錄 (Shanghai: Shanghai guji chuban she, 2002), 5.

12. Hayden White, "The Value of Narrativity," 5–27.

vocalized by the envoys empower the empire imagined in *Strange Realms* and influence the narratives of historical events. For instance, he recounts the narrative of the murdered Chinese envoy in 1377 as follows:

> Third year: [In response to the tributary mission sent by Hongwu], a mission sent by the Javanese king Xilibada came to pay tribute. They presented the two edicts issued by a former Yuan emperor. Xilibada was appointed as the king.
>
> Ninth year: The Hongwu emperor made Malayu-Jambi independent. The king of Java, Hayam Wuruk, outraged at the fact that Malayu-Jambi was declared Java's equal, murdered the Chinese envoy [sent to Sanfoqi] in Java.
>
> Thirteenth year: Java sent a mission to China with a gold-leaf memorial and 300 "black slaves" to atone for the dead envoy. One month later, the emperor sent the mission back with an edict.

> 三年，其主昔裡八達遣使朝貢。納前元所授宣敕二道，詔封為國王。
>
> 九年，封三齊國。其王八達那巴那務怒朝廷待三佛齊與之埒，使臣過其境，邀殺之。
>
> 十三年，復遣其臣阿烈彝列時奉金葉表文，貢黑奴三百人。[13]

This narrative is written in the form of an annal, like the Ming official annals, *Veritable Records of the Ming*. But the account does not record the murder of the envoy, nor do the official annals form a narrative pivoting on a central event. Nonetheless, the emperor's authority is unequivocal in both histories, as manifested by the inclusion of the same imperial edicts in both annals. The edict on the murder included in both *Veritable Records of the Ming* and *Strange Realms* reads as follows:

> "I rule the Chinese and the barbarians, and in my arrangements I do not distinguish between those near and those far away. Your land is isolated on an island in the ocean, and recently you have frequently sent envoys to China. Even though you claimed to be offering tribute, but were in fact seeking profit, I promoted loyalty by receiving the envoys with appropriate ritual. Previously, the envoy sent by the king of the country of Sanfoqi presented a memorial and requested a seal and tassels. I was pleased with their admi-

---

13. Yan Congjian, *Shuyu zhouzi lu*, 292.

ration for righteousness and then sent an envoy to confer these upon him, in order to manifest my concern for distant peoples. Who would have expected a villainous plot by which the envoy was enticed away and killed? How could you, relying on your location in a dangerous and distant place, dare to act in such a reckless and insulting manner? . . . If you assuage China's rage, then you will be able to protect your riches. If not, you will invite annihilation upon yourself, and regret will be of no use."

"朕君主華夷，按虛之道，遠邇無間。爾邦僻居海島，頃常遣使中國，雖去修貢實則慕利。朕皆推誠以禮待焉。前者三佛齊國王遣使奉表來請印綬朕嘉其慕義，遣使賜之，所以懷柔遠人。奈何設為奸計，誘使者而殺害之？豈爾恃險遠故敢肆侮如是與？. . . 幹怒中國，則可以守富貴。其或不然，自致殄咎，悔將何及！"[14]

The imperial edict emphasizes the dichotomy of Confucian moralism and barbarian materialism that is enunciated in the majestic tone of the Son of Heaven. Barbarians are merely "seeking profits" in the tributary system while China maintains it for reasons of loyalty and proper ritual. The final sentence is nearly a warning, implying the punitive potency of imperial "laws" embodied in Hongwu's edict.

But in *Strange Realms*' narrative, the edict is followed by other events:

In the thirtieth year, the emperor, considering that Java's subordinate state Sanfoqi deceitfully retained [Chinese envoys], blocked its commerce and travels [with China]. The Department of Rites took a detour to deliver official documents to Java via Siam. Later, the kingdom of Java was separated into East and West Java.

三十年，上以爪哇所屬三佛齊國挾詐，阻絕商旅。禮部移文暹羅轉達其國諭之，後其國分為東西。[15]

Even though the dated facts are arranged chronologically, they are without a noticeably coherent narrative. However, the list of Java's misfortunes after the insertion of the imperial edict perhaps gains momentum from it. *Veritable Records of the Ming* does not indicate any consequences after the edict's issue. While the edict is collected in volume 134 of *Emperor Taizu's*

---

14. Yan Congjian, *Shuyu zhouzi lu*, 292.
15. Yan Congjian, *Shuyu zhouzi lu*, 292–93.

Veritable Records (*Taizu shilu* 太祖實錄), Java's presentation of tributes as a plausible response to the edict is not recorded until volume 139. Nor does *Veritable Records of the Ming* mention the division of Java. Further, *Strange Realms'* account of Sanfoqi contradicts the narrative on Java. The reason China made a detour to deliver official documents was not to penalize Java but to protect intelligence from being intercepted by spies, resulting from Hu Weiyong's 胡惟庸 betrayal at the Ming court in 1380.[16] These two prominent pieces of evidence suffice to prove that Yan Congjian's narrative of the commercial and political paralysis of Java manifests the sacred power of the edict.[17]

The emperor's oral words and instructions also manipulate the actions of the Javanese. In dealing with the incomplete payment submitted as compensation for the deaths of the 170 Chinese embassy personnel in Java in 1406, Yongle waived the remainder of the penalty: "It is only to let the distant people be aware of their crimes. We do not covet their gold! Since they already feel guilty, the gold owed should all be exempted" 遠人欲其畏罪則已，豈利其金耶！且既能知過，所負金悉免之.[18] Yongle's benevolence is expressed again in a letter (*chiyu* 敕喻) to the Javanese king five years later. He consoled the king and asked him to ignore the rumors that China had granted Sanfoqi to Malacca. The Javanese king sent tribute envoys the next year to express his gratitude to Yongle. The account in *Strange Realms*, however, reveals that Yongle did in fact grant Sanfoqi to Malacca in order to protect the seaport from Siam's encroachment. Moreover, he conferred numerous titles on the descendants of the first Malacca king appointed by Zheng He during his first trip in 1406.[19] This might also explain why Yongle tolerated the homicide and lightened the penalty.

In Yan Congjian's view, China's tributary order lays the foundation for the distinction between Chinese transplants (with hometowns in China) and non-Chinese peoples. For the Chinese migrants and maritime merchants who want to be independent of the Chinese state, Yan Congjian values the call for pacification policy, as if returning to China is the Chinese sojourners' only choice. He applauds the overseas merchant Liang Daoming—a native of Guangdong who resided in and ruled Sanfoqi—for

---

16. Edward Dreyer, *Zheng He*, 17–18.

17. O. W. Wolters also notes that we should not read too much into the comment that Sanfoqi "became increasingly weak" after the envoy-murder incident. See O. W. Wolters, *The Fall of Śrīvijaya in Malay History*, 65.

18. *Ming Shilu leizhuan: shewai shiliao juan* 明實錄類纂：涉外史料卷 (Wuhan: Wuhai chuban she, 1990), 987; Yan Congjian, *Shuyu zhouzi lu*, 297.

19. Yan Congjian, *Shuyu zhouzi lu*, 287.

his submission to the Yongle emperor in 1405[20] and pities the rebellious "Japanese" pirate Wang Zhi's insubordination. In contrast to Yan Congjian's emphasis on diplomacy in dealings with foreign countries, diplomacy is not seen as a necessary strategy when dealing with Chinese "traitors." The "pirate" leader Chen Zuyi's capture and decapitation is presented as a victory in Yan's account. In this incident, 5,000 people were killed, ten ships burned, and seven captured.[21] The Chinese sojourners in Southeast Asia are consistently marked as Chinese, their only identity.

Yan's inflexible binary of Chinese and non-Chinese parallels an ethnographic categorization of Javanese peoples that he presents in *Strange Realms*. Like other sixteenth-century ethnographers, he uses the measure word *zhong* 種 to identify peoples. *Zhong* can be translated as types, kinds, seeds, descendants, or classes. This word is interchangeable with *deng* 等 (group, class), a measure word that Ma Huan, Zheng He's Islamic translator, uses in his travelogue *Survey of Oceanic Shores* (*Yingya shenglan* 瀛涯勝覽, hereafter *Shores*, 1451), one of the historical sources upon which *Strange Realms* is based. The equivalence between *zhong* and *deng* shows that ethnic and racial hierarchies fuse with social differences. *Strange Realms* classifies the first group of Javanese people as Arab and Persian merchants who have lived in Java for a long period of time, and does so in a manner identical to *Shores'* categorization of communities in Java. Yan's second group comprises Chinese immigrants who have converted to Islam, while his third group is made up of "black-skinned Javanese indigenes who sit and sleep on the ground, eat and drink without utensils, eat snakes and worms, and sleep and eat with dogs" 土人顏色黝黑，坐臥無椅塌，飲食無食著，啖蛇蟻蟲蚓，與犬同寢食.[22] The indigenous Javanese are marked as inferior because of their dark skin color, animal-like behavior, and customs. Racial and ethnic differences overlap with religious, cultural, and social differences. Yan's characterization naturalizes these differences as if there is an intractable barrier between the three types of communities.

Yan Congjian's portrayal of Javanese as unassimilable to other cultures and communities corresponds to his advocacy of the kind of diplomacy that at once maintains the imperial policy of "cherishing men from afar" and manipulates these foreign states. In contrast with the accounts in

---

20. Edward Dreyer, *Zheng He*, 41–42.
21. Geoff Wade, "The Zheng He Voyages: A Reassessment," *Journal of the Malaysian Branch of the Royal Asiatic Society* 78, no. 1 (2005): 37–58.
22. Yan Congjian, *Shuyu zhouzi lu*, 295.

Shores, wherein the Javanese are fully clothed (with one exception—in which the bride is naked during marital ceremonies), the Javanese in *Strange Realms* are described as living in relative nakedness: "ape-headed, barefooted, wearing nothing but a loincloth" 男子猱頭裸身，赤腳，腰圍單布手巾. The women are similarly portrayed, but with a slight difference: they wear gold-beaded necklaces and insert rolled tree leaves in their ears. Emma Teng points out how the degree of nakedness and physical grotesqueness in the portraits of indigenous Taiwanese in *Qing Imperial Tribute Illustrations* (*Huangqing zhigong tu* 皇清職貢圖, 1751) manifests the scale of cultural backwardness and the nature of belligerence embodied in the "other."[23] For Yan Congjian, nakedness signifies as much cultural primitivism as moral and ethnic inferiority.

In short, Yan Congjian's narrative of imperial authority and official tributary order evinces a rhetoric of chauvinism that seeks to manipulate rather than to communicate with the Javanese. Yan's personal advocacy of diplomacy is associated with his cultural identity as a demoted Confucian scholar aspiring for a successful career in public service.

The Empire of Morality: The Moral Scholar and the Deceitful Javanese

An erudite scholar from Jiangxi, He Qiaoyuan (1558–1632) spent over twenty years compiling *Hidden under the Mountain,* his unofficial biographical history of the Ming dynasty. After obtaining the *jinshi* degree in 1586, he was appointed secretary of the Bureau of Yunnan at the Ministry of Justice; he was later promoted to the supernumerary of the Bureau of Provisions at the Department of Rites and to director of the Bureau of Ceremonies. During Hideyoshi's invasion of Korea, He Qiaoyuan submitted a memorial to criticize the Department of War for its delinquency in strategic planning. He further advised the influential court official Wang Xijue 王錫爵 (1534–1614) to reestablish the tributary relationship with Korea and Japan as the solution to Japanese aggression.

Although He Qiaoyuan actively influenced the drafting of late Ming foreign policy, *Emperors' Tributes* (contained in *Hidden under the Mountain*) does not regard international relations as necessary. The empire in *Emperors' Tributes* is self-enclosed, constructed by the ethos of a self-sufficient agricultural society. The Hongwu emperor's words are cited at the beginning of the preface: "A vast territory cannot accommodate per-

---

23. Emma Teng, *Taiwan's Imagined Geography*, 168.

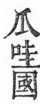

Figure 6. The country of Java in the Ming daily-used encyclopedia *Wuche bajin* 五車拔錦 (Beijing: Huaxia chuban she, 1999), 196.

manent peace; toilsome people are the origin of social turbulence" 地廣非
久安之計，民勞乃易變之源.[24] The same words are repeated at the end of
the preface. Hongwu's concern for social instability is as powerful as his
rhetoric, based upon which He Qiaoyuan would form his ethical understanding of the Ming empire.

In He Qiaoyuan's narration of Ming–Java relations, the moral power of
benevolence immanent in the emperor's words also saliently contrasts
with the immoral character innate to the Javanese rulers' actions. Explaining why he does not kill the Javanese envoy as retribution for the murdered Chinese envoy's life, Hongwu says: "I wished to imprison you, but I
thought about your attachment to your parents, wife, and children. Such
feelings are the same for both Chinese and foreigners" 欲拘爾使念父母
妻子之戀夷夏一也.[25] The Hongwu in *Emperors' Tributes* assumes the
universality of human feelings and human relationships, and his consideration of these further establishes him as a benevolent ruler. Similarly, Yongle shows mercy. The narrator says that after learning that the Western
Javanese king had only submitted 10,000 ounces of gold, "The emperor
said, 'It is only to let the distant men know they are guilty.' Thus, the
emperor forgave them and did not bring up the case again" 上曰要使遠
人知罪則已赦不問. The Javanese, nonetheless, are represented as deceitful and conflicted. The Western Javanese king cheated Yongle and the
Eastern Javanese king: "The Eastern king had not sent tribute to China for
a long time. It was because he was previously defeated by the Western king
who deceitfully said he would establish the Eastern Javanese king's son as
the ruler. Since this promise never materialized, the Eastern Javanese king
stopped sending missions to China" 而東王竟久不至。蓋先是為西王所
破，詭言欲立其子，竟不果，而遂滅.[26] The Javanese king's betrayal is
incommensurate with the moral principles by which Yongle and Hongwu
live and rule.

The images of Javanese as untrustworthy and violent imply the notion
of environmental determinism. The land-based Chinese civilization is
superior and antithetical to maritime cultures. He Qiaoyuan narrates, "I
used to go to Canton to ask various maritime merchants about the Javanese. They said that the Javanese were poor, alcoholic, materialistic, and
addicted to drugs and robbery. How could they prosper? The reasons they

---

24. He Qiaoyuan 何僑遠, *Mingshan cang* 名山藏 (Yangzhou: Jiangsu guanglin guji
keyin she he, 1993), vol. 8, 6039.
25. He Qiaoyuan, *Mingshan cang*, 6190.
26. He Qiaoyuan, *Mingshan cang*, 6191.

are called 'ferocious savages' have persisted for a long time" 余嘗至粵下，博問諸賈胡，謂爪哇窮儉酗酒，嗜財好毒劫，豈隆窳良，悍夷亦有時也.[27] The term "ferocious savages" identifies Javanese peoples and Javanese cultures with the natural environment in which they live. The culture of the land is deemed honorable and civil, while maritime culture is considered unethical and truculent. Nonetheless, He Qiaoyuan does not make fundamental distinction between Javanese and Chinese.

The same kind of Confucian morality characterizes He Qiaoyuan as a moral Confucian scholar, which legitimizes his composition of Ming dynastic history. In his preface to He's book, the well-known scholar Qian Qianyi 錢謙益 (1582–1664) notes three difficulties encountered by a scholar in compiling an unofficial history. First, compiling a history on the "contemporary dynasty" (*zhaodai zhi shi* 昭代之史) is dangerous because various social and political taboos will compromise the objectivity of any history writing. Second, historiography is not as important as the Confucian canon nor does the government sponsor unofficial history writing. Third, the authenticity of the collected historical sources is questionable. However, in Qian Qianyi's view, an imperial history is the identity of an empire (*guojia* 國家) with which its scholar-officials are all affiliated. Thus, the absence of a Ming history signifies the absence of a collective identity, which "brings shame upon scholar-officials" (*shidafu zhi ru ye* 士大夫之辱也).[28] Qian Qianyi attaches much greater importance to imperial histories than to gazetteers. With a view to legitimize He Qiaoyuan's composition, he portrays the scholar as honest, diligent, humble, and erudite. Cleverly reiterating that He Qiaoyuan never treats his composition as history, Qian Qianyi categorizes his book as belonging to the genre of *ji* 記 (records) to protect him from potential political criticism. The image of He as a scholar of broad learning naturalizes the politics of his writing.

In summary, He Qiaoyuan regards actions as having moral consequences. Underestimating commerce and the sustainability of tributary order, he places higher value on culturalism and ethics. It is, similarly, this morality that legitimizes his composition of unofficial history, which construes him as a scholar of broad learning rather than a man of political ambitions.

---

27. He Qiaoyuan, *Mingshan cang*, 6192.
28. He Qiaoyuan, *Mingshan cang*, 4.

The Empire of Revenge: The Erudite Scholar and Poisonous Javanese Women

Luo Yuejiong (*juren* 1585), a native of Nanchang of Jiangxi, published *All Guests* in 1591. He preferred erudition and personal opinions over the objectivity of history writing and the authenticity of historical sources: "As to whether the events and the discourses are false or not, this is not my concern" 至於事之真偽說之詭正非所較也.[29] In his opinion, history writing is a critical process during which a wide scope of sources must be consulted, including those lesser-known sources that lie beyond standard histories and the Confucian canon. Leo Shin points out that Luo Yue-jiong's passion for knowledge leads him to varied sources that support his open-minded view of non-Chinese peoples, through which he recognizes human diversity and commonality.[30]

But Luo Yuejiong's erudition also shapes his loyalist political conservatism. His narrative of Ming-Java exchanges in *All Guests* assumes the authority of early imperial history to channel his call to arms in the face of Hideyoshi's threat to China. He compares the genocide in Java in 1406 with the murder of Han-dynasty envoys in Zhizhi 郅支 and Loulan 樓蘭—the Xiongnu 匈奴 kingdoms to the northwest of the Han empire. Drawing upon the example of the Han emperor who summoned two assassins to murder the emissaries of the Xiongnu to avenge the man-slaughter, Luo comments that a military campaign against Java might have been a better response to the 1406 incident.[31]

Luo Yuejiong's nationalistic sentiments affect the tone of Yongle's words. An intimidating emperor appears in his explanation: "Had the emperor become angry, Java would have flowed with blood and corpses. That is why the sacred ruler demanded a penalty of gold instead" 第帝王一怒，必浮屍流血故聖主重行之罰之以金.[32] The emperor's benevolence reflects his inviolability and sanctity. Further, Yongle sounds formidable: "Do I need the gold? I only want the distant people to fear [me]" 朕利金耶欲遠人知畏爾.[33] The particle *er* 爾 replaces the phrase *zeyi* 則已 that appears in the same sentence cited in *Strange Realms* and *Emperors' Tributes*. While *zeyi* signifies a sense of compromise, *er* accentuates assertion.

---

29. Luo Yuejiong 羅曰褧, *Xianbin lu* 咸賓錄 (Beijing: Zhonghua shuju, 1983), 12.

30. Leo Shin, "Thinking about Non-Chinese in Ming China," 289–305.

31. Luo Yuejiong, *Xianbin lu*, 146.

32. Luo Yuejiong, *Xianbin lu*, 144.

33. Luo Yuejiong, *Xianbin lu*, 148.

Luo's preference for warfare is associated with his deprecation of maritime commerce. He ascribes Japan's aggression to the maritime merchants and immigrants from Guangdong and Guangxi who have "fled foreign states like Japan." In other words, Luo believes that the Chinese emigrants colluded with and helped Japan assault China's coasts. His active defense of Ming national security also results in his opposing the call for pacification policy. Unlike Yan Congjian, He opines that Zheng He should have decapitated the Chinese pirate and migrant in Sanfoqi Shi Jinqing 施進卿 (1360–1423) who betrayed the pirate leader Chen Zuyi and divulged information to Zheng He, who in turn appointed him as Palembang's chief.[34]

Luo's stress on military force in his semi-imaginary comment reinforces the Yongle emperor's acculturating power in his narrative. Acculturation distinguishes assimilable barbarians from unassimilable ones. For instance, Luo Yuejiong notes that the Tartars 韃靼 and Tufan 吐蕃 descend from King Jie 桀 of the Xia 夏 dynasty, the notoriously cruel and debauched ruler, and that the three Miao 苗 ethnicity groups are not assimilable. The description of the barbarians' avowed bellicosity is determined by Luo Yuejiong's knowledge of history, but it is not so much that his scholarship of the past constructs his understanding of human diversity as that his sensitivity to the weakened late Ming imperial identity influences his approach to knowledge of antiquity.

The subjectivity of Luo Yuejiong's narrative is reflected in his inclusion of noncanonical sources in history writing, which at times stigmatizes non-Chinese peoples. For instance, a tale included in his account of Java details that intercourse with Javanese women is deadly to Chinese and that their bodily fluids cause vegetation to wither.[35] This mystification of Javanese women's sexuality draws an ontological line between the Chinese and Javanese.

On the other hand, Luo Yuejiong, like Yan Congjian, tends to demystify foreign peoples in his appropriation of the sources. One example is the legend about the origin of Javanese people that first appears in Ma Huan's *Shores*. Ma recounts the Javanese people's originary fight with bloodthirsty demons and concludes that this is the reason the Javanese *hao* 好 (love) ferocity. He exhibits a tendency to explain what he defines as the Javanese people's immoral character by means of their origin legend. But Yan Congjian and Luo Yuejiong discontinue the rhetoric of demonization in their versions of this legend. Neither draws a direct connection between the

34. Edward Dreyer, *Zheng He*, 42.
35. Luo Yuejiong, *Xianbin lu*, 145.

myth and the Javanese people's nature and characteristics. As to the Java-nese people's belligerence, Yan Congjian uses *su* 俗 (culture or custom) instead of *hao*: "its culture prefers belligerence and fighting" (*qisu shangqi haodou* 其俗尚氣好鬥).[36] Luo Yuejiong further removes the Buddhist vocabulary that describes the demons as having "black face, red body, and red hair." Both Yan Congjian's and Luo Yuejiong's narratives show human continuity between Chinese and Javanese.

In summary, Yan Congjian, He Qiaoyuan, and Luo Yuejiong, writing at a time when the Ming imperial order was under assault, construct narra-tives of Ming–Java relations to reflect their own multivalent visions of the Ming empire as empires of diplomacy, morality, and revenge. Tapping into the emperors' verbal authority–their edicts, their remonstrations, and their remarks—the authors rearrange sequences of events, reconstruct narratives, and appropriate the emperors' comments on the events. While all three authors show a tendency to moralize Ming China's tributary economy and positional authority, they also show emotions and subjectiv-ity in history writing as demonstrated by the rhetoric of manipulation, denunciation, and revenge. Knowledge of antiquity and the "other" is val-ued, but maritime commerce, immigrants, and Javanese people are regarded as unethical. Collectively, the three unofficial histories show the authors' self-consciousness about their own socialcultural positioning and their nationalistic sentiments evoked by deep anxiety over the late Ming empire's position in the maritime world.

The Empire of Cannibalism: Military Conquest, Magical Barbarians, and the Vernacular World in *Voyages*

The vernacular novel *Voyages* offers a fictional account of Zheng He's voy-ages on the Indian Ocean. It narrates that the Yongle emperor dispatches Zheng He to seek the imperial jade seal that disappeared after the Ming conquest of China and the Yuan emperor Shun's flight into the western regions. In the novel, the Chinese army sails through tropical archipela-gos, following Zheng He's historical routes all the way to Mecca and then to an infernal hell before they return to China. The Chinese army ends up fighting upon every landing, in every foreign kingdom except Mecca. It is the Chinese who are victorious in every battle and demonstrate Chinese munificence and cultural superiority toward the defeated kingdom. The

36. Yan Congjian, *Shuyu zhouzi lu*, 295.

foreign countries each submit tributes and a written declaration to acknowledge China as the dominant empire of the world. Nonetheless, at the end of the story, the imperial jade seal is still nowhere to be found.

Anthony Yu notes that Chinese historical fiction has a generic tendency to simulate history.[37] Literatus Qian Zeng 錢曾 (1629–1701) believed that *Voyages* was adapted from late Ming popular tales and legends on Zheng He's voyages.[38] Modern scholars evaluate *Voyages* as a textual mix of fantastical imaginings and historical facts. Insomuch as the novel simulates the narrative structures and fantastical storylines in historical and religious romances such as *Romance of Three Kingdoms, Journey to the West* (*Xiyou ji* 西遊記), and *Canonization of Gods* (*Fengshen yanyi* 封神演義), it also contains geographical and historical records of Southeast Asia, South Asia, the Middle East, and the Indian Ocean.[39]

But the vernacular novel demonstrates itself to be a far more competent medium in representing historical realities than the unofficial narrative. While the three unofficial narratives' homogeneous historiographical act accentuates the ideal of Confucian culturalism, *Voyages* shows a more realistic late Ming society by fusing imperialistic ideology with ideologies of religion, commerce, and vernacularity. *Voyages* displays the expansionist nature of an imperial ideology that is more violent than the tributary policy of "cherishing men from afar." The dominant and overarching trope of religious and military combat is a common one in such religious romances as *Canonization of Gods,* which originated from Daoist rituals for territorial protection.[40] In *Voyages,* this trope signifies conquest as the Ming empire's fundamental ideology.

But *Voyages'* vernacular time-space reveals the tension between the everyday and the purported expansionist imperial image. The novel's view of an expansionist empire is articulated in vernacular Chinese through the rhetoric of object listing. *Voyages* begins with the following sentences:

---

37. Anthony Yu, "History, Fiction, and the Reading of Chinese Narrative," *CLEAR* 10 (July): 1–19, 1988.

38. Qian Zeng 錢曾, *Dushu minqiu ji* 讀書敏求記 (Beijing: Shumu wenxian, 1983).

39. The novel is discussed in Lu Xun 魯迅, *Zhongguo xiaoshuo shilue* 中國小說史略 (Tianjin: Baihua wenyi chubanshe, 2002), 128; Ma Youheng 馬幼恆, *Shishi yu gouxiang: Zhongguo xiaoshuo shi lunshi* 事實與構想—中國小說史論釋 (Taibei: Lianjing chuban sheye youxian gongsi, 2007); and Guo Zhenyi 郭箴一, *Zhongguo xiaoshuo shi* 中國小說史 (Beijing: Shangwu yinshu guan, 1939), 382–423.

40. Mark Meulenbeld, *Demonic Warfare: Daoism, Territorial Warfare, and the History of a Ming Novel.*

Ever since Heaven was created at midnight, there have been a Gold Goat, a Jade Horse, a Gold Snake, a Jade Dragon, a Gold Tiger, a Jade Tiger, a Gold Crow, an Iron Horse, a White Dog, a Hornless Dragon, an Intertwining Dragon, an Elephant, a Goat Horn, and a Phoenix Spirit. The universe was wet, murky, damp, and freezing.

粵自天開於子、便就有個金羊、玉馬、金蛇、玉龍、金虎、玉虎、金鴉、鐵騎、蒼狗、鹽螭、龍纏、象緯、羊角、鶉精，漉漉㕠㕠、瀼瀼稜稜。[41]

The various animal names in this paragraph come from the twelve calendrical signs that represent the twelve earthly branches, references to the Chinese conception of time. But why are there two Tigers, one in gold and the other in jade? Why is the list of the twelve signs incomplete, with the Rabbit and the Ox signs missing? Furthermore, why is the sun referred to twice, by the terms Gold Crow and White Dog? The cosmos is conceived as a collection of disparate images. The vernacular phrase *bian jiu you ge* 便就有個 (then there are) renders the remaining classical-language terms casual, loosening the logical binding between each listed term.

The listing of the names of heavenly bodies parallels the counting of exotic tributes submitted to the Ming emperor Yongle. Hormuz offers a pair of dark blue lions, Khmer brings four white elephants, Samarkand delivers ten purplish-scarlet horses with black manes and tails, and the Ryukyu Islands contribute a pair of white parrots. Each tribute is accompanied by a separate poetic eulogy that praises the animals' remarkable appearance, but every episodic description uses the same vernacular grammatical structures: "*The second foreign official is* from Khmer to the South of China. *He presents a memorial and pays tribute of* four white elephants" 第二個是正南方真臘國差來的番官番吏，進上了一道文表，貢上四隻白象.[42] The italicized phrases recur in every sentence that describes "which country submits what." The formulaic pattern heightens the quotidian characteristics of a vernacular world that imagines a tributary world order.

At the same time, *Voyages* elucidates the absence of imperial identity in late Ming China. Literary scholars have long considered the novel a failure because of the seemingly illogical absence of the imperial jade seal even

---

41. Luo Maodeng 羅懋登, *Sanbao taijian xiyang ji tongsu yanyi* 三寶太監西洋記通俗演義 (Beijing: Huaxia chuban she, 1995), 1.

42. Luo Maodeng, *Sanbao*, 71.

after the Chinese armada successfully defeats every country in the West-ern ocean.[43] Late imperial narratives in drama and fiction tend to have traveling objects return to their place of origin after a full-circle journey.[44] *Voyages* is an exception to this generic rule. The loss of the imperial jade seal spells out the insignificance of the tributes as a political symbol and the absence of an imperial identity in a vernacular world.

Voyages' emphasis on the absence of imperial identity divulges anxiety over the suspended official tributary system in an age of private maritime commerce. In history, the exotica serve both as political symbols of the tributary system and as economic goods. Economist Takeshi Hamashita points out that early Ming tributary relationships were largely commercial transactions, and the link between trade and tribute was disconnected to ensure the Ming's border security.[45] The Yongle emperor's sponsorship of Zheng He's voyages in history was mainly due to political and military concerns. But when private trade flourished in the late sixteenth century, exotica were mainly exchanged as commodities.

The absence of imperial identity is further reified in *Voyages* by its fetishizing of "treasures," weapons, and exotica. Zheng He's invincible navy finds its fundamental source of power in the capacity to discern and employ "treasure" (*baobei* 寶貝). The characters' attachment to their mili-tary apparatus corresponds to the devastating power and magic inherent in matter. A pair of swords can fly like shooting stars, a bell can destroy humans, a monk's bowl can contain oceans, and a flag can overthrow the cosmos. This magic of weapons is best illustrated in the words of Witch Wang, a female warrior from Bolin 浡淋 and wife of the Javanese soldier Gnaw Sea Dry:

> Relying upon the lightning and wind-chasing horse beneath me, relying upon the sun sword and the moon sword in my hands, even if it is the Western Ocean, I will open a road; even if they are iron fruits and silver mountains, I will thrust through.

---

43. Claudine Salmon and Roderich Ptak, eds., *Zheng He: Images and Perceptions* (Harrassowitz: Verlag, 2005).

44. Tina Lu, *Accidental Incest, Filial Cannibalism, and Other Peculiar Encounters in Late Imperial China* (Cambridge, MA: The Harvard University Asia Center, 2008).

45. Takeshi Hamashita, *China, East Asia and the Global Economy: Regional and His-torical Perspectives* (London: Routledge, 2008), 17.

憑著我坐下的閃電追風馬，憑著我手裡的雙飛日月刀，饒他就
是西洋大海，我也要蕩開他一條大路；饒他就是鐵果銀山，我也
要戳透他一個通明。[46]

The vernacular phrases "relying upon" (*pingzhe* 憑著), "even if" (*raota jiushi* 饒他就是), and "I will" (*woyeyao* 我也要) recur twice in this short paragraph. Repetition and vernacularity mutually reinforce each other, creating a forceful rhetorical effect of boasting. This touting of powerful and magical equipment is simultaneously a flaunting of the subject's ability. The object substitutes for the subject.

The objects' unparalleled power underlines quotidian concerns about materialism and commercialism, which undercut the aim of the official mission to retrieve the Ming's imperial identity. *Voyages* relates that by the time Zheng He's armada reaches its penultimate stop, Aden, its lengthy sea voyage has already run up a huge financial deficit. In order to compensate for the military costs, Zheng He's female general Yellow Balsam (Huang Fengxian 黃鳳仙) promises him to get a million bullion of silver. On the ship, she magically changes a pinch of yellow soil into an earthen hill, draws a city gate on a piece of paper, and pastes it at the foot of the hill. She thereby creates a magical shortcut to the Aden treasure storehouse where she "sees tens of thousands in gold and silver" 眼面前就是無萬的金銀.[47] She then loads the ship with mountains of wealth. But when she enters the storehouse again, the soldiers of Aden come looking for the thief. She hides in a porcelain jug, falsely claiming that she, the Mother of Silver and Gold (*jinmu yinmu* 金母銀母), expects them to present her as tribute to the Chinese emperor. The king is awed by the fact that even the god of money would go to China. This fantastical episode resembles a vernacular folktale in its depiction of encountering treasure. The fusing of Yellow Balsam as the god of money with the porcelain jug symbolizes the international porcelain trade at the time. Robert Finlay points out that the Chinese porcelain trade saw an unprecedented growth in the sixteenth century after Europe gained direct access to Asian markets.[48] But the parodic lie of Yellow Balsam and the comical fantasy of plundering money by esoteric magic contradicts the very principle of free trade. The novel's nonrealistic and supernatural outlook evinces a sense of economic imbalance, corresponding to its

46. Luo Maodeng, *Sanbao*, 299.
47. Luo Maodeng, *Sanbao*, 675.
48. Robert Finlay, *The Pilgrim Art: Cultures of Porcelain in World History* (University of California Press, 2010), 13.

recurrent rhetoric of vernacular hyperbole. The plebeian overstatement conjures the vulnerable image of the Ming state.

Voyages' gratifying fantasy of self-fulfillment projects the Chinese literati's criticism of Zheng He's voyages. Gu Qiyuan 顧起元 (1565–1628) and Yan Congjian once criticized the Yongle emperor's obsession with collecting exorbitantly priced exotica from the Western Ocean. They question whether exotica had political value and whether maritime voyages were critical to Ming China's imperial identity. In his geographical account *Guangzhi yi* 廣志繹 (*Expedition of Erudite Records*), Wang Shixing 王士興 notes that Zheng He departed China with more than 70 million taels of silver. When he returned from the Western Ocean, only 10,000 taels of silver remained.[49] *Voyages'* fictional compensation for the Ming empire's financial deficit shows apprehension of Ming imperial identity, subverting the official discourse on Zheng He's voyages.

While the magical weapons and treasures rendered in vernacular language in *Voyages* are a synecdoche of an everyday commercialized society, the magical barbarians symbolize the multiethnic communities and the transnational slave trade in the maritime world. The Javanese general Gnaw Sea Dry is represented as a Kunlun slave, a category of dark-skinned people living in Southeast Asia.[50] In *Voyages*, Gnaw Sea Dry is a superhuman in his swimming abilities: he can identify sea creatures, grind his teeth (probably to show his great strength) underwater, and does not need to come up for air for seven days and seven nights.[51] This fantastic imagination of Kunlun slaves' physical capacity can be traced back to the Tang dynasty. In the Tang romance tale (*chuanqi* 傳奇) "Kunlun Slave," a loyal and chivalrous Kunlun slave Mole 磨勒 intelligently helps his master to decipher his lover's riddle. As light as a feather and swift as an eagle, he is able to jump over high walls, carrying both his master and his lover. In the late Ming variety play (*zaju* 雜劇) dramatic adaptation of the Tang tale, "The Chivalrous Kunlun Slave-Warrior Becomes an Immortal" (Kunlun nu jianxia chengxian 崑崙奴劍俠成仙) by Mei Dingzhuo 梅鼎祚 (1549–1615), the image of a magical Kunlun slave overlaps with the image of a Daoist immortal. His racial and ethnic differences are replaced by religious and supernatural ones. This ethnic erasure contrasts with the intense

---

49. Wang Shixing 王士性, *Guang zhiyi* 廣志繹 (Beijing: Zhonghua shuju, 1997), 5.

50. Don Wyatt, *The Blacks of Premodern China* (Philadelphia: University of Pennsylvania Press, 2010); Marc S. Abramson, *Ethnic Identity in Tang China* (Philadelphia: University of Pennsylvania Press, 2008), 11.

51. Luo Maodeng, *Sanbao*, 283.

racial and ethnic depictions of foreign others in *Voyages,* which reflects a different world—the maritime world.

The image of Gnaw Sea Dry as a Kunlun slave reflects the slave trade's ongoing activity in the late sixteenth century. Literatus Wang Shixing notes that, in the Wanli reign, many Kunlun slaves, nicknamed "black demons," were traded in Canton: "One black slave's price is fifty to sixty pieces of gold" 买之一头，值五六十金.[52] In Wang's text and in contemporaneous discourse, "Black demons," like Kunlun slaves, was a flexible category that may have included Africans. The African slave trade was a significant aspect of Indian maritime trade, and representations of Africans appear in works across genres. In the late Chosŏn official painting "Painting of the Ming Army's Departure for China" (1599), the court painter Kim Suun 金守雲 includes four black figures in his portrayal of a Korean banquet for Chinese generals departing for home after fighting against Hideyoshi's army in the Imjin War (1592–1598). While unidentified, they might be African divers transported by Portuguese merchants from Macao.[53]

Gnaw Sea Dry's magical slave body is also juxtaposed with the body of a merchant master. He is also depicted as a Muslim, a Persian, or an Arab who has "deep-set eyes, broom-like eyebrows, a high nose, and curly hair" 兜凹眼，掃帚眉，高鼻子，卷毛鬚.[54] A late Ming pictorial illustration of *Voyages* likewise portrays Gnaw Sea Dry as a Muslim or a Persian.

This trope, however, is not a mere fabrication of late sixteenth-century seaborne commerce. It corroborates accounts in travelogues and histories such as *Strange Realms, Emperors' Tributes,* and *All Guests,* in which Arab and Persian Muslims are ranked as the most prestigious class in Java, which was their settlement. As a Dutch merchant observed in the 1590s, among the Arabs and Pegus, Malays, and Klings on the seas, some Persian merchants came from Java.[55]

Further, the magical character of barbarian warriors, especially female barbarian warriors as exemplified by Witch Wang, Gnaw Sea Dry's wife, indicates a Chinese racist fantasy of barbarians as dangerous, debased, and fake. In her rivalry with Wolf Teeth Zhang, Witch Wang creates

---

52. Wang Shixing, *Guang zhiyi,* 100–101.

53. Hyangsoon Yi, conference paper, "African 'Sea Monsters' and Barbarian Nuns in the Kingdom of Morning Calm: Discourse of Black Exotica in Late-Chosŏn Korea." Second Annual International Conference on Africa and its Diaspora. Athens, Georgia, 2014, 3.

54. Luo Maodeng, *Sanbao,* 287.

55. Anthony Reid, *Southeast Asia,* 67.

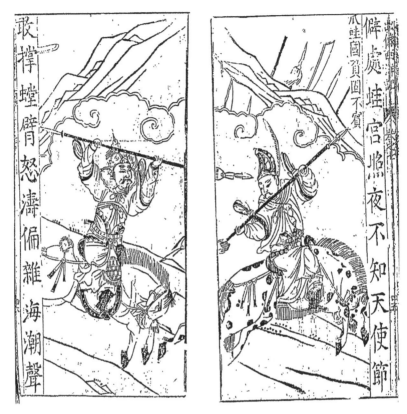

Figure 7. A Persian-looking military general with a moustache, wearing a feathered dome-shaped hat and riding a leopard-spotted horse, in a late Ming illustration of the Java episode in *Voyages*. The Chinese characters read: "The country of Java stubbornly resists submission. The palace of frogs in the remote region is ignorant of the envoys of the Heavenly Kingdom; how dare they extend their mantis arms to defend—waves of anger mix with sounds of oceanic tides" 僻處蛙宮照夜不知天使節，敢撐螳臂怒濤偏雜海潮聲. Source: *Sanbao taijian xiyang ji tongsu yanyi* (xinke quanxiang), Taibei: Tianyi chuban she, 1985]

seventy-two illusory selves to bewitch him. The seventy-two Witch Wangs remark on a wonderland where everyone is physically identical:

> You Chinese gave birth to 72 sages in 500 years; we barbarians do not read and do not understand the principles, so we 72 female warriors came into being in 500 years. Your 72 sages gathered together to follow Confucius's teaching; we 72 female warriors are born from the same egg. You and we follow the same principle.

彼此你中國五百年生出七十二個賢人;我西洋不讀書,不知道
理,五百年就生出我們七十二個女將。彼此你中國七十二賢人,
聚在一人門下; 我西洋七十二女將, 出在一個胞胎。彼此俱是
一理。[56]

The repetition of vernacular phrases such as "give birth to 72 . . . in 500 years" 五百年就生出 again shows the rhetorical effect of hyperbole that simultaneously exaggerates the Chinese fantasy about barbarians and subverts that fantasy. On the one hand, Chinese and Javanese are both characterized using the numbers 72 and 500—numbers reminiscent of Monkey King who has 72 magic transformations and has been imprisoned under a mountain for 500 years in *Journey to the West*. Witch Wang's self-deprecating comparison of her society with the Chinese one highlights the ontological difference between Chinese and non-Chinese as intellectuals and sexual beings. On the other hand, the seventy-two Witch Wangs bitterly justify their fraudulent existence by comparing themselves with the Confucian disciples. By drawing such a blasphemous equivalence, they mock Chinese civilization and thereby tarnish the Chinese imperial image.

Witch Wang's subversive language and debased nature reflect the historical reality of Chinese immigrants' settlement in Southeast Asia and their resistance to official cultures in China. Her exogamous marriage with Gnaw Sea Dry reverberates with the theme, commonly seen in travelogues, of barbarian women having sex with Chinese men—a common trope that points to Chinese sojourners' happy settlement in Southeast Asia. As discussed in chapter 1, the sexual relations between Southeast Asian women and Chinese men are recorded in contemporary accounts such as *Shores*: "If a married woman is very intimate with one of our men from the Central Country, wine and food are provided, and they drink and sit and sleep together."[57] With her common Chinese surname, Witch Wang reverses this common trope of travelogues in her marriage to Gnaw Sea Dry. Her unruliness points to the history of Chen Zuyi's rebellion and the Japanese pirate Wang Zhi's revolt from the government's campaigns to eliminate pirates.

The magical weapons and verbally blasphemous barbarians correspond to *Voyages'* author Luo Maodeng's repudiation of warfare. When Hideyoshi invaded Korea, news of the warfare circulated in Nanjing where

56. Luo Maodeng, *Sanbao*, 213.
57. Ma Huan, *Ying-yai sheng-lan*, 104.

Luo Maodeng resided.[58] Gauging the late Ming empire's weakened strength in the face of Japan's aggression, Luo Maodeng stresses the danger of overreach and the need for restraint.[59]

But the amplified violence and imperialistic discourse in *Voyages* bespeaks Luo Maodeng's literary revenge for the historical murders in Java, emerging from Luo's intensified nationalistic sentiments in the face of Japanese aggression. The novel's Zheng He flagellates the Javanese officials for their mistakes and demands that the Javanese king write a confession of his crimes and pay tribute to Yongle in person as an apology. Further, in Sanfoqi, Zheng He decapitates the pirate Chen Zuyi.[60]

At the end of the Witch Wang episode, the Chinese warriors engage in cannibalism, an extreme version of nationalistic imagination that corresponds to the trope of military conquest and celebration of Chinese dominance. Together with his Chinese soldiers, Zheng He kills Gnaw Sea Dry and eats the flesh of the Javanese soldiers. Their engagement in cannibalism is anachronistic. In the historical accounts *Yuan History* (*Yuanshi* 元史, 1370), *Shores*, *Strange Realms*, and *All Guests*, the event related to cannibalism is attributed to the Yuan army during its invasion of Java in 1292. In *Shores'* account, the Yuan soldiers are struggling to conquer Java even after fighting bravely for several months. Worst of all, water and food are exhausted. The generals then pray to Heaven, "We received the imperial order to attack the barbarians; if Heaven is with us, let a spring of water rise up; if [Heaven] is not with us, then let there be no spring.[61] They then thrust their swords into the sands by the briny sea. Magically, water gushes out—it is fresh and sweet. Only thus do the warriors survive. Fei Xin's 費信 *Overall Survey of the Star Raft* (*Xingcha shenglan* 星槎勝覽, 1436, hereafter *Star Raft*) furthers the narration by describing how, because of the miracle of the water, soldiers are able to defeat millions of barbarians. They claim territory, capture the Javanese, and eat the cooked flesh of the conquered. The narrator then concludes that this incident is still remembered in Java: "The Javanese today still say that Chinese eat human flesh" 至今稱中國能食人也.[62] Incongruous with the official

---

58. *Wanli dichao* 萬曆邸抄 (Nanjing: jiangsu guangling chuban she, 1991), 1063, 1065.

59. Luo Maodeng, *Sanbao*, 1.

60. Luo Maodeng, *Sanbao*, 372.

61. Ma Huan, *Ying-yai sheng-lan*, 89.

62. Fei Xin 費信, *Xingcha shenglan jiaozhu* 星槎勝覽校注 (Beijing: Beijing zhonghua shuju, 1954), 13–17.

Yuan History, which records that the Yuan army was defeated, *Star Raft*'s narrative sublimates failure into triumph. *Voyages* further fuses this Yuan-Java anecdote with its own narrative of Zheng He's voyages to channel late sixteenth-century nationalistic sentiments about Japanese aggression.

The nationalistic intensification of the imperialistic discourse, however, is challenged vigorously by the "subaltern" Ming empire in *Voyages*, showing the dialogical and polyphonic nature of a vernacular novel.[63] In the Infernal Hell, the last stop on Zheng He's overseas journey before the navy reaches home, a large group of wandering ghosts consisting of animals, soldiers, and women—altogether thirty-two groups—approach Judge Cui 崔判官 to accuse Zheng He and his armada of genocide. Among them are the 3,000 Javanese soldiers who were eaten by the Chinese, Witch Wang, and Gnaw Sea Dry. The judge dismisses the crowd by concluding that their miserable deaths are karmic retribution for their previous lives. But in the end, five ghosts remain. They ask the judge what they have done wrong in fighting for their own countries in the face of the encroaching Chinese armada. Judge Cui responds:

> "When did the Chinese destroy your state, annex your territory, or take away your goods? How can you say that you were facing a peril that was as dangerous as stacking eggs?" Old Star Jiang said, "If there was no danger to my country, why did I kill people ceaselessly?" The judge said, "When the Chinese came, all you were supposed to do was to sign the surrender paper. When did they threaten you? It was all because you insisted on fighting. Isn't this your murderous nature?" Gnaw Sea Dry said, "You are wrong, judge! In Java, 500 fish-eye soldiers were cut into pieces. 3,000 navy soldiers were boiled in a broth! Is this also because we insisted on fighting?" The judge said, "It was all your fault."

> 崔判官道: "南人何曾滅人社稷，吞人土地，貪人財貨，怎見得勢如纍卵之危?" 姜老星道: "既是國勢不危，我怎肯殺人無厭?" 判官道: "南人之來，不過一紙降書，便自足矣，他何曾威逼於人? 都是你們偏然強戰。這不是殺人無厭麼?" 咬海幹道: "判官大人差矣! 我爪哇國五百名魚眼軍，一刀兩段; 三千名步卒，煮做一鍋。這也是我們強戰麼?" 判官道: "都是你們自取的。"[64]

---

63. Mikhail Bakhtin, "Discourse in the Novel."

64. Luo Maodeng, *Sanbao*, 714.

The grammar of these rhetorical questions—"when did they" (*ta heceng* 他何曾), "isn't this" (*zhe bushi* 這不是), and "is this also" (*zhe yeshi* 這也是)—reinforces the self's own position and evinces a reluctance to engage with the "other's" perspective. Lu Xun notes that this disturbing episode was adapted from two closely related late Ming popular stories, "Five Ghosts Arguing with the Judge" (*Wugui naopan* 五鬼鬧判) and "Five Mice Wreaking Havoc in the Eastern Capital" (*Wushu nao Dongjing* 五鼠鬧東京).[65] The late Ming versions of these stories unfortunately no longer exist, although the 1879 novel *Three Heroes and Five Gallants* (*Sanxia wuyi* 三俠五義) is partially based upon this topos. *Voyages*' adaptation of this literary topos is thus valuable for not only preserving late Ming textual and literary materials but also bringing to light self-other antagonism as a literary motif in response to historical cross-border conflicts in warfare, immigration, and maritime trade.

The rhetorical questions raised in the passage specifically manifest the irreconcilable nature of some late Ming intellectuals' conflicting ideologies. The Javanese ghosts' rebellion emphasizes Confucian values of benevolence and justice. The judge, however, contradicts the entrenched Confucian ideology of "cherishing men from afar" with his nationalistic justification of violence. Like the story sources that have disappeared, the reaction of the Ming audience to the scene—whether they were sympathetic to the Southeast Asians or to the judge—is impossible to know. Nonetheless, the plot tells us that the narrator is sympathetic with the ghosts and expects the reader to be like him. The five ghosts rebel and claim that the judge "selfishly" (*si* 私) discriminates against them. But such narrative sympathy is represented only through another round of confrontation, showing a persistent tension between the two contending ideologies.

The irreconcilable tensions between violence and benevolence, between the vernacular and the official, between maritime commerce, immigration, and foreign peoples and the tributary system echo the eternal absence of the imperial jade seal in *Voyages* and the profound sense of uncertainty regarding imperial identity shared by the four authors. While the illusion of a coherent identity is confirmed by the historical narratives, *Voyages* shows a disillusioned reality.

In conclusion, this chapter has examined three unofficial historical narratives (*Strange Realms*, *Emperors' Tributes*, and *All Guests*) and one vernacular novel (*Voyages*) to dissect the construction of the late Ming

---

65. Lu Xun, *Zhongguo xiaoshuo shilue*, 180–82.

empire's self-image in the discourse of Japanese piracy and Yuan/Ming-Java foreign relations. In such discourse of desire, the four authors imbue their narratives with personal anxieties and nationalistic sentiments. While the historical narratives tend to moralize and idealize China's tributary world order, the vernacular fiction paints a more realistic picture of the late Ming state by involving heterogeneous voices of the "other." Collectively, the four narratives represent differing images of the Ming empire, revealing the intellectuals' deep apprehension of the Ming's identity, their political criticism of the state, and divergent and even self-conflicted views toward maritime commerce, the tributary system, immigrants, and foreign peoples.

II

Japan

CHAPTER THREE

Learning the Barbarian Tongue

This chapter delineates how rampant Japanese piracy problems in the coastal Zhejiang region prompted local scholar-officials to compile military geographical treatises, bilingual glossaries, and translations of *waka* poetry. These became significant discursive practices of the late Ming discourse on Japan. Such discursive practices continued the Neo-Confucian tradition of philology, phonology, and evidential scholarship and the long history of Chinese transcription and translation of foreign languages. These discursive practices show a rising attention to the dichotomy of Chinese and Japanese languages and literatures and of vernacular and classical Chinese.

In 1566, Zheng Shungong 鄭舜功, an envoy and spy in Japan, compiled a geographical encyclopedia of the country titled *Riben yijian* 日本一鑑 (*A Mirror of Japan*). In the preface, he first confirms the superiority of Chinese language; but then, anxious about the linguistic diversity and confusion in China that may obstruct Chinese eloquence, he at last defends the value of Japanese language.

> The edict proclaims that the Japanese language has forty-seven phonograms to transliterate Sinitic scripts. They created these to transcribe and translate Chinese. Isn't this evidence that these barbarians have long admired Chinese civilization? Our sages' writings are esteemed. The sounds of Chinese and of foreigners are beautiful. As for Chinese pronunciation, Wu and Chu topolects are too glib. Yan and Ji topolects are too heavy and muddy. Qin and Long topolects render the falling tone as the entering tone. The flat tone in the Liang and Yi topolects sounds like the falling tone. The vowels in Hebei and Hedong differ greatly. Wu people pronounce *rao* as *du*, *wu* as *lao*, *ru* as *yu*. Some even cannot differentiate *you* and *zhi*, *wang* and *yang*. Even the language of China is like this. As for those

strangers with sparrow-like tongues, when they want to imitate Sinitic sounds, how can it be an easy thing for them? Therefore, I selected their daily words and classified them into eighteen categories. Underneath each character is its transcription. This is to understand their language.

宣諭得知，倭字四十七數，以志華文調定，寄音翻譯，具備今此之。夷久崇文教，匪不知乎？聖賢文章為貴也。華夷聲音為美也。若夫華夏聲音也。吳楚有傷於輕浮，燕翼有失於重濁，而秦隴去聲為入，梁益平聲似去，河北河東取韻尤遠，吳人呼堯讀武為姥，說如近魚，切...之類，及有知之不辯王揚不分者，華夏之音有如此，況夷舌骹，欲為華夏之音者，夫豈而易言之哉，故採日用文字類，分十八凡字之下以為寄音，庶通其言。[1]

For Zheng Shungong, various Chinese dialects cannot showcase the ideal accent of *Huaxia* 華夏 (China). He cites the passage on topolects from the preface to *Zhongyuan yinyun* 中原音韻 (*Sounds and Rhymes of the Central Plain*, 1324). That text states that although the poet Xin You'an 辛幼安 (1140–1207) moved from the north to the south during the Southern Song dynasty and the poet Yuan Yuzhi 元裕之 (1190–1257) lived at the end of the Jurchen Jin dynasty and the beginning of the Mongol Yuan dynasty, scholars adopted their accent because their verses follow "the pronunciation of Zhongzhou, which is the most proper" 音節則為中州之正. "Proper pronunciation" (*zhengsheng* 正聲) is "capable of manifesting the strength of the empire" 足以鳴國家氣化之盛.[2] But Zheng Shungong deftly skips over defining the authentic language of *Huaxia*, focusing instead on the value of learning the barbarian tongue, Japanese. He categorizes the Japanese language under the rubric of "One Hundred Barbarians [Languages]" (*baiyi* 百夷), differentiating Japanese from other foreign languages, including Tartar, Jurchen Jin, Indian, Islam, Uyghur, and Burmese. Zheng emphasizes the usefulness of learning the "sound of barbarian tribes" (*manmo zhi yin* 蠻貊之音).[3]

Chinese script had long been considered as a prestigious written form in premodern China and Sinosphere.[4] In Japan, for example, *kanshi* 漢詩

---

1. Ōtomo Shin'ichi, *Nihon ikkan: honbun to sakuin* 日本一鑑本文と索引 (Tokyo: Kasama Shoin, 1974), vol. 5: 7.

2. Zhang Yulai 張玉來 et al., *Zhongyuan yinyun* 中原音韻 (Beijing: Zhonghua shuju, 2013).

3. Hou Jigao, *Zensetsui*, 6.

4. For the meaning of "Sinosphere," see Joshua A. Fogel, *Articulating Sinosphere:*

(Sinitic poetry) had continuously been an important literary genre in the court and a form of cross-cultural communication with monks, envoys, and literati in East Asia.[5] The Chinese educated elite generally did not expect to learn non-Chinese languages until the twentieth century. Bilingual individuals who served as translators and interpreters in premodern China usually had foreign or ethnic backgrounds. The Buddhist scripture translators in early China were Indians, Sogdians, Tocharians, and Yuezhi who traveled the Silk Road and came to reside in Dunhuang 敦煌. The dictionaries compiled during the conquest dynasties, such as the Yuan and Qing, were written by non-Chinese. For example, Muslim Shaikh Muhammad (Masha Yihei 馬沙亦黑) and Mongol Huo Yuanjie 火原潔 compiled the Sino-Mongol bilingual manual *Huayi yiyu* 華夷譯語 (*Sino-Foreign Words Translated*, 1382).[6] The Tang monk Xuanzang 玄奘 (602–664) is among the few Chinese who diligently learned Sanskrit and traveled to India in order to translate them into Chinese.[7]

The Chinese considered the Chinese script and literary education system superior. Hou Jigao writes of the Japanese scripts:

Sino-Japan Relations in Space and Time (Cambridge, MA: Harvard University Press, 2009), 4.

5. See Wiebke Denecke, "Anthologization and Sino-Japanese literature," in *The Cambridge History of Japanese Literature,* eds. Haruo Shirane, Tomi Suzuki, and David Lurie (Cambridge: Cambridge University Press, 2016), 89.

6. For studies on *Huayi yiyu*, see Marian Lewicki, *La Langue mongole des transcriptions chinoises du XIVe siècle: Le Houa-yi yi-yu de 1389*, Traveux de la Société des Sciences et des Lettres de Wrocław, ser. A, 29 (Wrocław: Nakładem Wrocławskiego Towarzystwa Naukowego, 1949); and Antoine Mostaert, *Le matérial mongol du* Hua i i iu de Houng-ou, *1389*, ed. Igor de Rachewiltz, with the assistance of Anthony Schönbaum, Mélanges chinois et bouddhiques 18 (Brussels: Institute des hautes Études Chinoises, 1977). Victor Mair's journal article "Buddhism and the Rise of the Vernacular in East Asia" mentions the text with an illustration of it. See Victor H. Mair, "Buddhism and the Rise of the Written Vernacular in East Asia: The Making of National Languages," *Journal of Asian Studies* 53, no. 3 (August 1994): 715.

7. About Xuanzang and his translation of Buddhist scriptures, see Tansen Sen, "Military Concerns and Spiritual Underpinnings," in *Buddhism, Diplomacy, and Trade: the Realignment of Sino-Indian Relations, 600–1500* (Honolulu: University of Hawai'i Press, 2003), 15–54; and "The Spread of Buddhism," in *The Cambridge World History, vol. 5, Expanding Webs of Exchange and Conflict, 500 CE–1500 CE*, eds. Benjamin Z. Kedar and Merry Wiesner-Hanks (Cambridge: Cambridge University Press, 2015), 447–79. On early Chinese translation of Buddhist scriptures, see Max Deeg, "Creating Religious Terminology: A Comparative Approach to the Early Chinese Translations," *Journal of the International Association of Buddhist Studies* 31 (1–2): 83–118.

In high antiquity, they absolutely had no written language. They only incised wood and knotted rope to mark events. Ever since the Wei and Jin dynasties, they acquired Buddhist sutras from China. They believed in Buddhism. Although now they know a little writing and composition, they do not have a schooling system. . . . The primers are called *yilu* (hiragana). They have forty-eight phonetic letters. The forty-eight hiragana syllabary phonograms are differentiated by voiced and voiceless sounds. They can be applied to all kinds of writing styles. People are all familiar with the cursive writing style. Japanese people who can recognize authentic Chinese characters are very rare.

上古絕無文字，惟刻木結繩以為憑劑。自魏隋時，五經佛法得自中國，酷信佛經，今雖略知文賦，尚無學校開科之設，啟蒙所讀者名曰以路法，共四十八音，四十八字有清濁之分，可以通用一應字體，皆以草書為熟。呼音與中國大異。民間子弟識中國真字者甚鮮。[8]

Hou Jigao still emphasizes that Chinese scripts are "authentic." Much as Japan received Buddhism transmitted from China and needed a Chinese literary education system, its scripts were also derived from Chinese originals.

Tao Zongyi 陶宗儀 (1329–1410) of Huangyan 黃岩 in Zhejiang noted the functional and aesthetic significance of Japanese hiragana. Comparing Japanese scripts to Mongolian scripts, the author of *Shushi huiyao* 書史會要 (*Essentials in the History of Calligraphy*, 1376) points out the immediacy of vernacular writing as uniquely embodied in hiragana: "[The Japanese monk] says that his country has its own language. They only have forty-seven phonographs. If one grasps them all, one can know their meaning and sound. This is because once the script is written, the meaning is known" 雲彼中自有國字，字母僅四十有七，能通識之，便可解其音義，因索寫一過，就叩以理。[9] He also praises Japanese calligraphy as "dragon flying and snake moving" 龍蛇飛動, comparing its style to the eminent Tang calligrapher Crazy Su's 顛素 (725–785) "wild brushwork" (*kuangcao* 狂草).[10]

---

8. Hou Jigao, *Zensetsu*, 34.

9. Tao Zongyi 陶宗儀, *Shushi huiyao* 書史會要, *Qinding siku quanshu* 欽定四庫全書, 366.

10. Tao Zongyi, *Shushi huiyao*, 366.

It was not until the Ningbo incident (Song Suqing 宋素卿 incident) in 1523 that the Ming government and more Chinese scholar-officials began to think it essential to learn the Japanese language to better understand China's rival and to obtain intelligence. The notorious incident caused immense destruction to the Ningbo region. According to Hou Jigao, shogun Ashikaga Yoshiharu 足利義晴 (1511–1550), unable to control his rivals, let his vassal daimyo Ōuchi Yoshioki 大內藝興 (1477–1528) dispatch an embassy headed by a Zen monk named Kendō Sōsetsu 謙導宗設 to China to conduct the "tally trade" (*kanhe* 勘合貿易) and to seek China's support. Meanwhile, Hosokawa Takakuni 細川高國 (1484–1531) sent a separate embassy led by a Zen monk named Rankō Zuisa 鸞岡瑞佐 and Chinese merchant Song Suqing (1445–1525) to Ningbo to seek China's support. They arrived in Ningbo and "condemned and slandered" (*dihui* 詆毀) each other.[11]

Published in the same year as the Ningbo incident, Xue Jun's 薛竣 (1474–1524) *Riben jiyu* 日本寄語 (*The Japanese Dictionary*, 1523) is the earliest Chinese study of the Japanese language. It is included in his geographical account of Japan *Riben kaolü* 日本考略 (*A Survey of Japan*, 1523). This glossary is further included in *The Edited Collection of Maps of Japan* (*Riben tuzuan* 日本圖纂, 1561) by Zheng Ruozeng 鄭若曾 (1503–1570)—a private secretariat of the Zhejiang Provincial Touring Censor (*Xun'an yushi* 巡按御史), Hu Zongxian 胡宗憲 (1512–1565) and in *Huangming yuwo lu* 皇明馭倭錄 (*Imperial Ming's Control of Japanese Pirates*) by Wang Shiqi 王士騏 (b. 1557). The Institute of Foreigners (*Siyi guan* 四夷館) housed in the Department of Rites compiled the Ming official account of the Japanese language, *Riben guan yiyu* 日本館譯語 (*Translation of Japanese Language*) (1548), collected in *Huayi yiyu* 華夷譯語 (*Sino-Foreign Words Translated*). Further, besides Zheng Shungong's *A Mirror of Japan*, Li Yangong 李言工 (1541–1599), a commandant of Linhuai 臨淮, and Hao Jie 郝杰, junior guardian at Nanjing, published *Riben kao* 日本考 (*A Study of Japan*) in 1592. At the same time, Hou Jigao 候繼高 (1533–1602) published *Riben fengtu ji* 日本風土記 (*The Geography and*

---

11. Hou Jigao, *Zensetsu*, 24. Japanese sources show a slightly different story. In 1521, the young Japanese shogun Ashikaga Yoshitane broke with Hosokawa Takakuni and expelled Takakuni from the capital. Takakuni then overthrew Yoshitane and enthroned Ashikaga Yoshiharu (1511–1550) as shogun. Both Takakuni and Yoshiharu wanted Yoshitane's tributary privileges, but Ashikaga Yoshitane refused to grant them. So both of their embassies arrived in Ningbo to claim their legitimacy as the representative of the king of Japan. For a survey of the Ningbo incident, see Peter D. Shapinsky, *Lords of the Sea*, 206–14.

Customs of Japan, 1592–1593). This contains content identical to content in *A Study of Japan*, both of which include, adapt, and expand the glossary in *The Japanese Dictionary*.

These compilers attributed the Ningbo incident to Chinese ignorance of the Japanese language. In his preface to *A Survey of Japan*, Xue Jun clearly states:

> Japan is one kind of eastern barbarian. The seas separate them from China. Its customs and culture are ugly. Therefore, they are unimportant. [But] Japan repeatedly betrays; Japanese people are deft at deception. If we do not translate their language, it is impossible to know whether they will betray or submit. If we do not know facts, we cannot detect any falsehood in our intelligence. If we do not plan well, we will lose control of our frontiers.

> 日本乃東夷一種，遐隔大海，習俗妍醜，固不足為軒輊，第叛服不常，巧於用詭，語音不寄，則向背罔知，事體不諳，則情偽莫測。計禦不密，則邊陲失守。[12]

Xue Jun further relates that the two Japanese embassies reached Ningbo and then "mocked and laughed at each other" 互相詆笑. The conflict between them soon brought disaster to the local people: "Had such havoc not been anticipated, they would have eliminated Ningbo" 籍使不蚤為之計，寧波幾為所屠矣.[13]

Based on Xue Jun's *Japanese Dictionary*, Zheng Shungong's *A Mirror of Japan* rationalizes similarly about Xue's compilation of the dictionary, though it seems Zheng's own bilingual glossaries are more accurate in terms of Japanese scripts:

> When the two factions of the Japanese envoys fought with each other, a scholar named Xue Jun from Ningbo compiled *A Survey of Japan*. *The Japanese Dictionary* is in the book which classifies Japanese vocabulary into fifteen categories and collects more than 300 words. I speculate that at that time, he did not know Japanese scripts

---

12. Hamada Atsushi, *Nihon kigo no kenkyu* 日本寄語の研究 (Kyoto: Kyoto Daigaku Bungakubu, 1965), 5.

13. Xue Jun 薛俊, *Riben guo kaolue yijuan buyi yijuan* 日本國考略一卷補遺一卷, in *Siku quanshu cunmu congshu* 四庫全書存目叢書 (Jinan: Qilu shushe, 1996), vol. 255, 276.

and only roughly knew Japanese sound. It is inevitable that he made mistakes. Now the Japanese bandits are inextinguishable, their sparrow-like tongue is hard to understand. Our soldiers and generals make mistakes in communicating with them.

日本國兩起貢使警殺之時，鄞有上舍薛俊者，作為考畧，於中寄語分聚一十五類，三百餘條。推原當時未知倭字，彷彿倭音，不免有訛。抑今賊寇東滅西生，鴃舌莫辯，兵有誤聽，將有誤。[14]

Zheng also reveals that the Japanese found that Chinese interpreters "only roughly knew Japanese speech and were not skilled at Japanese scripts; therefore, they could not thoroughly comprehend them" 通事粗通倭音，不精譯字，故不儘識其說.[15]

Eighteenth-century readers of the sixteenth-century geographical treatises on Japan understood their authors to be exercising the Neo-Confucian discourse of practical learning. The writer of the epilogue to *The Edited Collection of Maps of Japan* compares the work's author, Zheng Ruozeng to Wang Yangming who applied the Confucian principle of investigation to his military administration in quelling the rebellion of the Ming prince Zhu Chenhao 朱宸濠 (d. 1521):

In the past, the Neo-Confucian sage Wang Yangming brought the riot of Chenhao to peace. He was then given the title of *xijue* [duke]. His name has been known to posterity. Our *Canjun* used to travel with him and discourse on the Confucian *li* with his peers. The world called him Master [Zheng] Kaiyang. In the *renzi* year of the Jiajing reign [1552], the Japanese island pirates spread venom into the southeast. Master Kaiyang introduced his military strategies and exterminated the enemies. His achievements were no smaller than Wang Yangming's. . . . We have never had books and pictures on Japan, except *A Survey of Japan*. But we do not have evidences to eliminate errors and rumors. Our minister obtained a secret map from Nan'ao. He broadly collected various opinions and composed this cartographical treatise.

昔陽明王先生以理學矩儒平宸豪之亂，誓封錫爵，名垂不朽。先參軍公嘗從之遊，與師門諸同志闡明理奧，世稱開陽先生。嘉靖

14. Ōtomo Shin'ichi, *Nihon ikkan*, vol. 5: 6.
15. Ōtomo Shin'ichi, *Nihon ikkan*, vol. 5: 7.

王子，日本島寇，流毒東南，出其方略，殲滅無遺，功不在陽明先
生下。...日本向無圖籍，止有考畧一書，殲訛無徵，參軍公得南
澳秘圖，博採群說，著為圖論。[16]

The emphasis on empirical knowledge is manifested by the fact that Zheng Ruozeng diligently sought new information from unofficial channels such as purchasing the maps of Japan from a maritime merchant in Ningbo. Further, the study of Japanese language and geography is considered "erudite learning" (*boxue* 博學) or "broadly collected various opinions." Learning foreign languages, therefore, will not only broaden the learner's epistemological horizon but also strengthen Ming China's imperial identity through military defense.

The former envoy to Ryukyu, Chen Kan 陳侃 (b. 1507), also states the importance of knowing truth through investigation and learning foreign languages in his *Record of Diplomatic Missions to Ryukyu* (*Shi Liuqiu lu* 使 琉球錄, 1534).

> The accounts of Ryukyu in *The Comprehensive Compendium of Du*, *The Ocean of Collected Events*, *The Naked Creatures*, and *The Star Raft* are all not true. Why is it so? It is because Ryukyu people do not learn Sinitic scripts. Thus, they do not have historiography. Since the Chinese have never been there themselves, how could they know the truth? This is how accounts were made of falsehood based upon falsehood.... Therefore, I collected various accounts to revise them. This is based upon the concept of skepticism. Besides, given that barbarian speech and scripts are not known to Chinese, I have attached an appendix to the book.

《杜氏通典》、《集事淵海》、《贏蟲錄》、《星槎勝覽》等書，凡載琉
球事者，詢之百無一實。若此者，何也？蓋琉球不習漢字，原無
誌書，華人未嘗親至其地。胡自而得其真也？以訛傳訛，遂以為
誌何？以信今而傳後，故集羣書而訂正之。此《質異》之所以作
也。兼以夷語、夷字恐人不知，並附於後。[17]

Chen Kan advocates empiricism, "seeing is believing." He fetishizes Chinese characters, associating scripts with truth and historical reality. But he

---

16. Zheng Ruozeng 鄭若曾, *Riben tuzuan* 日本圖纂, in Hamada Atsushi, *Nihon kigo no kenkyu*, 65.

17. Chen Kan 陳侃, *Shi Liuqiu lu* 使琉球錄 (Beijing: Zhonghua shuju, 1985).

also sees the necessity of knowing foreign languages, because this is how he is able to "interview" (*xun* 詢) native people and know facts.

The Chinese scholar-officials' compilation of Chinese-Japanese dictionaries constituted an early phase of the Neo-Confucian discourse of philology, phonology, and evidential scholarship that culminated in the eighteenth century. Benjamin Elman has pointed out a trend in phonological studies of ancient texts emerging in the Lower Yangzi in the seventeenth century. The pioneer of evidential scholarship (*kaozheng* 考證), Gu Yanwu 顧炎武 (1613–1682), proposed to study ancient rhymes, phonological changes, and glosses. Gu Yanwu believed that he could restore the classical world order by studying the way Confucius spoke in the classics.[18] Philologists and evidential scholars like Huang Zongxi 黃宗羲 (1610–1695) and Gu Yanwu studied military geographical treatises, mathematics, and astronomy, emphasizing experiential knowledge and empiricism (*shixue* 實學). Elman observes that evidential scholarship reflected "a heightened awareness of the irregularities and incongruities of the natural world" in the Qing dynasty.[19] This chapter proposes that this intellectual trend can be pushed back earlier to the sixteenth century in the coastal Zhejiang region. Local scholar-officials' compilation of military geographical treatises, bilingual glossaries, and translations of *waka* poetry evince an early philological and phonological scholarly trend.

Transcribing Japanese Sounds in Wu Dialect

A Survey of Japan, *A Mirror of Japan*, and *The Geography and Customs of Japan* all contain bilingual glossaries. These are the earliest and most comprehensive Sino-Japanese dictionaries. The Japanese words in hiragana are transliterated in Chinese scripts pronounced not in Mandarin but rather in Wu dialect. Using dialect phonology to transcribe foreign sounds is typical in the Chinese corpus of systematic transcriptional materials of foreign languages such as Tibetan and Uyghur. Historical linguists have long followed the convention of using the Chinese transcriptions of Buddhist terms in Sanskrit and Indian languages to reconstruct early Chinese dialectal varieties of Chinese spoken languages. Daniel Boucher notes that

---

18. Benjamin Elman, *From Philosophy to Philology: Intellectual and Social Aspects of Change in Late Imperial China* (Cambridge, MA: Council on East Asia Studies, 1984), 254; 32–33.

19. Elman, *From Philosophy to Philology*, 90–91.

in the process of reconstruction, linguists should also consider the complicated regional history of Indian Buddhist texts.[20] The 'Phags-pa script, an alphabet designed in 1269 for Kublai Khan by the Tibetan monk and state preceptor Drogön Chögyal Phagpa, transcribes the Chinese southern sound system.[21] The three Sino-Japanese dictionaries similarly become linguistic materials for studying pronunciations of Japanese and Chinese.

A Survey of Japan (1523) contains fifteen categories of vocabulary: astronomy, seasons, geography, directions, treasure, people, actions, body, utensils, clothes, food, plants, animals, numbers, and general words. *A Mirror of Japan* (1566) also has the fifteen categories but replaces *A Survey of Japan*'s "directions" and "actions" with "literature and history" and

TABLE 1: Sample Terms Selected from the Three Travelogues

Term	*A Survey of Japan* (1523) 357 words	*A Mirror of Japan* (1566) 3,404 words	*The Geography and Customs of Japan* (1592) 1,114 words
天	天帝 (tiandi; tiendi)	梭剌 ソラ (suola, su[bis]lha) 押邁 アマ (yamai, ngame)	同音又所賴 (suola; sulha)
子	莫宿哥 ムスコ	課 コ	莫宿哥 ムスコ
丈夫	壽山 (shoushan; zeu/ziu san)	[夫] 阿烏大 ヲウト (aniaoda; adieudou) 阿大課 ヲトコ (adake; adaku)	禿那俄 (tuna'e; tuna'e [tones differ])
倭		歪 ワ	
九	个个乃子 ココナツ (gegenaizi; gigignazi)	課課奈滋 ココナツ (kekenaizi; kukugnazi)	姑 (gu; gu)
夜	搖落 ヨル (yaoluo; yaulo)	欲路 ヨル (yulu; yuelo)	搖落
回來	慢慢的阿耶里 モドツテオヤレ (manmande'ayeni; manmangegnayeni)		慢慢的耶俚

---

20. Daniel Boucher, "Gandhari and the Early Chinese Buddhist Translations Reconsidered," *Journal of the American Oriental Society* 118, no. 4 (1998): 417–506.

21. W. South Colin, *A Handbook of Phags-pa Chinese*, ABC Chinese Dictionary Series (Honolulu: University of Hawai'i Press, 2007), xiv.

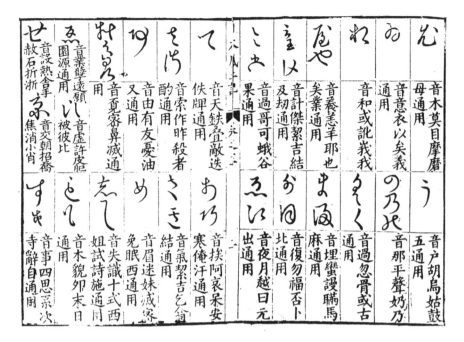

Figure 8. A chart of hiragana with phonetic annotations in Chinese scripts, from Hou Jigao 候繼高, *Zensetsu heisei ko Nihon fudoki* 日本風土記 (Kyoto: Kyoto University, 1961), 38.

"sound and color." *A Survey of Japan* has 364 words. *A Mirror*'s number of words is a dramatically increased 3,404. *The Geography and Customs of Japan* (1592) contains 1,114 words sorted by an extensive system with fifty-three categories.[22] It also usefully provides hiragana in handwriting style to accompany each word.

The dictionaries at times differ in the pronunciations they give for the same Japanese lexicons. Here, I compare the pronunciations of ten sample words (see Table 1).

The compilers' accents influence the Chinese transcriptions. *A Mirror of Japan* adopts Wu dialect, rather than Mandarin, to transcribe the Japanese words. Consequently, for the Japanese word 子 (child), there is con-

---

22. The added categories include days and nights, months, dates, days, five phases, heavenly branches, earthly branches, fire and coal, cities and towns, countries and states, rulers and subjects, officials and servants, solders and people, teaching and professions, craftsmanship, outcasts, disabled, relatives, greetings, bedding, silk and cloth, colors, grains, cooking, mathematics, toilette, farming tools, ships, vegetables, wild grass, spices, medicine, and fruits.

siderable difference in the pronunciation of 課 (Mandarin kè; Wu dialect, kū), which the compiler uses to designate the Japanese pronunciation ko (コ). He also notes that the use of the character 搖 (yao; yau) to designate ヨ (yo) is mistaken and uses 欲 (yu; yue) instead. Further, tones make a difference. Mandarin Chinese tones sound sharper and stronger, whereas the tones in Wu dialect are softer and less distinctive. In *A Study of Sino-Japan Trade* (*Huayi tongshang kao* 華夷通商考, 1695), Nishikawa Joken 西川如見 (1648–1724) notes that Beijing and Nanjing lingua franca sound similar, but differ in tonal strength, and that the Nanjing pronunciation system was the most common in China and influential to Japanese pronunciation.[23] However, not every Chinese transcription of the Japanese lexicon can be reconstructed. For instance, in consultation with a Japanese-Portuguese dictionary published between 1603 and 1604 in Nagasaki, Hamada Atsushi notes that the Sinitic scripts 慢慢的 in 慢慢的阿耶里 is indecipherable. This might be a mistaken form of 慢陀的 or モドツテ.[24] It also remains unclear why the original Japanese pronunciation of 壽山 designates 丈夫.

To help its Chinese readers to understand Japanese pronunciation, *The Geography and Customs of Japan* further includes the "Song of Proper Pronunciation" to describe different character groups' similar utterances that correspond to each Japanese hiragana. The song reads as follows:

切音正舌歌	The Song of Proper Pronunciation
俗曰鄉音處處別	It is customary that hometown accents differ everywhere.
古聖先賢難校切	Ancient sages can hardly change and correct the accent.
挨哀界蓋總依稀	It is always hard to differentiate *āi* and *āi*, *jiè* and *gài*.
耶陽養也通彷彿	It seems *yē*, *yáng*, *yǎng*, *yě* all sound the same.
鐵天疊敵語非殊	*Tiě*, *tiān*, *dié*, *dí*, they do not sound different.

23. Zhang Shenyu 張昇余, *Riben tangyin yu Ming Qing guanhua de yanjiu* 日本唐音與明清官話研究 (Xi'an: Shijie tushu chuban gongsi, 1998), 54.
24. Hamada Atsushi, *Nihon kigo no kenkyu*, 110.

地席帝齊音似鴉	*Dì, xí, dì, qí*, they similarly sound like a crow cawing.
路而落賴懶蹉跎	*Lù, ér, lùo, lài*, one cares least to differentiate them.
他拖陀篤多無隔	*Tā, tuō, tuó, dǔ*, they sound alike.
革各客骨開口音	*Gé, gè, kè, gǔ*, they all have mouth-opening vowels.
多和打里言難撇	*Duō, hé, dǎ, lǐ*, the pronunciation is hard to differentiate.
活法拔尾宜啓唇	*Huó, fǎ, bá, wěi*, it is best to open your lips.
擺排白敗齒微合	*Bǎi, pái, bái, bài*, slightly close your teeth.
氣吉結計總難分	*Qì, jí, jié, jí*, hard to differentiate them.
所索達答休辨出	*Suǒ, suǒ, dá, dá*: hard to tell the difference.
搖邀要耀不差池	*Yáo, yāo, yào, yào*: same pronunciation.
淡淡旦帶無可釋	*Dàn, dàn, dàn, dài*: hard to explain.
脉蠻埋買沒清渾	*Mài, mán, mái, mǎi*: no difference in consonance.
粘牙帶齒何清白	Sticky and dragging teeth, where is the pure and clear sound?
若然認字怪呼音	If one utters a strange sound when reading a script,
十有五分他未識	Likely he does not know the character.
對答要句與徐徐	If one can slow down the speed of the conversation,
自然音正無差迭[25]	Naturally, one's pronunciation will be corrected.

The compiler Hou Jigao annotates: "I ordered him to write in Japanese cursive writing to show the vocal accuracy of the transcriptions" 令書其本國草書以見音語確也. The "him" presumably refers to the bilingual Japanese speaker and writer who helps Hou Jigao to compile the book.

---

25. Hou Jigao, *Zensetsu*, 59.

TABLE 2: A Transliteration Table for the "Song of Proper Pronunciation"

Characters	Wu dialect (huangyan)*	Mandarin	Possible corresponding Japanese hiragana
挨,哀,界,蓋	nian, ai, ga, gall	āi, āi, jiè, gài	あ　か
耶,陽,養,也	ye, yang, yang, ya	yē, yáng, yǎng, yě	や
鐵,天,疊,敵	tie, tie, dia, die	tiě, tiān, dié, dí	て
地,席,帝,齊	dii, xih, dii, xi	dì, xí, dì, qí	ち
路,而,落,賴	lou, er, lo, la	lù, ér, luò, lài	ろ　ら
他,拖,陀,篤	Gie, tou, dou, do	tā, tuō, tuó, dǔ	と
革,各,客,骨	ge, gei, ke, guo	gé, gè, kè, gǔ	が　こ　く
多,和,打,里	Dou, hu, dang, li	duō, hé, dǎ, lǐ	お　た　り
活,法,拔,尾	huo, fa, ba, mi	*Huó, fǎ, bá, wěi*	は
擺,排,白,敗	Ba, ba, be, ba	*Bǎi, pái, bái, bài*	ば
氣,吉,結,計	qi, jie, jie, ji	*Qì, jí, jié, jì*	き
所,索,達,答	Su, suo, da, da	*Suǒ, suǒ, dá, dá*	す
搖,邀,要,耀	yao, yao, yao, yao	*Yáo, yāo, yào, yào*	よ
淡,淡,旦,帶	dan, dan, dan, da	*Dàn, dàn, dàn, dài*	だん
脉,蠻,埋,買	ma, mai, ma, ma	*Mài, mán, mái, mǎi*	ま

*For a study of Huangyan dialect, see Chen Liyao 陳理堯, *Huangyan fangyan yuyin yufa chutan* 黃岩方言語音語法初探 (Beijing: Zhongguo wenshi chubanshe, 2017).

This pronunciation song serves as a phonetic orthography to help Chinese readers with different accents to understand Japanese hiragana pronunciation by classifying Chinese characters with similar utterance in a Wu dialect. The song classifies a group of Chinese characters with approximate pronunciations to designate the same Japanese hiragana (table 2).

This chart shows some inconsistent transcriptions. These characters do not differentiate nasal sounds from non-nasal sounds. For example, the graph 賴 is used to designate ら, whereas it is classified together with 落, which designates ろ. Similarly, 革 signifies が, whereas 骨 transcribes both こ and く.

This Chinese phonetic orthography song mirrors the Japanese-annotated Chinese-language textbooks that circulated in premodern Japan. The pronunciation of Japanese kanji can be roughly differentiated as ごおん (Go'on 吳音), かんおん (Kan'on 漢音), and とうおん (Tōon 唐音). Chinese translators (*Tang tongshi* 唐通事) in Nagasaki used to annotate Chinese in the Chinese-language textbooks with Tōon. Dialects were also crucial for the practice of translation and interpretation. Chinese translators in Japan had to learn Nanjing and Zhangzhou dialects from the time they were children. They held meetings to practice conversations in Fuzhou dialect, Zhangzhou dialect, and Nanjing dialect.[26] Such phonological and philological practice among the Chinese translators in Japan has been recorded:

> Sinophone translation was the most difficult discipline. Children must learn to speak local dialects, to chant classics, history, and poetry, to examine the four tones and all types of rhymes. If they speak one script or one word that does not match the original pronunciation, then their speech is vulgar and incomprehensible. Therefore, the descendants of the translators' lineages aim to study academic writings.[27]

In Buddhist and Daoist ritualistic performances, chanting scriptures in Sanskrit, for instance, requires accurate transliterations of Sanskrit. Incorrect pronunciation was believed to reduce the sutras' efficacy.[28] Because Sanskrit sounds might not have a corresponding sound in Chinese characters, many Chinese characters are used to introduce and convey foreign sounds. For instance, the Buddhist term *sheli* 闍梨 means *guifan shi* 軌範師 or *zhenghang* 正行, an honorific address to a respected monk or teacher. The sound of the character 闍 corresponds to the exotic sound "cha" in the original Sanskrit word acarya. It has been suggested that this word was chosen because of its rareness, so that it could prevent readers from spontaneously perceiving the conventional meaning of a familiar word.

Phonetic orthography in *The Geography and Customs of Japan* further stresses the accuracy of pronunciation by recognizing the varieties of Chinese accents. As to the fact that all three Sino-Japanese dictionaries adopt Wu dialect to transcribe Japanese sound, we can reason that, first, they may be intended for the southeast coastal people who spoke the language, and second, this may be a natural choice. The dialect as the mother tongue

---

26. Xie Yuxin 謝育新, *Riben jinshi tangyin: yu shiba shiji Hangzhou hua he Nanjing guanhua duibi yanjiu* 日本近世唐音：與十八世紀杭州話和南京官話對比研究 (Beijing: zhongguo chuanmei daxue chuban she, 2016), 5.

27. Xie Yuxin, *Riben jinshi tangyin*, 5.

28. Joshua Capitanio, "Sanskrit and Pseudo-Sanskrit Incantations in Daoist Ritual Texts," *History of Religions* 57, no. 4 (May 2018): 348–405.

and constant and stable source of pronunciation system comes naturally to the transcriber. A standardized spoken Mandarin did not yet exist. Nonetheless, this phonetic orthography rehearses modern-day language reform movements. Linguist Zhou Youguang 周有光 (1906–2017) invented pinyin as romanization of Chinese scripts to standardize Chinese pronunciation.[29]

In the twentieth century, the complex tensions between dialects and national language under the People's Republic of China were manifested in the promotion of Mandarin in schools, the cultural prestige of Cantonese and Wu dialects, and the minimal representation of hundreds of dialects and minority languages in China. In the seventeenth century, however, dialects were the only phonological means one adopted to annotate foreign languages. The precursor of modern national language is classical Chinese—the "sages' words." In this seventeenth-century linguistic hierarchy, the so-called "inferior" vernacular Chinese corresponds to foreign tongues. Nonetheless, vernacular speech, just as a foreign tongue, can demonstrate the speaker's genuineness and sincerity. Xue Jun in *A Survey of Japan* says,

> Gentlemen dare not to speak any words except the sages' words. Dialects are indeed not worth bothering one's lips and teeth. Nonetheless, speech is the voice of the heart, and if you understand their speech, you will be able to see through to the sincerity or falsehood of their hearts. Thus, I have compiled common expressions, emulated their pronunciations, categorized and translated them. This may help our soldiers with listening and understanding the foreign tongue. This is also one method of defense. These rudimentary writings do not have any profound meaning. Readers do not have to explain them.[30]

> 士君子非先王之法言不敢言，而方言固不足煩唇齒。言者，心之聲得其言或可以察其心之誠與偽，故特寄其常所接談字，仿佛音響，而分繫之。似以資衛邊將士之聽聞，亦防禦之一端也。初無義理，觀者不必字為之釋。[31]

---

29. Zhou Youguang 周有光, *Zhongguo yuwen de shidai yanjin* 中國語文的時代演進 (Columbus, Ohio: National East Asian Languages Resource Center, Ohio State University, 2012).

30. Translation modified based upon the translation of Joshua A. Fogel, "Chinese Understanding of the Japanese Language," in *Sagacious Monks and Bloodthirsty Warriors: Chinese Views of Japan in the Ming-Qing Period* (Norwalk, CT: East Bridge, 2002), 69.

31. Hamada Atsushi, *Nihon kigo no kenkyu*, 5.

The astute attention to the genuineness of vernacular speech and dialects corresponds to the late Ming literatus Feng Menglong's advocacy of Wu-dialect mountain songs. In the preface to *Mountain Songs* (*shange* 山歌), he writes:

> Moreover, having come to the end of the world, there is much false verse and prose, but false mountain songs do not exist. The mountain songs do not compete with poetry; there is no falsehood in them. As there is no falsehood, we can preserve the genuine by collecting mountain songs. Incidentally, when we see that the songs noted by ancient officials (songs from the *Shijing*) were like that and that songs sung by contemporary common people are like that; mountain songs can be used as materials for understanding the world. If I borrow the true feeling of men and women and am able to uncover the falsehoods of Confucianism, the effect will be the same as that of *Hanging Branches*. Thus, I publish *Mountain Songs* after publishing *Hanging Branches*.[32]

且今雖季世，而但有假詩文，無假山歌。則以山歌不與詩文爭名，故不屑假。苟其不屑假，而吾藉以存真，不亦可乎？抑今人想見上古之陳於太史者為彼，而近代之留於民間者如此，倘亦論世之林雲爾。若夫借男女之真情，發名教之偽藥，其功於《掛枝兒》等，故錄《掛枝詞》而次及《山歌》。

The feeling of genuineness is manifested as much as through the songs' rhymes and lyrics as through dialects.

Shu-mei Shih points out that Han Chinese communities overseas were also Sinitic language communities who spoke Mandarin, Cantonese, Fukienese, Hakka, and Teochiu, among other dialects.[33] Jing Tsu further proposes the notion of "literary governance" to summarize how modern intellectuals' efforts at standardization, orthography, and the technology of writing aimed for global access to power.[34] The premodern use of dialects as a means of phonetic annotation was an integral part of the long history of translation and transcription in East Asia. The late Ming astute awareness of phonetic orthography and varieties of Chinese dialectic pronunciations in

---

32. Translation from Oki Yasushi and Paolo Santangelo, *Shan'ge, the Mountain Songs: Love Songs in Ming* (Leiden: Brill, 2011), 5.

33. Shu-mei Shih, "Introduction," *Sinophone Studies*, 1–15.

34. Jing Tsu, *Sound and Script in Chinese Diaspora* (Cambridge, MA: Harvard University Press, 2010), 2.

the wake of the importance of learning Japanese language anticipated the modern discourse of Chinese national languages and dialects.

Translation and Transcription of *Waka*

The Geography and Customs of Japan includes thirty-nine handwritten *waka* poems carefully transcribed, analyzed, and translated into Chinese. Hou Jigao studies the pronunciation of the Japanese kanji, introduces two grammatical concepts—*zhuyu* 助語 and *zhengyin* 正音—and translates the *waka* into Chinese verses.

It can be concluded that when transcribing the *waka*, the compiler copied down Japanese poems without any direct understanding of the texts—he garbled parts of them. He then transcribed syllable-by-syllable readings and provided translations, presumably based on oral recitation by a native Japanese (accompanied by an interpreter) or a bilingual individual.[35] For example, the text in the complete register is a typical classical *waka* titled "Pine Wind Awakens Me from Sleep" 松風攪睡. Its Japanese scripts and romanization are as follows:

よもすがら	*yomosugara*
おもひたりけり	*omoitarikeri*
我心	*wagakokoro*
松ふく風に	*matsu fuku kaze ni*
おとろかされて	*odorokasarete*

The English translation is: "All night I was lost in thoughts of love, my mind awakened by the wind blowing in the pines." This poem might come from a Heian or medieval *waka* anthology.

The *huyin* 呼音 (pronunciation) section transcribes the *man'yōgana* 万葉仮名, the origin of *kana*, into Chinese. The *dufa* 讀法 (transcription) section presents a complete syllable-by-syllable transcription. The *shiyin* 釋音 (explaining the sound) section is a mix of accurate and inaccurate explanations of the meanings of the Japanese words, but the *qieyi* 切意 (translation) section is more a Chinese reinvention of the poem.

It is apparent that these transcriptions must be pronounced in either Jiangsu or Zhejiang dialect. Mandarin Chinese, or *guanhua* 官話, would

---

35. Translation is always a team collaboration, whether in premodern or modern times. For early translation of Buddhist scriptures into Chinese, see Victor H. Mair, "Buddhism and the Rise of Written Vernacular in East Asia," 707–51, 716.

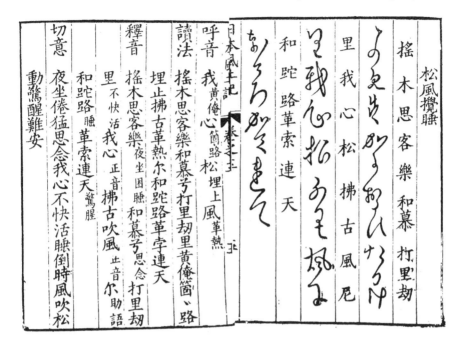

Figure 9. A waka poem titled "Pine Wind Awakens Me from Sleep," from Hou Jigao, *Zensetsu*, 39.

sound both harsher and inaccurate to the original Japanese sound. If we transliterate the poem according to Zhao Yuanren's 趙元任 "common Wu dialect" romanization system based upon a local dialect in the Taizhou region, where piracy problems were most severe during the Ming,[36] then the transcription is as follows on the left. On the right is the Mandarin pronunciation's *pinyin* romanization for comparison.

搖木思客樂	*Yiau mu si ke la*	*Yáo mù sī kè lè*
和慕亦打里劫里	*Hu mu yi dang li jie li*	*Hé mù yì dǎ lǐ jié lǐ*
黃俺箇箇路	*Wang ye die die lou*	*Huáng ǎn gè gè lù*
埋止拂古革熱尔	*Ma zi fe gu ge nie er*	*Mái zhǐ fú gǔ gé rè ěr*
和跎路革索連天	*Wu du lu ge so lie tien*	*Hé túo lù gé sǔo lián tiān*

---

36. Zhao Yuanren 趙元任, *Xiandai wuyu yanjiu* 現代吳語研究 (Shanghai: kexue chuban she, 1956).

Below is the Chinese translation of the *waka*.

夜坐倦	At night, I sat in weariness.
猛思念	Suddenly, I thought of him/her.
我心不快活	I was unhappy at heart.
睡倒時	When I was asleep,
風吹松動	Wind blew through the waving pines.
驚醒難安	Awakened, I was stirred.

The poem maintains a structure similar to the *waka*: the first three lines as the upper verse, and the last three lines as the lower verse. The language is highly vernacular, demonstrated especially by such words as *meng* 猛 (suddenly) and *shuidaoshi* 睡倒時 (fall asleep). This may suggest that the translation, similar to the earliest type of translation on Buddhist scriptures, was done orally through interpretation.[37] This vernacular translation brings out an emotional moment of disturbance that, however, is a bit too strong for the subtle emotional sensibility in the original poem.

Another *waka* titled "Picking Flowers in the Springfield" 春野採花 from the *Kokin wakashū* 古今和歌集, reads as follows:

君 がため	*kimi ga tame*
春の野に出でて	*haru no no ni idete*
若菜つむ	*wakana tsumu*
わが衣手に	*waga koromode ni*
雪はふりつつ	*yuki wa furi tsutsu*

The English translation is "For you, I walked the fields in spring. Gathering green herbs, while my garment's hanging sleeves are speckled with falling snow." The poem's Chinese transcription, *Wu* dialect romanization, and *pinyin* romanization are as follows:

吉密革答密	*Jih mieh ge dah mieh*	*Jí mì gé dá mì*
發而那那尼一迭	*Fa er na na ni yii die*	*Fā ěr nà nà ní yī dié*
法乃和多而	*Fa nai yu du er*	*Fǎ nǎi hé duō ěr*

---

37. Victor H. Mair, "Buddhism and the Rise of Written Vernacular in East Asia," 707–51.

黃俺遇路木鐵外	*huang ye yu lou muh tieh way*	*Huáng ǎn yù lù mù tiě wài*
挨迷尼奴里子子	*ai mi nii no lii tzyh tzyh*	*Āi mí ní nú lǐ zǐ zǐ*

In this transliteration, the Japanese *kanji* 君 (きみ) is transcribed as 吉密 (*Jih mieh; jimi*)，春 (はる) as 發而 (*fa'er*), 野 (の) as 那尼 (*nani*), 花 (はな) as 法 (*fa*), 出 (いでる) as 一迷 (*yii die; yi die*), 我 (われ) as 黃俺 (*huang ye; huang an*), 衣 (ころも) as 過路木 (*go lou muh; guolumu*), and 雨 (あめ) as 挨迷 (*aimi*). The author explains that these words are all *zhengyin* 正音 (*seion*), by which he probably means that these *kanji* have different Japanese pronunciations. Since the author transcribes 出 as 一迷 (いで) without referring to its other forms including the dictionary form, we can deduce that the author has not paid enough attention to the conjugation of Japanese verbs. In terms of pronunciation, we can detect its errors in its misprinting of 過路木 as 遇路木, mis-transcribing 野 (の) as (nani) 那 尼 by mistakenly identifying the adverb に as part of the pronunciation of 野 (の), and incorrectly transcribes に as (way/wai 外), and other similar mistakes.

The Chinese poem paraphrased from the Japanese is as follows:

春野為君出，	Going out to the spring field for you,
纔把花枝折。	I just bended a blossoming twig.
採花遇春雨，	Picking flowers in spring rain,
我手衣袖濕。	My hands and sleeves were all wet.

In the Chinese poem, which follows the pentasyllable form, the image of flowers replaces the *waka*'s "green herbs" (*wakana*), and rain substitutes for snow (*yuki*). Spring rain rather than spring snow better fits the springtime climate of lower Yangzi River. Although many Chinese poems and folk songs describe picking tea leaves or herbs in spring rain, the translator still replaces "green herbs" with "flowers." This channels the romantic sentiment commonly seen in Chinese folk songs familiar to the Chinese reader. For example, in Feng Menglong's *Mountain Songs*, a ditty named "Picking Flowers" (*caihua* 採花) reads:

隔河看見野花開，	The girl saw some wild flowers blooming across the river.
寄聲情哥郎聽我采朵來。	She asked her lover to pick one for her.
姐道郎呀，	She said to him:
你采子花來，	"Go fetch some blossoms,
小阿奴奴原捉花謝子你，	Your little slave would like to thank you for them.
決弗教郎白采來。[38]	She would not let you do it for nothing."

But the translated poem conveys emotional sensitivity unseen in most dynamic and straightforward Chinese folk songs and *waka*'s oral or vernacular feature is absent in most Chinese classical poetry. In this regard, the translated poem captures the essence of the original *waka* from *Kokin wakashū*. As Motoori Norinaga (本居宣長, 1730–1801) summarizes, *waka* poetry with its effort to use native Japanese language shows emotional sensibility to phenomena in the natural world and objects of poetic beauty.[39]

The Geography and Customs of Japan's *waka* collection is the earliest Chinese study of Japanese poems. It took almost three hundred years until such conscious Sino-Japanese translingual translation emerged again in the late nineteenth century. Liang Qichao published his translation of the Japanese author Tōkai Sanshi's 東海散士 (1883–1922) political novel *Kajin no kiguro* 佳人之奇遇 (*The Lady's Marvelous Encounter*) in 1898. The Chinese mainly used Japanese as a medium to assimilate Western modern concepts. The Chinese began to import numerous Japanese loanwords in the form of *kanji* (they appear in premodern Japanese, modern Japanese compounds that have no equivalent in classical Chinese phrases, or classical Chinese phrases adopted by Japanese to translate Western terms).[40] *The Geography and Customs of Japan*'s translation of *waka* with its attention to Japanese language itself anticipated the translation movements of the late nineteenth and early twentieth century.

---

38. Feng Menglong 馮夢龍, *Shange* 山歌 (Shanghai: Zhonghua shuju, 1962), vol. 2: 8.

39. Haruo Shirane, "Eighteenth-Century Waka and Nativist Study," *Early Modern Japanese Literature: An Anthology, 1600–1900* (New York: Columbia University Press, 2002), 599–630.

40. Lydia Liu, *Translingual Practice: Literature, National Culture, and Translated Modernity—China, 1900–1937* (Stanford: Stanford University Press, 1995), 32–34.

CHAPTER FOUR

Turning Pirates

There are only three pirates who feature in late Ming Chinese vernacular stories. The first two are the valiant and dissolute Chinese pirate kings Wang Zhi and Xu Hai who appear in Zhou Qingyuan's *Second Collection of the West Lake*, Lu Renlong's *Model Words to Shape the World*, and Qingxin Cairen's *The Romance of Jin, Yun, and Qiao*. The third pirate is Old Eight Yang (Yang Balao 楊八老), the miserable Chinese merchant and captive who is forced to turn into a Japanese pirate in Feng Menglong's short story "Old Eight Yang's Strange Encounter in the Country of Yue" (hereafter "Strange Encounter"), included in his first short story collection *Stories Old and New*.

The two types of pirates—Chinese pirate kings and Chinese captives turned Japanese pirates—highlight different aspects of the term *wokou*, which could signify Japanese of the archipelago's western rim and Satsuma, Chinese smuggler lords, unlicensed maritime merchants, captives, slaves, and even overseas Chinese.[1] This chapter discusses the story of Old Eight Yang and how it illuminates Japanese racial and ethnic differences and the fluid boundary between captives, slaves, pirates, traders, and migrants in a rapidly evolving maritime world. Chapters 5 and 6 discuss stories of the pirate kings.

Pirates as Japanese, Japanese as Pirates

"Strange Encounter" caters to contemporary anxiety over pirates, Japanese people, and Japanese language, piqued by the presence of maritime

---

1. Peter D. Shapinsky, "Envoys and Escorts," 40–41. Also see *The Cambridge History of Japan*, vol. 4, *Early Modern Japan*, eds. John W. Hall et al. (Cambridge: Cambridge University Press, 1991), 235–300.

renegades on China's eastern seas. This Chinese fear of Japanese maritime power is comparable to the early modern English fear of "turning Turk" as manifested in Shakespeare's *Othello*. Following Stephen Greenblatt's positioning of Shakespearean drama in the historical context of an emerging colonialism triggered by Columbus's cross-Atlantic voyage to the Americas, scholars have started historicist study of early modern dramas through a global lens. By the beginning of the seventeenth century, "Turkish" privateers operated in the Mediterranean and the northeastern Atlantic to develop trade. They captured and enslaved British subjects and forced them to convert to Islam from Christianity.[2] Reflecting this transnational maritime history, the "Moor of Venice" in *Othello* embodies English fascination and fear of sexually jealous and physically violent Turks, depicted with dark skin and thick lips.[3] Written in the same time period, "Strange Encounter" tells a Chinese man's enslavement by Japanese pirates. It is a Chinese racial and ethnic fantasy of Japanese pirates.

"Strange Encounter" expresses late Ming Chinese anxieties about Japanese pirate aggression in a transnational world of cultural, social, and racial instability. In stark contrast to the pivotal importance of religious conversion in English narratives, "Strange Encounter" emphasizes the signification of learning Japanese language and customs in the Chinese narrative of "turning *wonu*" 倭奴 (Japanese dwarf slave). Old Eight Yang, a petty merchant from Zhouzhi 盩厔 County in Shaanxi Prefecture, travels to Fujian, Guangdong, and Guangxi to trade, leaving behind his wife and six-year-old son. After he settles down in Zhangpu 漳浦 and takes one more wife there, he hopes to travel back to his hometown to see his family. When he passes by Tingzhou 汀州 of Fujian, he is abducted by Japanese pirates and transported to Japan, where he is forced to shave his hair, bare his feet, and learn how to use a Japanese sword and fight in a Japanese manner. After a year and a half, he adapts to the environment of Japan and grasps the Japanese language. "Then, he is indeed no different from a true Japanese" (*yu zhenwo wuyi* 與真倭無異), the narrator explains.[4]

---

2. See Daniel J. Vitkus, "Turning Turk in *Othello*: The Conversion and the Damnation of the Moor," *Shakespeare Quarterly* 48, no. 2 (Summer 1997): 145–76; Sir Godfrey Fisher, *Barbary Legend: War, Trade, and Piracy in North Africa 1415–1830* (Oxford: Clarendon Press, 1957).

3. See Ania Loomba, "*Othello* and the Racial Question," in *Shakespeare, Race, and Colonialism*, 91–111.

4. Feng Menglong 馮夢龍, "Yang Balao yueguo qifeng," 楊八老越國奇逢 in *Yushi mingyan* 喻世明言 (Beijing: Zhonghua shuju, 2014), 271; Shuhui Yang and Yunqin Yang, trans., "Yang Balao's Extraordinary Family Reunion," in *Stories Old and New: A*

Figure 10. A Japanese pirate blowing a sea conch. From Qiu Ying's *Wokou tujuan*, stored at the Institute for Advanced Studies on Asia, Tokyo University. Reproduced with permission.

In describing the pirates who abduct Old Eight Yang, Feng Menglong associates Japanese language and people with the ocean: "With a wailing sound of a sea conch, a host of pirates, waving their katana swords, jumped out from goodness knows where and surrounded them" 把海匝 羅吹了一聲，吹得嗚嗚的響，四圍許多倭賊，一個個舞著長刀，跳躍 而來，正不知那里來的。[5] The wailing sound created by the conch shell, the onomatopoeia "wuwu," could be made to function as a honk to frighten the enemy. The conch shell also symbolizes a kind of mysterious sea body, the pirates' foreign speech, and their untraceable family background. In *The Painting Scroll of Japanese Pirates* (*Wokou tujuan* 倭寇圖 卷) attributed to the famous artist Qiu Ying 仇英 (1494–1552), one of the pirates holds a sea conch, signifying them as the opposite of the Chinese people based on land. In his southern *chuanqi* play, *Crying Phoenix* (*Mingfeng ji* 鳴鳳記), Wang Shizhen 王世貞 (1526–1590) describes the

Ming Dynasty Collection (Seattle: University of Washington Press, 2000), with modification, 308.

5. Shuhui Yang and Yunqin Yang, trans., "Yang Balao's Extraordinary Family Reunion," 207.

Japanese as amphibians: "bald-headed, barefooted, imitating frogs' croaking" 科頭跣足學蛙鳴.[6]

"Strange Encounter" goes further to argue that adopting foreign speech and customs has the power to produce visible physical differences. Old Eight Yang himself abhors his own Japanese appearance: "This entire body is an image of a *wonu*. Even when he looks at himself in the mirror, he will be surprised. How can other people recognize him" 此身全是倭奴形象，便是自家照著鏡子，也吃一惊，他人如何認得?[7] After he returns to China, his former servants, wives, and sons cannot recognize him.

In order to trace Japanese somatic and cultural differences in Chinese records, let us turn to the linguistic terms *wo* and *wonu* themselves. The earliest meaning of the graph 倭 is "small" or "bent." *Shuowen jiezi* 說文解字 (ca. 100 CE) informs us that "Wei (the graph) is a concordant appearance. [The graph] follows *ren* 'person' and takes '*wei*' 'bend' as phonetic. *Book of Songs* says, 'The roads of Zhou are winding'" 倭, 順兒。從人委聲。詩日周道倭遲. The first use of 倭 (*wo*) to designate Japanese people appears in the "Geography" section of *Han shu* 漢書 (the *Book of Han*) compiled by Ban Gu 班固 in 82 CE: "It is said that in the seas off Lelang are the *Wo* people; that they are divided into some one hundred kingdoms and at harvest time come to offer tribute and appear in audience [at court]" 雲樂浪海中有倭人，分為百餘國，以隨時來獻見雲.[8] When used to signify Japanese people, the graph 倭 is rendered with a sound (*wo* or *wa*) different from the earlier sound (*wei*).[9] Linguists have argued that such pronunciation difference could imply that *wo* and *wonu* could be phonetic loanwords of an early Altaic language used during the Yayoi 弥生 period (300 BCE–300 CE), resulting from the intermingling of migrants from Asian mainland with indigenous Jōmon 繩文 people.[10]

Old Eight Yang's visual transformation into a Japanese pirate resonates with Ming popular perception associating the Japanese with pirates. The view that Japanese are "by nature cunning and deceptive" was persistent in Ming historiography.[11] An account in the "Various Barbarians" (*zhuyi*

---

6. Wang Shizhen 王世貞, *Mingfeng ji* 鳴鳳記 (Shanghai: Zhonghua shuju, 1960), 62.

7. Yang and Yang, trans., "Yang Balao's Extraordinary Family Reunion," 316.

8. The term Lelang 樂浪 is itself a loanword, designating Goguryeo. For the citation, see Wang Yuansun 汪遠孫 ed., *Hanshu dili zhi jiaoben* 漢書地理志校本 (Zhengqi tangyuan, 1887), 2/43, 87.

9. Translation modified based upon Jonathan Smith's unpublished paper "Wo 倭."

10. Wang Yuansun ed., *Hanshu dili zhi jiaoben*, 2/37, 73.

11. For a study of Ming dynasty perceptions of the Japanese, see Wang Yong, "Realis-

men 諸夷門) section of the Ming everyday encyclopedia *Wuche bajin* 五車拔錦 records:

> The country of *Riben* is the country of *Wo*. It is in the midst of the ocean southeast of the country of *Xinluo {alt: Xinlao}*. On the oceanic islands spanning more than nine hundred *li*, the Japanese live along the coast and make a living by pirating. The Chinese call them *wokou*.

> 日本國即倭國。在新羅國東南大海中。依山島而居。九百餘里，專一沿海為寇生活中國呼為倭寇.[12]

The accompanying illustration shows a half-naked and half-bald man, a cloth wrapped around his waist. He has a protruding forehead and a big belly. He looks martial and menacing and carries a long sword over the shoulder.

The word *wo* became increasingly associated with buccaneers in the sixteenth and seventeenth centuries. Between 1504 and 1527, with the consent of the shogun, Japanese *ronin* (wanderers or drifters), joined by fishermen and bandits, pillaged cities and towns along the coasts of China, Korea, and Southeast Asia.[13] *The Painting Scroll of Battling Japanese* (*Kangwo tujuan* 抗倭圖卷) by an anonymous Ming artist highlights the images of Japanese as pirates. They are barefoot, half bald, and nearly nude. Some pirates are clothed in thigh-length robes with red bands tied around their waist; their legs are unclothed. Some pirates are nearly nude, wearing only underwear. They use bows, katana swords, and long spears as weapons.

The Painting Scroll of Japanese Pirates associates the marauders with the Japanese race in additional ways. These skillful mariners have a masculine and wild appearance. Two have darker skin than their peers; they are heavily bearded, and their bodies are covered in hair from head to toe.

---

tic and Fantastic Image of Dwarf Pirates: The Evolution of Ming Dynasty Perceptions of the Japanese," translated by Laura E. Hess, edited by Joshua A. Fogel, *Sagacious Monks and Bloodthirsty Warriors: Chinese Views of Japan in the Ming-Qing Period*, 17–41.

12. Xu Sanyou 徐三友, *Wuche bajin* 五車拔錦 (Beijing: Huaxia chuban she, 1999), 189–90.

13. Robert Antony, "Nanyang fengyun: huoyue zai haishang de haidao, yingxiong, shangren" 南洋風雲：活躍在海上的海盜、英雄、商人, ed., Li Qingxin 李慶新, *Haiyang shi yanjiu* 海洋史研究 (Beijing: shehui kexue wenxian chuban she, 2010), vol. 1, 153–70.

Figure 11. Japanese portrayed as pirates, in the Ming daily-used encyclopedia *Wuche bajin*, p. 189.

Frank Dikötter notes that the term *wonu* was an approximate transliteration of Ainu, the name of the indigenous Jōmon people of Hokkaido. Ainu people tend to have thick body hair, big beards, and baldness.[14] The pirates in the painting wear Japanese-style clothes with Japanese patterns and colors that unambiguously associate Japanese with pirates. The two figures wearing flamboyant red silk gowns are pirate chieftains.[15] But portraying

14. Frank Dikötter, *The Discourse of Race in Modern China* (Hong Kong: Hong Kong University Press, 1994), 106.
15. Robert Antony, *Like Froth*, 141.

Figure 12. Japanese pirates portrayed in *Kangwo tujuan*. Image from Harvard University. Reproduced with permission.

Japanese and pirates with Chinese imagination, the author of the painting was still unfamiliar with the extent of the cultural diversity of both Japanese people and "Japanese" pirates.[16]

Although pirates were imagined as Japanese, historically, the majority of pirates were in fact Chinese. Old Eight Yang's name may indeed allude to the Chinese pirates who wreaked havoc in coastal Fujian and Taiwan. A memorial submitted by Wang Zhichen 王之臣, minister of the Department of the Army, in 1627 (during the Tianqi 天啓 reign, 1621–1627) reveals that pirates always used pseudonyms such as Yang Number Six 楊六 and Yang Number Seven 楊七 to spread rumors in coastal Fujian where they pillaged.[17] Further, the well-known pirate leaders Lin Xinlao 林辛老 and Yang Number Six 楊六, who were highly active in early seventeenth century when "Strange Encounter" was published and circulated, led their

---

16. Zennosuke Tsuji 辻善之助, "wakowutokiki" 倭寇圖卷記, preface to *Wakowuzumaki* 倭寇図卷, The University of Tokyo.

17. "Binbu shangshu Wang Zhichen wei Zheng Zhilong" 兵部尚書王之臣為鄭芝龍進攻銅山中左官兵禦戰失敗事題行稿, from The Second National Historical Archival Collection (Di'er Lishi dang'an guan 第二歷史檔案館), Beijing.

Figure 13. Japanese race portrayed in *Wokou tujuan*.

pirate gangs to camp in Dongfan 東藩 in Taiwan and to pillage thousands of miles along coastal China. Old Eight Yang's name might have drawn inspiration from these legendary pirate leaders.

The majority of late Ming pirates were Chinese bandits and outcasts. Literatus Zheng Duanjian 鄭端簡 (1499–1566) from Haiyan 海鹽 in Zhejiang observed that "the pirate incident was caused by Chinese bandits. Officials who lost their jobs and scholars who could not get degrees through the increasingly competitive civil examination system joined the freebooters to become their spies and local guides" 倭奴之變，多由中國不逞之徒，如衣冠失職書生不得志者，投其中，為之奸細，為之鄉導觀.[18] These Chinese disavowed their original loyalties to society and the state by becoming outlaws, bandits, and pirates. Additionally, members of inland bandit gangs and sworn brothers maintained close ties with pirates and assisted them in raiding villages and markets.[19]

From Negative Perception to Scholarly Naming: Portraying Japanese in *The Pictures of Eastern Barbarians*, *A Survey of Japan*, and *The Geography and Customs of Japan*

In contrast to the popular representation of the Japanese as vile buccaneers, Cai Ruxian's 蔡汝賢 *The Pictures of Eastern Barbarians* (*Dongyi tuxiang* 東夷圖說, 1589) describes Japanese people's geography, customs, nature, knowledge of Chinese language, and their kings' bloodline and lineage. The graphic image included in the compendium features a Japanese man in Japanese-style attire and with a samurai hairstyle. In contrast to *Wuche bajin*, Cai Ruxian's language is more explicitly respectful of Japanese culture, and his ethnographical portrayal of Japanese is more extensive. But he nonetheless draws on a negative vision of Japanese shaped by the rampant piracy problem in coastal China. He specifically employs the rhetoric of comparison to represent the Japanese:

> In its customs, men shave their hair and bare their head, tattoo their faces and bodies. They tie their clothing horizontally without sewing them together. Women's clothes resemble quilts and blankets. They put on the garment by pulling it over their head. They paint

---

18. Cai Jiude, 采九德, *Wobian shilue* 倭變事略, in *Yanyi zhilin* 鹽邑志林 (Shanghai: Shangwu yinshu guan, 1937), vol. 29, 6.

19. Robert Antony, *Like Froth*, 135–36.

Figure 14. A Japanese image in Cai Ruxian's *Dongyi tushuo*.

their bodies in vermilion color. This resembles Chinese women applying powder on their face.

其俗男子魁頭斷髮，黥面紋身，裙襦橫結，不施縫綴。女人衣如單被，貫其首而穿之，以丹塗身為飾，如中國之敷粉也。[20]

For Cai Ruxian, rituals and customs, such as clothing, hairstyle, and cosmetics, are essential for defining a culture and a people. In comparing the sartorial and physical appearance of Japanese men and women with that of Chinese men and women, Cai Ruxian constructs a vision of Japanese

---

20. Cai Ruxian 蔡汝賢, *Dongyi tushuo* 東夷圖說, in *Siku quanshu cunmu congshu* 四庫全書存目叢書 (Jinan: Qilu shushe, 1996), vol. 255, 429.

culture at odds with Chinese culture whose everyday ritual practices are prescribed by *The Book of Rites* (*Li ji* 禮記). The Confucian text stipulates that when men reach the age of twenty, they will perform the coming-of-age ceremony by tying their hair into a bun on top of their head and wearing a cap.[21] Thus, men who shave their hair and bare their head are not Han Chinese. Similarly, the practice of tattoos was prohibited in Chinese culture because the physical marker generally served as an index of alterity. Before the Yuan dynasty, a face tattoo was legal punishment for a crime. Tattoos could also signify status as a slave.[22] Tattoos might, however, be willingly adopted by some Chinese. Soldiers and generals could use tattoos to mark their loyalty. Tattoos could also signify martial strength, outlawry, and masculinity.[23] Eight bandits in *The Water Margin*, including Lu Zhishen 魯智深, Shi Jin 史進, Zhang Shun, and Ruan Xiaowu, sport splendid tattoos. Nonetheless, the practice was generally seen as signifying otherness. Many Ming–Qing travel writers discovered that indigenous peoples in southern China, Taiwan, Ryukyu, and Japan tattooed their faces and bodies. For these writers, describing these physical markers functioned both to objectively record the non-Han Chinese cultural practice and to designate the non-Han as bestial.[24]

Cai Ruxian's descriptions betray that he was not fully cognizant of the complexity of the sixteenth-century Japanese sartorial system. For Cai, the women's pullover garments and the men's nonsewn robes signify Japanese primitivism because simple pullover garments were typically worn in the prehistoric era.

> The Japanese are addicted to alcohol and believe in sorcerers. They take life lightly and love killing. Greedy by nature, they live on plundering. Their swords, spears, bows, and arrows are extremely fine. Adept at swords, they fight in battles with bared bodies. Jumping around effortlessly, one Japanese can vanquish a crowd. As to pillaging camps and setting up traps, Chinese always fall for their tricks.

---

21. James Legge, trans. *The Sacred Books of China. The Texts of Confucianism, Part IV. The Li Ki, XI-XLVI* (Oxford: Clarendon Press, 1885), 425.

22. Carrie Reed, "Tattoo in Early China," *Journal of American Oriental Society* 120, no. 3 (July–September 2000): 360–68.

23. Reed, "Tattoo," 368–71.

24. Teng, *Taiwan's Imagined Geography*, 106–7. Also see Abramson, *Ethnic Identity*, 27.

其人嗜酒信巫，輕生好殺，性貪且惟以劫掠為生，刀槍弓矢極其
犀利，裸身赴關，慣舞雙刀，輕依跳躍，能以寡勝眾，至劫營設
伏，華人每隨其術中。[25]

Composed immediately after the Ningbo incident (1523), Xue Jun's *A Survey of Japan* (1523) employs the rhetoric of anarchy and archaism to represent Japan and Japanese. Drawing on sources from the *Jiu Tangshu* 舊唐書 (*Old Book of Tang*, 945) and *Xin Tang shu* 新唐書 (*New Book of Tang*, 1060), he extensively describes the history of Japan's origins, monarchy, and civil wars. The section "Historical Evolution" (*yange* 沿革) is the first of seventeen sections listed in the work's second volume. The section reads:

> The country of *Riben* is the ancient country of *Wonu*. Amenominakanushi (Heavenly Ancestral God of the Original Heart of the Universe) established the capital at Tsukushiand built the Himukaidai Jingū shrine. He ruled such countries as *Yamatai, Touma, Yindu,* altogether some one hundred countries. They were governed by the major Japanese king. The kingship was passed down to the twenty-third ruler who was called Hikonagisa no Mikoto (ひこなぎ さのみこと). His fourth son, Emperor Jimmu, from Tsukushi, entered the Yamato no kuni and the Kashihara Shrine. He still named the country Wo. During the times ruled by the Huan Emperor and the Ling Emperor of the Han Dynasty, the *Wonu* wreaked havoc. They fought against each other. For years, they did not have a ruler. There was a woman who called herself Himiko. She remained unmarried. She used sorcery to bewitch people who then appointed her the ruler. Her laws were very strict. She died a few years after she ascended to the throne. The people did not trust her son, so they began killing each other. Once again, they appointed Himiko's daughter Iyo as the ruler. The country was then appeased. It was hence named the Country of Women. During the Tang, they began to learn the Chinese language. Ashamed that their name was disgraceful, they changed the name to Nihon, meaning that the country was close to where the sun rose. In the time of the Qin, the First Emperor of Qin dispatched Daoist Xu Fu to send one thousand boys and girls into the ocean to seek the elixir of immortality on Penglai Island. Daoist Xu failed the mission. Fearing that he will

---

25. Cai, *Dongyi tushuo*, 429.

be executed, he landed on Yi and Chan Islands and called his kingdom the country of the Qin Emperor. Therefore, China always called Japan "Xu Wo (Wo surnamed Xu)." This is not the proper name of Japan. In addition, most Japanese are by nature treacherous, wicked, and greedy. They often spy on us, and if they find we are divided, then they will plunder and pillage at will. Hence, coastal people again regard them as Japanese pirates, worrying about their invasion and taking extreme precaution to defend the coasts.

日本國者，古倭奴國也。天御中主都築紫日向宮，主邪魔維國、尹都、投馬種類，百有餘國。奄為所屬。號大倭王，傳二十三世，日彥瀲尊，第四子神武天皇，自築紫入都大和州橿原宮，仍以倭為號。迄漢桓靈間，倭奴作亂，互相攻伐，歷年無主。有一女子，名卑彌呼者，年長不嫁，以妖惑眾，乃共立為王，法甚嚴峻，在位數年死。宗男嗣，國人不服，更相誅殺，複立卑彌呼宗女壹與，國遂定，時稱女王國。逮唐咸亨初，賀平高麗。稍習夏音，惡其名不善，乃更號曰日本，蓋取近日始升之義也。先秦時，遣方士徐福將童男女千人入海求蓬萊仙不得，懼誅止夷，澶二州號秦王國屬倭奴國，故中國總呼曰徐倭，非日本正號也。又其性多狙詐，狼貪，往往窺伺得間，則肆為寇掠，故邊海復以倭寇目之，苦其來防甚密也。[26]

Tracing the origin of Japanese people back to Qin China, Xue Jun fuses Japan's monarchic history and civil wars with the Chinese legend of the First Emperor's quest for immortality. Japan may be fairly civilized, but it inhabits China's past. The rhetoric of anarchy and anarchism fuses with the perception of Japanese as treacherous and vile, continuing the popular narrative of Japanese in daily-used encyclopedias. With such rhetoric, Japan's actual history remains unknown. What is known is that the exonym's apparent derogatory meaning (slave) eventually caused the Japanese to change their country's name to the endonym Riben 日本.[27]

Xue Jun further details the sartorial practices of men and women with the rhetoric of archaism and association:

With regard to their appearance, men shave their hair and bare

26. Xue Jun, *Riben guo kaolue yijuan buyi yijuan* 日本國考略一卷補遺一卷, in *Siku quanshu cunmu shibu* 四庫全書存目史部 (Jinan: Qilu shushe, 1997), vol. 255: 267.

27. It has been suggested that the Japanese ambassador Awata no Mahito to Tang China contributed to Japan's nominal transformation in Chinese records. Joshua A. Fogel, *Articulating the Sinosphere*, 19.

their head, tattoo their faces and bodies. The positions and sizes of the tattoos mark their social statuses. Women pull their hair down and comb their side hair back behind the ears. They disguise their bodies with vermilion. This is because in their custom, they are worried about water demons. They make themselves resemble juvenile dragons to evade them.

其形體，男子斷髮魁頭、黥面文身，以文左右大小為尊卑之差。婦女被髮屈紒，以丹扮身，蓋夷俗患水妖，象龍子以避之也。[28]

The line "The positions and sizes of the tattoos mark their social statuses" is cited verbatim from *Dongyi liezhuan* 東夷列傳 (*Biography of the Eastern Barbarians*) of *Hou Han shu* 後漢書 (*Book of the Later Han*).[29] The line "This is because in their culture, they worry about water demons. They make themselves resemble juvenile dragons to evade them" appropriates the description of the indigenous people of the Yue 越 region in the *Dili zhi* 地理志 (*Geography*) of *Han shu* 漢書: "The people of Yue tattooed their bodies and cut off their hair to avoid the harm of dragons" 粵（越）地文身斷髮，以避蛟龍之害. Ying Zhao 應劭 (153–196) explains this line in his comments: "[the indigene people] often work in water, so they shave their hair and tattoo their bodies to make themselves resemble juvenile dragons to avoid injury by dragons" 常在水中，故斷其髮，文其身，以像龍子，故不見傷害也。[30] In associating the Japanese people with the indigene people of Yue in China, Xue Jun means to rationalize and understand the non-Han Chinese cultural practice.

Xue Jun's effort to rationalize and understand the Japanese continues in his detailed description of sartorial customs:

With regard to their apparel, men wear shirts and skirts, the garments are tied together horizontally, without being sewn together. They often bare their feet. Occasionally, they wear shoes which resemble sandals, with painted uppers and tied around the feet. They do not wear hats or gold or silver jewelry. Women's garments resemble quilts and blankets. They put them on by pulling them over the heads. They also wear shirts and skirts. The clothing all has embroidered borders. They make thin bamboo strips into combs.

---

28. Xue, *Riben guo kaolue yijuan buyi yijuan*, 271.
29. Fan Ye 范曄 ed., *Hou Hanshu* 後漢書 (Beijing: Zhonghua shuju, 1965), 1803.
30. Wang Yuansun 汪遠孫 ed., *Hanshu dili zhi jiaoben* 漢書地理志校本, vol. 2: 44.

其服飾，男子衣裙襦，橫幅結束，不施縫綴。足多跣，間用履，形如屨，漆其上而繫之足。首無冠，不用金銀為飾。婦女衣如單被，穿其中貫頭而着之，亦衣裙襦，裳皆有襈。攝竹聚以為梳。[31]

The descriptions of shoes, jewelry, embroidered borders on clothing, and combs are all appropriated from *Sui shu* 隋書 (*Book of the Sui Dynasty*) and *Taiping yulan* 太平御覽 (*Imperial Reader of the Taiping Era*). Xue Jun expresses his respect for Japanese culture and challenges the existing view that barbarians do not have culture:

> *Baihu tong* says, "the graph *yi* (barbarian) means squatting, suggesting that they do not have manners or ritual." I believed this view. But *Wang zhi* writes, "The graph *yi* signifies emergence. This means that barbarians are trustworthy and love life. Since ten thousand sentient beings can emerge from underneath the earth, by nature, they are gentle and submissive. They can be easily acculturated by the Way." Alas, why are these views different?

白虎通曰: "夷者，蹲也，謂無禮儀。" 即是而觀，信矣。王制乃云: "夷者，抵也，言信而好生，萬物抵地而出，故天性柔順，易以道禦。" 噫，是何見之左邪？[32]

Reading these descriptions based on historical texts, sixteenth-century readers of *A Survey of Japan* were unsatisfied with its archaic information and omissions:

> However, [Xue Jun's] knowledge is not broad enough. The two sections "The History of Japan" and "Territory" only roughly outline Japan. It contains many mistakes and omissions. Japan's subordinate states include Silla and Paekche. But he does not know that Xinluo {alt: Xinlao} and Baiji had already been absorbed by Korea during the Song. When Xue Jun composed the travelogue, these countries no longer existed. Further, he only listed the [Japanese] kings before the emperor Yongxi in the Song and did not list any kings after the Yuan.

然見聞未廣，所輯沿革，疆域，二略，約舉梗概，掛漏頗多。屬國

---

31. Xue Jun, *Riben guo*, 271.
32. Xue Jun, *Riben guo*, 272.

中兼及新羅百濟等國，不知新羅百濟，在宋時已為朝鮮所並，其
時並無是國矣。又序世係但及宋雍熙以前，而不載元以後，國王
名號亦疏漏也。[33]

Hou Jigao's 1592 *The Geography and Customs of Japan* updates and
revises *A Survey of Japan* and expands its fifteen categories to thirty-
three.[34] With the rhetoric of naming and classification, he points out how
clothing and self-presentation can be markers of class and age:

Rich Japanese women will put down their hair and comb their hair
back behind the ears. Poor women will tie up their hair for work's
convenience. Baby girls will be painted with vermilion to resemble
baby dragons in order to avoid water demons. They do not wear
jewelry or earrings. Their cosmetics include face powder and lip
balm. Rich women will use gold and silver to make precious hairpins to fix their hairdo, which is called *gemeisu* (カミサシ). Poor
women will use copper, tin, or bone to make hairpins; their names
are the same. Sometimes they wear rings, which are called *yipijieni*
(イビカネ). Their garments are like quilt covers. They pull them
over their heads. Silk clothes are named *gucong* (コソデ). Cotton
cloth is named *jiermuna* (キルモノ). They also wear skirts, which
are called *jiafu* (キャフ).

女子富貴者，批髮屈紒，貧常以髮束髻，以便工用。初生以丹扮
身，象龍子以避水妖。首不用金銀為飾，耳無環，梳粧面粉唇脂。
富貴以金銀造簪，寶物挽髮，名曰革眉素。若貧者，以銅錫骨用
造簪，其名同。手閒用戒指，名曰衣皮揭泥。衣如單被，穿其中貫
頭，而着之段絹衣，名曰骨從。地布曰吉而木那。下身亦衣裙襦，
名曰加福。[35]

Men's clothing items are also listed and all transcribed into Chinese: ハキ
モノ 法吉木那, タビ 単皮, ハダノオビ 法檀那和皮, オビ 和皮, カミサシ革
眉素若, イビカネ 衣皮揩泥, コソデ 骨聳地, キルモノ 吉而木那, and キャ
フ 加福. This is the most detailed and updated account on sixteenth-
century Japanese costumes. Such detailed classification of Japanese gar-

33. Xue Jun, *Riben guo*, 294.
34. For details of the content of the categories, see footnote 22 of chapter 3.
35. Hou Jigao, *Zensetsu*, 28–29.

ments and accessories does not come with an awareness of Japanese clothing's evolution over time. However, the social hierarchy that receives keen attention in Hou Jigao's work may reflect the salient social function of clothing in contemporaneous Ming society. Overall, *The Pictures of Eastern Barbarians*, *A Survey of Japan*, and *The Geography and Customs of Japan* show a gradual shift from negative depictions of Japanese as pirates to the scientific naming of Japanese objects and rationalizing of Japanese customs.

Overseas Chinese: Captives, Traders, Spies, and Converts

"Strange Encounter" adds another layer of meaning to the term *wonu* by showing Chinese captives *turning* into "fake Japanese pirates" (*jiawo* 假倭). Some Chinese captives were traders. A fisherman named Su Ba 蘇八 from Linhai 臨海 in Taizhou 台州 was captured in 1581, together with seven fellow fishermen, when they were navigating from Haimen 海門 to the Yucheng archipelago 于撑礁洋 to fish. Abducted to Satsuma, Su Ba was sold to a temple as a slave for four taels of silver. Later, he was able to redeem himself and make a living by selling fabric and fish on the island of Hisejima 飛瀨島 of the Satsuma in southern Japan. Another man named Zhu Junwang 朱均旺 from Jiangxi went to trade textiles at Fujian seaports of Zhangzhou 漳州, Haicheng 海澄, and Badu 八都 in 1577. From there, he took a ship to Vietnam to trade porcelain, copper, and iron. Because the commodities were hard to sell, he took another ship to Tình Quảng Nam. When the ship cruised in the middle of the ocean, Japanese pirates abducted him together with other Chinese merchants and sold him to the Japanese temple Fukushōji 福昌寺 to transcribe Buddhist scriptures.[36] A Chinese businessman named Xu Yi 許儀 was abducted by the Japanese when he sailed across Guangdong Province in 1592 on the eve of the Imjin War.[37]

The phenomenon of captured Chinese traders residing in Japan resonates with the thriving early seventeenth-century maritime trade, which

---

36. *Quanzhe bingzhi sanjuan* 全浙兵制三卷, 176–77. Zheng Jiexi 鄭潔西, "Wanli nianjian de renchen woluan he Fujian haishang tigong tde riben qingbao" 萬曆年間的壬辰倭亂和福建海商提供的日本情報, trans., Matsuura Akira 松浦章, *Mingshi yanjiu congkan* 明史研究叢刊 (July 2010): 198–215.

37. *Quanzhe bingzhi sanjuan*, 176–77.

had expanded since the early sixteenth century. The Chinese traders who had come to live in Japan became overseas Chinese who were required to know both Chinese and Japanese. This shift is evident in the fact that while *A Survey of Japan* does not include any information on commerce, *The Geography and Customs of Japan* adds two trade-related sections, "Maritime Trade" 出海通商 and "Seaports for Commercial Ships" 商船所聚. These sections are based upon Mao Yuanyi's 茅元儀 (1594–1640?) *Treatise on Armament Technology* (*Wubei zhi* 武备志) published in 1621. The travelogue tells that Japan has three major seaports. First is Saikaidō (West Sea Route さいかいどう西海道). The second is the Satsuma islands and the port of Hakata (はかた 花旭塔). The third one is Tōkaidō (East Sea Route とうかいどう 東海道) and Anotsu (Cave Port 洞津), called Anotsu no tsu 阿乃次以津 by local Japanese, in the province of Ise (いせ 依勢州). Many Chinese maritime merchants lived in Hakata and were said to love living in the port, which had a Chinatown street (*datang jie* 大唐街). "Although they used to be Chinese, now they are Japanese" (*wo* 倭), *The Geography and Customs of Japan* concludes.[38]

Some overseas Chinese claimed loyalism to China and became spies. They reported military intelligence back to China's coastal local governments. On the eve of Hideyoshi's invasion of Korea, on the island of Hisejima, Su Ba overheard the daimyo's plan of invading China and saw his face, which "had several moles and resembled a dog's face" 顊上有黑痣數點，面似犬形.[39] Hideyoshi even commanded a Chinese captive named Xuan 玄 to be his guide for his planned entrenchment of China. The most salient example of Hideyoshi's use of Chinese captives is the Chinese informant Xu Yi. On the eve of the Imjin War, he wrote two letters divulging Hideyoshi's planned attack and requested Chinese merchants sojourning in Japan to deliver them to the Ming government. But the Ming government did not respond to his intelligence. Xu Yi then "wailed day and night; heaved sighs facing the sky" 日夜憂哭，仰天長嘆. Later, Zhu Junwang, a fellow from his hometown whom he had rescued from the Japanese pirates, volunteered to return to China. Zhu composed an intelligence report of 5,000 words to inform China of Japan's geography, the reasons for Japanese piracy, strategies for defending against Japanese piracy, Hideyoshi's reasons for invasion, and the names of Japan's sixty-six "kingdoms" (provinces).[40]

---

38. Hou Jigao, *Zensetsu*, 33–34.

39. *Jinbao wojing* 近報倭警, appendix to Hou Jigao's *Riben fengtu ji* in *Siku quanshu zongmu* 四庫全書總目 (Jinan: Qilu shushe, 1997), vol. 31, 176.

40. Zheng Jiexi, "Wanli nianjian."

Some Chinese regarded overseas Chinese who served the Japanese ruling elite as traitors. Xu Yi states in his intelligence report that he resented those villains who led Japanese to harass China's coast. As a result, he successfully requested the Satsuma king to kill more than ten of those Chinese pirates. The remaining Chinese pirates then escaped to Cambodia, Siam, and Luzon. When Hideyoshi conquered Satsuma, part of his campaign to command control over all of Japan, Xu Yi also persuaded Hideyoshi to behead Chinese pirates. He argued it would be futile to consult with "the Chinese who lived a long time in Japan because they are on the same side as the Japanese enemy. No single one of them will speak truth" 唐人久住日本者，皆賊寇之黨，想無一人肯言真者.[41]

In other instances, some Chinese captives who had turned to piracy-plundered China in order to escape from the Japanese. Cai Jiude observes that many pirates who plundered Jiangnan were themselves from the region. Previously abducted by the Japanese, they returned to pillage to make a living: "Unwilling to follow the Japanese to sail into the ocean, these captives escaped back to China for life" 舊為擄去者，今不欲從彼入海故逃生耳.[42] These Chinese captives also seldom went back to Japan after seizing an opportunity to return to China.[43]

"Strange Encounter" draws on the Chinese loyalist vision and reinforces the racial and ethnic differences between Japanese and Chinese. Its readers undoubtedly sympathized with Old Eight Yang who *is forced* into becoming Japanese. Such sympathy is yoked with a sense of national and cultural belonging, which the pirates in the story utilize to plead for legal leniency. In mid-eighteenth-century China, a large number of captives were forced into committing crimes together with true pirates. Although these captives had been under duress, they were still punished on the ground that they had committed crimes.[44] "Strange Encounter," however takes a different position: it advocates absolute leniency for the captured pirates based upon their Chineseness. Old Eight Yang's ethnic and linguistic transformation does not indicate that he is an "authentic Japanese" (*zhenwo* 真倭). He and his fellow abductees are as much "false Japanese" as authentic Chinese. His insuppressible desire for "going back" (*chonghui* 重回) to his hometown to reunite with his wives and sons manifests his Chinese identity. His sojourn in Japan is phrased as "floating in an alien

---

41. *Jinbao wojing*, 178.
42. Cai Jiude, *Wobian shilüe*, 22.
43. *Jinbao wojing*, 178.
44. Robert Antony, *Like Froth*, 17.

country" (*yiguo piaoling* 異國飄零). The Chinese identity entails his place of birth, family bonds, and dialect.

"Strange Encounter" finds a compromise between the instability caused by the piracy problem, the conflicts between the pirates and the Ming government, and the conflicts between Chinese and Japanese identities. Because of the Ming government's on-and-off sea ban policies and the coastal ministry's volatile governance, the pirates kept switching their allegiance from the Ming empire to the high seas and back again. This aspect of the maritime problem—pirates' vacillating loyalties—was described with phrases such as "the barbarian situation keeps turning" (*yiqing fanfu* 夷情反覆), "turning without constancy" (*fanfu wuchang* 反覆無常), and "like mosquitos awakening one from sleep, making discomfort" (如蚊蟲警寢自覺不寧). "Strange Encounter," however, resolves this problem from an ethnic perspective, by helping the pirates claim their Chinese identity. Old Eight Yang and his fellow captives all tell the same story: they are all Chinese; they are all from Fujian: "All of them joined him in claiming their innocence. Assistant Prefect Yang carefully interrogated them and learned that they were all from Fujian, all taken captive by the pirates at the same time" 眾人又齊聲叫冤。楊公一一細審，都是閩中百姓，同時被擄的。[45]

It has been suggested that the story of a miraculous family reunion during dynastic transition is a narrative archetype in late imperial *huaben* vernacular stories.[46] These stories of wartime family reunions are generic also in the sense that the person who appears to be a lost family member cannot be distinguished from any other stranger encountered on the road. The stranger's generic appearance in this type of vernacular story corresponds to the indistinguishability of the gang of pirates in "Strange Encounter": they look the same and unanimously assert that they are abducted Chinese. Yet it is legitimate to doubt the truthfulness of these pirates' words. Historically, many pirates disguised themselves as local people by wearing the same clothes and uniforms as local commoners and soldiers.[47]

Profound anxieties over the incongruity between a person's appearance and interiority underlie "Strange Encounter." Old Eight Yang's inability to recognize himself in the Japanese pirate he sees in the mirror cor-

---

45. Feng Menglong, *Yushi mingyan*, 275; Yang and Yang, "Yang Balao's Extraordinary Family Reunion," 313.

46. Tina Lu, *Accidental Incest*, 66.

47. Tina Lu, *Accidental Incest*, 26.

relates with the difficulty in discerning the captured Chinese who uniformly appear as Japanese. Such anxiety over the incongruity between the outside and the inside was deeply rooted in a highly fluid and complex late Ming culture. Tina Lu has argued that *The Peony Pavilion* addresses the problem of personal identity: "Are characters who they claim to be? Can we trust their outward appearance?"[48] "Strange Encounter" likewise reveals the prevalent cultural anxieties. In his comments on *The Water Margin*, Li Zhi further highlights the contrast between an eloquent but phony person and a genuine person who may appear coarse and rude but is in fact trustworthy and true in feeling:[49]

"Those who speak decorative words and are proficient at courtesy, their mentality is like that of a bandit. Elderly Brother Li, although he is rude and socially awkward, he is truly genuine and sincere. He is the person one can entrust one's life to. Therefore, Confucius says, the person who speaks flowery words is rarely benevolent."

李生曰:"凡言詞修飾、禮數嫻熟的,心肝倒是強盜。如李大哥,雖是魯莽不知禮數,卻是情真意實,生死可托。所以孔夫子曰:巧言令色,鮮矣仁,君子不可小知而可大受也。"[50]

But a person's appearance cannot be commensurate with his interiority in the early modern transnational world in which commodities and people relentlessly circulated. Personal identity was fluid and multidimensional. Scholars on early modern Chinese material culture have pointed out that the circulation of luxury apparel such as python robes and ornamented garments among merchants, concubines, and prostitutes projects the sociality and upward mobility of non-elite people that contradicted the official social hierarchy.[51] In other words, appearance ceased to signify a fixed social identity. The most salient example is the sumptuary behaviors of the merchant Ximen

48. Tina Lu, *Persons, Roles and Minds: Identity in* Peony Pavilion *and* Peach Blossom Fan (Stanford: Stanford University Press, 2001), 106–13.

49. Zhang Jianye 張建業, ed., *Li Zhi quanji zhu* 李贄全集注 (Beijing: shehui kexue wenxian chuban she, 2010), vol. 19, 75.

50. *Li Zhi quanji zhu*, vol. 19, 16.

51. Sarah Dauncey, "Illusion of Grandeur: Perceptions of Status and Wealth in Late-Ming Female Clothing and Ornamentation," *East Asian History*, no. 25/26 (June/December 2003): 43–68; Sophie Volpp, "The Gift of a Python Robe: The Circulation of Objects in *Jin Ping Mei*," *Harvard Journal of Asiatic Studies* 65, no. 1 (June 2005): 133–58.

Qing's wife and concubines in *Jin Ping Mei cihua*. Their palace-style garments worn during the Lantern Festival may designate them to be simultaneously in the classes of royalty, courtesans, and nouveau-riche merchants.[52] These non-elites' manipulation of sartorial codes not only demonstrates the social mobility of the times but also corresponds to the transregional mobility and cross-cultural mutability between Japanese and Chinese identities in the turbulent sea world as represented in "Strange Encounter."

The Absence of Dialects and Foreign Speech: The Politics of Written Vernacular in "Strange Encounter"

"Strange Encounter" has multilinguistic registers ranging from classical language to semicolloquial and semiclassical idioms to early modern Mandarin with varying degrees of vernacular phrases. For example, "Strange Encounter" begins with a poem:

> Did not Wei Qing the slave rise to power overnight and marry Princess Pingyang? Wasn't the melon grower of Xianyang at one time an enfeoffed duke? Like spinning balls, fortunes turn round and round; the winds of change shift all too often. Those with wisdom and insight stay aloof and watch puppets dance on the stage of life.[53]

> 君不見平陽公主馬前奴，一朝富貴嫁為夫？又不見咸陽東門种瓜者，昔日封侯何在也？榮枯貴賤如轉丸，風云變幻誠多端。達人知命總度外，傀儡場中一例看。[54]

The poem, which uses semiclassical language and such colloquial idioms as "*junbujian*" 君不見 and "*youbujian*" 又不見 the narrator as an "ancient-style poem" (*gufeng* 古風). With its mixing of styles, it expresses the quick circulation of fortunes and transformation of a person's social status.

Such semiclassical and semivernacular language style corresponds to the story's propensity to adopt classical language to describe the time-space of the story. For example, the story begins by naming the ancient Chinese capital Xi'an to describe the place where Old Eight Yang lives:

---

52. David Roy, *Jin Ping Mei Cihua or Plum in the Golden Vase* (Princeton: Princeton University Press, 1993–2003), vol. 1, 204.

53. Translation modified based upon Yang and Yang, "Yang Balao's Extraordinary Family Reunion," 303.

54. Feng Menglong, "Yang Balao yueguo qifeng", 266.

The prefecture of Xi'an, being part of Yongzhou, according to "The Great Yu's Laws of the Land" in *The Classic of History*, was named Wangji in the Zhou dynasty, Guanzhong in the Qin dynasty, Weinan in the Han dynasty, Guannei in the Tang dynasty, Yongxing in the Song dynasty, Anxi in the Yuan dynasty."[55]

這西安府乃《禹貢》雍州之域，周曰王畿，秦曰關中，漢曰渭南，唐曰關內，宋曰永興，元曰安西。[56]

Xi'an's different names, whether it is the King's City, Inside the Pass, South of Wei River, or Eternal Prosperity, convey geographical and political meaning and carry the weight of history. But by associating the ancient capital with a petty merchant, the narrator means to challenge this official discourse of history, which he himself constructs in the vernacular story. As he argues in the preface, it is the age of the "rise of vernacular fiction and the decline of official history" (*shitong san xiaoshuo xing* 史統散小說興). The language of the narration is written vernacular Chinese mixed with classical Chinese. For example: "That very day, they made up their minds, and on, a *chosen* auspicious day, he bade his wife and son farewell and set out on his journey. *Taking with* him a page boy *called* Suitong, he *took* a boat and headed in a southeasterly *direction*" 當日商量已定，擇個吉日出行，与妻子分別。帶個小廝，叫做隨童，出門搭了船只，往東南一路進發。[57]

The narrator describes the characters' actions and the tense (past tense). This vernacular narrative's fluency and fluidity are impressive, involving spatial movement from inland China to the coastal area.

Victor Mair discerns that written Sinitic languages are highly elliptical in nature. The sound of Sinographs was difficult to represent in premodern times.[58] "Strange Encounter" manifests the rare presence of dialects and real-life speech in *huaben* fiction. For example, Old Eight Yang must speak the dialect of his hometown, Zhouzhi 盩屋 County. He also presumably knows Fujianese, because his second wife (whom he weds after settling in Zhangpu) and her mother speak in Zhangzhou dialect. He does business with people from Fanyu 番禺 of Canton, so he must also know

55. Feng Menglong, "Yang Balao yueguo qifeng", 266.

56. Yang and Yang, "Yang Balao's Extraordinary Family Reunion," 303.

57. Feng Menglong, "Yang Balao yueguo qifeng," 267; Yang and Yang, "Yang Balao's Extraordinary Family Reunion," 304.

58. Victor H. Mair, ed., "Introduction," *The Columbia Anthology of Traditional Chinese Literature* (New York: Columbia University Press, 1994). About the written vernacular, see Victor H. Mair, "Buddhism and the Rise of Written Vernacular in East Asia," 707–51.

some Cantonese. But the story does not represent these dialects. Instead, his first wife from Shanxi speaks only in classical language composed of four-character idiomatic phrases:

> It is said that thrift and hard work are the basic principles of maintaining a household. What good is there in waiting at home for some miracle to happen?[59]

> 李氏道：“妾聞治家以勤儉為本，守株待兔，豈是良圖？乘此壯年，正堪跋踄，速整行李，不必遲疑也。”[60]

Patrick Hanan points out a "particularistic realism" of Feng Menglong's vernacular fiction.[61] Feng Menglong is "daring" in portraying the fictional characters' personalities, emotions, motives, and natures. The language mode of his story enables such narrative style to achieve artistic purposes. Although the wife of Old Eight Yang's speech does not reflect reality, her classical Chinese denotes a sense of domesticity, privacy, and intimacy, in addition to her good education and exemplary wifely virtues.

Different characters speak in different modes of vernacular language. Old Eight Yang's speech is more vernacular and also more sincere: "Even this is so, it is that I am *still concerned* about my young child and gentle wife." 雖然如此，只是子幼妻嬌，放心不下。[62] His speech reveals his tender feelings for his wife and child, although the written vernacular Chinese still cannot represent his accent and dialect. Old Eight Yang's second mother-in-law speaks even more vernacularly.

> Madam Nie *repeatedly* offered the following argument: "Master Yang, being a traveler ten thousand miles from home with no kith and kin around, you have no one to take care of you. Now, my daughter is young enough to be a good match for you. Wouldn't it be nice if you could *set up two households? When you go back home you'd have your wife to serve you, and when you come to Zhangzhou, you'd have my daughter. In this way, you'd never get lonely, which would be good for your business, too.* I'm not asking that you go to a great deal of expense. My only wish is that my

59. Yang and Yang, "Yang Balao's Extraordinary Family Reunion," 303.
60. Feng Menglong, "Yang Balao yueguo qifeng," 266–67.
61. Patrick Hanan, *The Chinese Vernacular Story*, Harvard East Asian Monographs 94 (Cambridge, MA: Harvard University Press, 1981), 107.
62. Feng Menglong, "Yang Balao yueguo qifeng," 267; Yang and Yang, "Yang Balao's Extraordinary Family Reunion," 304.

daughter, my only child, marry a good man and have sons and daughters, so that I can have someone to fall back on in my old age. Your wife will not take it amiss even if she hears about this. *Goodness knows how many travelers throw away their money in brothels*, but what I am proposing is within the bounds of decency. Please consider what course would be best in the long run. Do not decline outright."[63]

被虔媽媽<u>再三</u>勸道：“楊官人，你千鄉万里，出外為客，若沒有切己的親戚，<u>那知</u>疼著熱？如今我女儿年紀又小，<u>正好</u>相配官人，做個‘<u>兩頭大</u>’。你歸家去有娘子在家，在漳州來時，有我女儿。<u>兩邊來往</u>，都不寂寞，做生意也是方便順溜的。老身又不費你大錢大鈔，只是單生一女，要他嫁個好人，日后生男育女，連老身門戶都有依靠。就是你家中娘子知道時，料也不嗔怪。<u>多少做客的</u>，娼樓妓館，<u>使錢撒漫</u>，這還是本分之事。官人須從長計較，休得推阻。”

The colloquial idioms, the adverbs, and the passive marker 被 all underline the vernacular nature of her speech. The peculiar jargon phrase 兩頭大 might also be a Fujianese lexicon. The highly colloquial characteristic of Madam Pi's speech not only suggests her relatively low social status and educational level but also her clever, shrewd, and pragmatic personality, her identity as an old experienced woman, and the easily communicable and social nature of her speech.

"Strange Encounter" does not represent Japanese, just as the fiction does not represent dialects. Old Eight Yang learns how to *speak* Japanese, as the original Chinese term *wohua* 倭話 means Japanese speech. The miserable captive lives in Japan for nineteen years, and he prays every night: "May the gods bless me and let me return to my native land to see my family again."[64] The reader is left uncertain of the language Old Eight Yang speaks—oral Japanese (presumably a kind of Japanese dialect), Mandarin Chinese, Zhangzhou dialect, or Zhouzhi county dialect? If Old Eight Yang speaks in Japanese, then the original term 神明 can be a Japanese phrase, しんみょう. Sinitic logographs, called *seion* in Japanese, are Chinese loanwords in Japan for which the characters and approximate pro-

---

63. Feng Menglong, "Yang Balao yueguo qifeng," 267–68; Yang and Yang, "Yang Balao's Extraordinary Family Reunion," 305.

64. Feng Menglong, "Yang Balao yueguo qifeng," 267; Yang and Yang, "Yang Balao's Extraordinary Family Reunion," 304.

nunciation have been adopted together.[65] It also remains uncertain to which gods Old Eight Yang prays.

Although accents are unrepresentable in vernacular fiction, "Strange Encounter" underscores how dialect or accent divulges a person's genuine and authentic identity. When the eastern wind takes Old Eight Yang and his fellow pirates back to China, on a raid, they land in Wenzhou 溫州, where a local army captures and transports them to Shaoxing 紹興. There, Old Eight Yang's former servant from Xi'an recognizes him based upon his accent: "Your Honor's accent is somewhat from Inside the Pass" 長官也帶些關中語音.[66] Coincidentally, the assistant prefect who interrogates him happens to be his first son, Yang Shidao 楊世道, whom he has not seen for nineteen years. After hearing the account of this strange old man who claims that he is from Zhouzhi County and tells a story that is suspiciously similar to his father's (which he obviously learned from his mother), Minister Yang seeks advice from his mother, who now lives with him in Shaoxing. She proposes: "I will eavesdrop from behind the screen; then the truth will be decided right away" 我在屏后竊听，是非頃刻可決.[67] Old Eight Yang's voice and accent, she suggests, will instantly reveal his true identity. Coincidentally, Old Eight Yang's second son (by his second wife from Zhangpu) is also a prefect in Shaoxing and likewise learns of his story. He similarly relates this strange story to his mother; she, however, proposes only to take a peek at him from behind a screen.[68]

Chapter 3 has mentioned Feng Menglong's advocacy of Wu-dialect mountain songs to promote human sincerity and authenticity. The feeling of genuineness is manifested as much through the rhymes and lyrics of regional songs as through dialects. For the *huaben* genre written in vernacular Chinese, it is impossible to achieve the same effect as Wu-dialect songs. In the preface to *Stories Old and New*, Feng notes that "vernacular fiction can make cowardly people brave, lustful people chaste, narrow-minded people open, and stubborn people sweat" 通俗小說可以是怯者勇，淫者貞，薄者敦，頑鈍者汗下.[69] As with mountain songs, the language of vernacular fiction could have revealed the falsehoods of Confu-

65. David B. Lurie, *Realms of Literacy: Early Japan and the History of Writing* (Cambridge, MA: Harvard University Asia Center, 2011).

66. Yang and Yang, "Yang Balao's Extraordinary Family Reunion," 311.

67. Feng Menglong, "Yang Balao yueguo qifeng," 276; Yang and Yang, "Yang Balao's Extraordinary Family Reunion," 314.

68. Feng Menglong, "Yang Balao yueguo qifeng," 277; Yang and Yang, "Yang Balao's Extraordinary Family Reunion," 316.

69. Feng Menglong, *Stories Old and New: A Ming Dynasty Collection*, 3.

cianism and the genuineness of human emotions. Nonetheless, Feng Menglong expects vernacular stories to convey meaning and moral values. In his preface to his mountain song anthology, Feng Menglong again discerns the dichotomy of dialects and classical Chinese:

> In [Suzhou] dialect, the characters *sheng, sheng,* and *zheng* all rhyme with *jiang* and *yang*. There are many other such examples, too numerous to quote here. The population of the Suzhou area sing in their local dialect. This is also the case in the "tile game" and "money game." These games are played in one area only, and not throughout the empire, whereas imperial decrees apply to the whole empire.[70]

> 凡生字，聲字，爭字，俱從俗談葉入江陽韻，此類甚多，不能備載，吳人歌吳，譬諸打瓦拋錢，一方之戲，正不必如欽降文規，須行天下也。

Presuming that "imperial decrees" (*qinjiang wengui*欽降文規) are sagely to be transmitted and understood throughout the empire, Feng Menglong does not further differentiate early modern Mandarin, written vernacular Chinese, and classical Chinese. He only differentiates regional dialects from classical Chinese. Nonetheless, the association between regional dialects and personal authenticity in "Strange Encounter" accords with the philological philosophy evinced in the compilation of Sino-Japanese dictionaries and *waka* poetry—learning the barbarian tongue through dialectic phonology is to know the mind of "the other."

Insomuch as script and sound are separated in Chinese language, vernacular stories and mountain songs are two divergent generic species. The mountain songs concern rhymes, pronunciations, and immediate colloquial expressions. Vernacular stories concern meaning and moral values, aiming for a much broader Sinitic audience. The circulation of the vernacular fiction defines the influence of Chinese scripts in the Sinosphere. Numerous Chinese vernacular stories and novels were read and annotated in Korea and Japan.

Overall, whereas the three works of travel writing demonstrate a shift from negative perceptions of Japanese race and ethnicity to scientific naming, race and ethnicity in the vernacular story are both reified and destabilized. Old Eight Yang's ethnic and visual transformation embodies

---

70. Oki Yasushi and Paolo Santangelo, *Shan'ge, the Mountain Songs: Love Songs in Ming* (Leiden; Boston, Brill, 2011), 10.

how the Chinese world denigrates and fantasizes the Japanese pirates. But the empire keeps assimilating exotic and foreign Japanese pirates and transforming them back to Chinese. Late Ming cultural anxieties over personal identity and authenticity influence this racial and ethnic discourse of Japanese. The separation of dialect from appearance corresponds to the nonequivalency between a person's exteriority and interiority. Correspondingly, the separation of sound and script in the genre of vernacular story results in its underrepresentation of foreign language and dialects and its promotion of genuine human emotions, or *qing*, to Sinitic readers. This generic feature contrasts with twentieth-century modern intellectuals' advocacy of vernacular writing across genres and the more reified notion of race and ethnicity, which operates in tandem with nationalism.

III

Jiangnan, China

CHAPTER FIVE

Historical Narratives of the Pirate Kings

Narratives of two heroic and debauched Chinese pirate kings, Wang Zhi and Xu Hai, widely circulated in the unofficial history writings on the pirate raids that took place between the 1540s and 1560s during the Jiajing reign. A native of Huizhou in Anhui Province, Wang Zhi was a pirate leader and maritime merchant who arrived in Japan and made his base on the Gotō Islands (in the East China Sea, off the western coast of Kyūshū) in the 1540s. Wang frequently visited Ōuchi Yoshinaga 大内義長 (1532–1557) and Ōtomo clan 大友氏, enlisted Japanese pirates into his band, and was a tur-ret shipbuilder with Japanese sea lords.[1] Together with his ally, Xu Hai, a former Buddhist monk affiliated with the Hupao Temple 虎跑寺 in Hang-zhou, Wang supervised the shipping networks between Japan, China, and Southeast Asia and collaborated with Japanese regional warlords.[2] The Ming government attributed the large-scale Jiajing-reign pirate raids to Wang Zhi, who was eventually captured and beheaded in 1559. Xu was cap-tured and executed by the Ming government three years before Wang.

Many historical and fictional accounts narrate the deeds of Wang Zhi and Xu Hai and the process the Zhejiang Provincial Touring Cen-sor Hu Zongxian 胡宗憲, the commander in chief who directed Ming's anti-piracy campaigns in Zhejiang, devised to capture the pirate kings. This chapter focuses on the historical accounts published between 1560 and 1615. Chapter 6 discusses the fictional narratives published between the 1620s and 1640s. Whereas the fictional narratives focus

---

1. Peter D. Shapinsky, "Envoys and Escorts," 54. Also see Peter D. Shapinsky, *Lords of the Sea*, 136, 156.

2. Shapinsky, *Lords of the Sea*, 136, 156; Jurgis Elisonas, "The Inseparable Trinity: Japan's Relations with China and Korea," in *The Cambridge History of Japan,* vol. 4, *Early Modern Japan,* eds. John W. Hall et al. (Cambridge: Cambridge University Press, 1991), 235–65.

more on the private space, zooming in on the romance between Xu Hai and his lover Wang Cuiqiao 王翠翹, the historical accounts pivot around the more public and authoritative sphere of the state, family clans, and local communities. In these narratives of the public and authoritative sphere, four events are central to the narration: (1) the Ming envoys' trip to the Gotō Islands, where the two pirate kings were based, (2) the pirate raids, (3) Hu Zongxian's strategies of capturing the pirate kings; and (4) Wang Zhi's submission to the Ming. This chapter discusses five varying narratives: Cai Jiude's *A Survey of the Japanese Pirate Raids* (1558, hereafter *The Pirate Raids*), Yan Congjian's *Strange Realms* (1574), He Qiaoyuan's *Emperors' Tributes* (ca. 1597–1620), Xu Xueju's *Thorough Records of the Quelling of Japanese Pirates in Southeast China in the Jiajing Reign* (ca. 1583, hereafter *Thorough Records*), and Zhang Nai's (*jinshi*, 1604) *Records of Pirate Raids in Wusong, 1554–1555* (1615, hereafter *Wusong Records*).

The historical narratives form distinct moral and imagined communities through different ways of perceiving the piracy raids, recording the events, and narrating the personalities and moral characteristics of Wang Zhi, Xu Hai, and their ally; through discussions of Ming China's imperial authority and diplomatic strategies, and through discerning the dynamics among the state and individual agency. Hayden White alerts us to the difference between a discourse and a narrative: "A discourse that openly adopts a perspective that looks out on the world and reports it and a discourse that feigns to make the world speak itself and speak itself as a story."[3] A narrative is a discourse in disguise. Benedict Anderson has already noted that "imagined community" is created through "print capitalism" which makes the print vernacular language the common reading medium for the majority of the nation's population.[4] In the case of the publications of the pirate raids in sixteenth- and seventeenth-century China, the common print language used in the published history is classical Chinese, and the published fiction used syncretic vernacular language in written form. These two types of the print language contribute to the construction of "imagined empire" among readers and authors alike in the event of the piracy raids. The classical-language historical accounts revolve around the authoritative space of the state, and the vernacular fictional accounts focus on the public and personal space. A trend of this ambivalent and fluid sphere of the "imagined empire" is that personal voices and

---

3. Hayden White, "The Value of Narrativity," 5–27.
4. Benedict Anderson, *Imagined Communities*.

non-state public space emerged toward the end of the Ming and during the Ming–Qing transition.

A Chinese Sojourner, an Outlaw, an Avenger: Wang Zhi in *Veritable Records* and *Pictorial Compendium of Governing the Seas*

In the Ming official annals, *Veritable Records of the Ming*, Wang Zhi's ambivalent identities as both a Japanese and a Chinese become a point of controversy. The official account records that in the fourth month of 1557, Hu Zongxian 胡宗憲 appointed two licentiate students as envoys to Japan to deliver an edict from the Jiajing emperor to the Japanese king. The edict requested the king to return Chinese maritime merchants or pirates to China. While on the Gotō Islands, the two envoys encountered Wang Zhi and his adopted son Mao Haifeng 毛海峰 (also named Wang Ao 王滶). Wang and Mao told the envoys that the Japanese kingdom was in turmoil, and the king was bound to die in the conflicts. Since the leaders of the Japanese factions lived on different islands, the envoys needed to deliver the imperial edict to every island to ensure the message would be communicated. Wang Zhi also asked the envoys to relay his message to the Jiajing emperor that he hoped China would open up seaports and support maritime trade. To further show his sincerity in collaborating with China, Wang promised that if China opened maritime trade ports, he would help China track down and eliminate merchant pirates.

According to the *Veritable Records of the Ming*, in gauging Wang Zhi's motivations, Hu Zongxian regarded Wang Zhi as a Chinese sojourner. Hu speculated that either Wang feared that delivering the edict to the king would bring him trouble because he was not a Japanese or, that as a Chinese, "he missed his homeland" (*huailian gutu* 懷戀故土) and wanted to take advantage of the occasion to return to China. Hu's sympathetic view of Wang Zhi—that he was a Chinese sojourning abroad—differed from the Senior Grant Secretary Xia Yan's 夏言 (1482–1548) opinion of Wang Zhi as no different from a deceptive "Japanese barbarian" (*woyi* 倭夷). According to Xia, Wang Zhi's "malevolence was hard to measure" (*qi jian wei yiliang ye* 其姦未易量也), and the Japanese were equally "treacherous, shifting, violent, and abusive" (*bianzhao xiongnüe* 變詐兇虐).[5]

Hu Zongxian's talented military strategist Zheng Ruozeng highlights Wang Zhi as a maritime outlaw through a narrative of retribution in the

---

5. *Shizong shilu* 世宗實錄, in *Ming Shilu leizhuan*, vol. 434, 500–501.

Figure 15. Chinese pirate Wang Zhi's statue in Nagasaki. Photo taken by Qian Jiang.

"Biography of Wang Zhi" (Wangzhi zhuan 王直傳) included in Zheng's compilation *Chouhai tubian* 籌海圖編 (*Pictorial Compendium of Governing the Seas*, ca. 1562). In explaining Wang Zhi's pursuit of treason and rebellion, Zheng Ruozeng recounts that Wang believed he was predestined for warfare: Wang learned from his mother that she had dreamed of shooting stars and icy woods on the day he was born. He interpreted the dream as a sign of his heavenly mandate. That is, heaven commanded him to revive the empire with military force, since the Chinese character *bin* 冰, meaning ice, is a homonymous pun of the script *bin* 兵, signifying wars, soldiers, and arms.[6] The concept of requital (*bao* 報) rationalizes Wang Zhi's treacherous actions as a pirate king. He submitted to the Ming government because "Wang Zhi used to feel unsatisfied with Japanese; therefore, he wanted to avenge and then dominate them with the hand of the Ming" 有宿憾于夷，欲藉手以報及以威懾諸夷。[7] After he helped the Ming eliminate the rebels on the Gotō Islands, he demanded a generous reward. But he felt "ill treated" (*yiweibo* 以為薄) after having been given only one hundred *shi* of rice. He held a "grudge" (*yuan* 怨) against China thereafter. The narrative's emphasis on *bao* by describing his ethical interactions with China and Japan justifies the occurrence of the pirate raids and crystalizes the reason Wang Zhi became a pirate.

According to Zheng Ruozeng's account, by then, Wang Zhi had already been a wanted criminal in China: "The capturer of Wang Zhi will be awarded with an official title and 10,000 in gold" 生擒王直者封伯予萬金。[8] To capture Wang, Hu Zongxian imprisoned Wang's mother, wife, and children at Jinhua 金華 and expedited the envoys Jiang Zhou 蔣洲 and Chen Keyuan 陳可願 to observe and defeat the pirate king through the mission of sending the emperor's edict to the Japanese king. Hu instructed the emissaries that "Wang Zhi lives beyond the seas. It is hard to defeat him on ships. We must lure him out, forcing him to lose his territorial strength" 王直越在海外，難與他角勝於舟楫之間，要須誘而出之，使虎失其負嵎之勢，乃可成擒耳。[9] At the banquet with Wang Zhi, the envoys greeted him and he responded humbly: "I, Zhi, am but a speck in an ocean, a servant who runs this way and that. Your lordship took the trouble to send messengers across great distances to find me, and I am disconcerted" 直海介逋臣，督公不尺

---

6. Zheng Ruozeng 鄭若曾, *Chouhai tubian* 籌海圖編 (Beijing: Zhishi chanquan chuban she, 2011), vol. 9, 29–30.

7. Zheng Ruozeng, *Chouhai tubian*, vol. 9, 31.

8. Zheng Ruozeng, *Chouhai tubian*, vol. 9, 32.

9. Zheng Ruozeng, *Chouhai tubian*, vol. 9, 31.

繾牟鞫之，远劳信使，死罪死罪. The envoys then praised Wang Zhi, "Your honorable made yourself the hegemon on the sea. This is indeed a great achievement" 總督公言足下稱雄海曲志亦偉矣. They then asked why Wang Zhi chose to become a pirate. Wang replied that Hu Zongxian misunderstood him: "I am vanquishing pirates for the country, and I am not a pirate" 為國家驅盜非為盜也. The envoys then admonished him:

> "What kind of words are these? You collaborated with gangsters and barbarians to murder and plunder, and then you say 'I am not a bandit?' Isn't this the same as a person who is fishing at night and says that I am not stealing fish, but protecting fish? Even a child of three *chi* tall knows that this is a lie."

> "是何言歟？足下招聚亡命，糾合倭夷，殺人剽貨，坐分攜獲而為之辭曰，'我非為盜者。'是何異昏夜操罟以臨人池上，執之則曰：'我非盜魚，為君護魚者。'三尺童子知不然矣。"[10]

When Wang Zhi was silenced (*yusai* 語塞), the envoys then persuaded him to make achievements for China in order to redeem himself and protect his family who had been imprisoned but were staying safe and sound under the surveillance of Hu Zongxian. After learning his family was well, Wang Zhi secretively rejoiced.

Throughout Zheng Ruozeng's account, Wang Zhi remained clear-headed about the facts that Hu Zongxian wanted to capture him and that surrender meant failure and death. The commander pressed Wang Zhi to surrender without weapons or soldiers. Hu even feigned to get drunk and spoke up in his dream, confessing that he hoped to "make [Wang Zhi] alive" (*yuhuo ru* 欲活汝) after his submission. He purposefully let Wang Ao overhear his words, and Wang Ao then relayed the message to Wang. However, he always remained suspicious of Hu Zongxian until he realized that Xu Hai was defeated, and he was completely isolated and besieged. Thus, he decided to submit, comparing himself to Liu Bang 劉邦, the first emperor of the Han dynasty: "In the past, the Han Emperor fought at the Hong Gate banquet. Kings shall not die. Even if General Hu is baiting me, he will not harm me" 昔漢高謝羽鴻門，當王者不死；縱胡公誘我，其奈我何！[11] So he requested Wang Ao, who was a hostage, be released in exchange for Wang Zhi turning himself in. Once he arrived at the Ming army's gate "insolently" (*jieran* 桀然), he was captured.

---

10. Zheng Ruozeng, *Chouhai tubian*, vol. 9, 32–33.
11. Zheng Ruozeng, *Chouhai tubian*, vol. 9, 36.

After summarizing the official accounts' narratives of the pirate raids and pirate kings, I will analyze the five authors' varying versions of the same history.

The Empire of Suspicion: Deceptive Pirates and the Anecdotal Narrative in Cai Jiude's *The Pirate Raids*

Cai Jiude, native of Haiyan 海鹽 of Zhejiang, composed *The Pirate Raids* five years after the Jiajing-reign pirate raids in his hometown. It is one of the earliest historical records of the pirate raids in Jiangnan. By associating his witnessing of wartime atrocity with the disasters that befell his lineage and fellow townspeople, Cai Jiude's account highlights how wars impacted people's emotions, memory, and ways of history writing as storytelling. In the preface, Cai Jiude laments his "witness" (*muji* 目擊) of the "turmoil of the times" (*shibian* 時變). Remembering vividly how houses were burned to ash and treasures became trash in ditches, the author mourns over those perished innocents and curses the "cannibalistic" "Japanese" pirates. Noting that some loyal men from his lineage sacrificed their lives for "imperial favor" (*guo'en* 國恩), he feels obliged to record the history and illuminate the deceased heroes' ideal for later generations of his lineage.[12] By stressing that his intended audience is his fellow lineage members, Cai Jiude converges the trauma of his fellow townspeople with the suffering of his family clan. Monika Fludernik observes that the narrator's "experientiality of the story resides not merely in the events themselves but in their emotional significance and exemplary nature."[13] Lynn A. Struve has used the term "Confucian PTSD [posttraumatic stress disorder]" to discuss Zhang Maozi's 張茂滋 memoir *Yusheng lu* 餘生錄 (*Record of Life beyond My Due*, ca. 1644–1661), arguing that the wartime historical record is filled with the author's oscillation between deep pain over the loss of his parents and grandparents and his self-blame and sense of failure for having survived the war.[14] *The Pirate Raids* similarly fuses history writing with the author's mourning over the loss of his compatriots.

The narrated events in *The Pirate Raids* concern the collective experience of a generation or a community. The many peculiar occurrences con-

---

12. Cai Jiude, *Wobian shilüe*, 1–3.

13. Monika Fludernik, "Natural Narratology and Cognitive Parameters," in *Narrative Theory and Cognitive Sciences*, ed. David Herman (Stanford: Center for the Study of Language and Information, 2003), 245.

14. Lynn A. Struve, "Confucian PTSD: Reading Trauma in a Chinese Youngster's Memoir of 1653," *History & Memory* 16, no. 2 (Fall/Winter 2004): 14–31.

Figure 16. The facade of a household in the fortified city of Taozhu 桃渚, built to defend against piracy raids in the Ming. Photo taken by author.

struct a collective memory of the war, which implies the events' temporal insignificance. The seemingly day-to-day documentary does not have a specific first-person narrative. The account builds an imaginary and abstract collective first person through the plural "we." This enables the narrator to recount various bizarre images and traumatic events on behalf of his lineage members and fellow townspeople.[15]

---

15. This is historian Reinhart Koselleck's second of the three genres of history writing—accumulation. Reinhart Koselleck, *Geschichtliche Grundbegriffe: Historisch*

These narrated events do not merely signify historical facts but more importantly connect to emotional and cognitive registers. First, the absurd and aberrant occurrences are described as unbelievable and surrealistic. The Japanese pirates were puzzling. A group of strangers, heads shaven, from the sea, spoke unintelligible "birds' language" (*niaoyu* 鳥語).[16] Numerous bamboo-like ship sails covered up the sky. A giant wood log and melted iron liquid were employed as weapons. A warrior set fire to a pirate boat, causing a pirate leader to be burned to death—his skin and hair both charred (*fumao jinjiao* 膚毛儘焦).[17] The wounds on the captured pirates' bodies were bizarrely bloodless 痕多無血人咸異之. The pirates displayed the heads of the beheaded soldiers on the village's bridge. They dragged captured people, whose ears and noses were penetrated with arrows, by the hair 執民以髮貫耳鼻曳而行.[18] Typical horrible wartime images abound: numerous women raped, countless infant corpses, and earth-shattering wailing. The rhetoric of these visual images is to elicit the reader's emotional response and to evoke feelings about the cruelty of war as "beyond description" 慘不可言. These typical and particular anecdotes relate the specific to the general.

The narrative of the traumatic pirate raids as a dramatic social "disruption" (*bian* 變) depicts pirates as deceivers, tricksters, and traitors. The Chinese character 變 not only means phenomenal transformation and warfare, but also deception and betrayal. Hiding out in the temple of Goddess Mazu, the pirates secretively turned the altar cloths into sailing canvas. They easily tricked townspeople into believing (*qingxin* 轻信) that they would surrender. But after the townspeople stopped besieging them, they fled into the ocean and vanished. Further, the pirates disguised themselves by dressing in the same clothing as local villagers (冒吾民服色，服色裝束與我為一) : "one cannot discern the differences" (*buke xibian* 不可细辨) and "when the enemies arrived, people still suspected that they

---

Lexikon zur politische-sozialen Sprache, vol. 2, eds. Werner Conze, Otto Brunner, and Reinhart Koselleck (Stuttgart: Deutschland, Klett, 1975). Reprinted in *L'Expérience de l'histoire*, ed. Michael Werner, trans. Alexander Escudier (Paris: Hautes Études-Gallimard et Seuil, 1997). Françoise Lavocat argues that this genre of history writing is related to the anecdote, which captures the very nature of peculiarity of something in a factual narrative. Françoise Lavocat, "Narratives of Catastrophe in the Early Modern Period: Awareness of Historicity and Emergence of Interpretative Viewpoints," *Poetics Today* 33, no. 3 (Fall–Winter 2012): 253–99.

16. Cai Jiude, *Wobian shilüe*, 2.
17. Cai Jiude, *Wobian shilüe*, 3.
18. Cai Jiude, *Wobian shilüe*, 4–5.

were fleeing residents" 賊既至前，猶疑為逃竄之民. Some pirates also used divination and "magic" (*huanshu* 幻术) to "delude people" (*huozhong* 惑眾). People often suspected (*yi* 疑) what they saw or heard, since it was "hard to tell what was real and what was unreal" (*mode xushi* 莫得虛實).[19]

There is no explanation of the piracy raids, although the war is narratively constructed as fact. A profound sense of insecurity about the raids and the unknowable pirates is evinced: "even the military defense department could not know the whereabouts of the unpredictable pirates" 軍門以海寇居島出沒無常，莫得虛實.[20] Under the sway of "our" emotional anxieties, the narrative constructs Hu Zongxian's strategy of "luring" (*you* 誘) as the only effective counterreaction to the deceptive pirates and the ruthless piracy raids.

The strategy of "luring" echoes Hu Zongxian's military vision: "The art of war values strategies and downplays competition of strength" 兵法代謀為上角力為下.[21] It is in this vein that Chinese envoys were sent to Japan in the second or third month of 1556 to persuade Wang Zhi to "turn inward" (*neifu* 內附)—that is, submit—to China. Jiang enticed him by showing him the glory that would come afterward and the disasters that would follow if he continued to rebel (*yi huofu you zhi xiang* 以禍福誘之降).

Further, Hu killed the plundering pirates by luring them into drinking poisoned alcohol. This resonates yet contrasts with the plotline in *The Water Margin*. Out of ultimate distrust of the bandits, the Song emperor gives Song Jiang poisoned wine to drink after the bandits have surrendered to the Song and fought devotedly against the Khitan Liao and the Hangzhou peasant uprising. Knowing the emperor's intention to have him commit suicide, Song and Li Kui drink the poison and announce that they "die for their country" (*wei guojia ersi* 為國家而死).[22] They choose to die because they do not want to "ruin the bandits' name of implementing heavenly justice and of loyalty and righteousness" 壞了我替天行道忠義之名.[23] By contrast, *The Pirate Raids* highlights only the bizarre appearance of the pirates' poisoned and blackened corpses, emphasizing the effectiveness of the strategy of "baiting."

The Pirate Raids evinces a deep sense of distrust of the surrendered bandits and the reasons for their capitulation. Xu was "cunning and unpre-

19. Cai Jiude, *Wobian shilüe*, 7.
20. Cai Jiude, *Wobian shilüe*, 68.
21. Cai Jiude, *Wobian shilüe*, 68.
22. Shi Nai'an 施耐庵 and Luo Guanzhong 羅貫中, *Shuihu quanzhuan* 水滸全傳 (Shanghai: Shanghai renmin chuban she, 1975), vol. 3, 1412.
23. Shi and Luo, *Shuihu quanzhuan*, 1411.

dictable" (*jijie pocei* 機械叵測); his "submission in exchange for an official rank was an excuse of observing the situation"; he "did not reveal his true intent" 投降取封，不過託言觀變，歸心未露.[24] Further, when Xu Hai again announced permanent submission to the Ming government, declaring that "he will purchase 3,000 *mu* of land in Shen Village of Ping Lake (*Pinghu Shenzhuang* 平湖沈莊), Cai Jiude reasons that Xu Hai purchased the lands to provide shelter for his soldiers and supporters in preparation for further combat. The minister and most officials concluded that only by eliminating this "traitor" (*neini* 內逆) can the root of calamity be eradicated.

The deceitful pirates were lustful. In *The Pirate Raids*, Xu Hai desired his collaborator Ye Ma's 葉麻 favorite concubine, Madam Du. The jealous Xu plotted to subjugate Ye, their distrust of each other continuing to grow. On the third day of the seventh month of the thirty-third year of the Jiajing reign (1554), Xu wangled for Ye an invitation for a false banquet. At the banquet, Ye was first offered a bonus reward and was then arrested. One of his thumbs was chopped off as a sign of subjugation. Ye cried out that he had regrettably fallen into Xu's trap. A devious plotter, Xu was not a real hero and soon brought death upon himself.[25]

While Xu Hai's lust led to his destruction, Wang Zhi's blind pursuit of kingship and material comfort gave rise to his downfall. Having received the emperor's edict to execute Wang Zhi, Hu Zongxian instructed the famous anti-piracy general Qi Jiguang 戚繼光 (1528–1588) to securely guard the strategic hubs in Zhejiang and again attempted to "bait" Wang Zhi by showing that an untrustworthy pirate can survive only by submitting. Surrender could help Wang "turn disasters into glory" 乃汝轉禍為 福之秋也, Hu spoke in an attempt to inveigle.[26] Xu Hai had already been eliminated, and Wang Zhi knew that he was on his own. Thus, he surrendered.

The appendix to *The Pirate Raids*, presented as a letter written by Wang Zhi himself, supplements the unofficial history's main narrative by describing Wang's arrival at the military headquarters "insolently" (*jieran*) in the eleventh month of the thirty-sixth year of the Jiajing reign (1556). All officials wished to seize him upon seeing his attitude. Concerned that this will provoke Wang's brigade, Hu "pretends to treat Wang with courtesy in order to detain him" 乃陰待以禮而羈留之. Hu set up a resting

---

24. Shi and Luo, *Shuihu quanzhuan*, 1411
25. Cai Jiude, *Wobian shilüe*, 82.
26. Cai Jiude, *Wobian shilüe*, 101.

camp for him, assigned him company, entertained him with banquets, and gave him an extravagant vehicle to ride. Ranked as Hu's most honorable subject, Wang took pride in himself and indulged in Hu's unbelievable favor. But all this munificence, the narrator says, was Hu's scheme to "ensnare his heart" (*yinshe qixin* 陰懾其心). On the twenty-fifth day of the first month of the thirty-seventh year of the Jiajing reign (1557), Wang Zhi was imprisoned.[27] In consideration of the maritime piracy trouble, the imperial court could not decide whether to execute him or not until approximately two years after.

In sum, *The Pirate Raids*'s anecdotal narrative of bizarre events constructs a collective and abstracted "we" first-person narrative, which also generalizes the characteristics of the pirate raids and the pirates. Such a narrative presumes that pirates as a type are deceivers and tricksters flawed with lust, so they can be easily tricked and avenged in return. The traumatic emotional experience of the warfare creates *raison d'être* for such vengeful perception of the pirates. Hu Zongxian's strategy of luring and "ensnaring pirates' hearts" manifests the logic of emotional retaliation.

The Empire of Bribery: The Destined Pirate King and the Allegorical Narrative in Yan Congjian's *Strange Realms*

Whereas *The Pirate Raids* presumes that pirates are swindlers, Yan Congjian's *Strange Realms* underlines the image of pirates as profiteers. In *Strange Realms*, he composes two substantial chapters on the history of the Ming dynasty's diplomatic relations with Japan, the history of the pirate raids, and the pirate kings Wang Zhi and Xu Hai. Yan interprets the pirates and the piracy war allegorically as indicators of the Ming empire's moral and political disintegration. This allegorical vision leads him to sympathize with the pirates and commoners alike.

Like Zheng Ruozeng's narrative of Wang Zhi in *Pictorial Compendium of Governing the Seas*, Yan recounts Wang Zhi's prophecy dream and elaborates on Wang's predestined kingship. When the envoys arrived at the Gotō Islands, Wang Zhi's adopted son Wang Ao 王澂 told them directly that it was useless to see the Japanese king, since Wang Zhi, "the King of An Hui of China" 徽王, was "the actual ruler of the barbarian islanders" (*daoyi suozong* 島夷所宗).[28] Thus Wang Zhi should receive the imperial

27. Cai Jiude, *Wobian shilüe*, 106.
28. Yan Congjian, *Shuyu zhouzi lu*, 84.

edict for the Japanese islanders.[29] The envoys praised his heavenly endowed talent: "Your Honor's talent is superior in the world. You cannot dive into dragons' pool; therefore, you ride on whales' waves. You have been forced to do so. This is not your original intent" 足下才略超世，未能奮跡龍池，故遂涉身鯨波，亦不得已焉耳，非足下本心也.[30] The controversial historical figure Cao Cao 曹操 (155–220) portrayed in *Romance of Three Kingdoms* exemplifies a type of talented man in Chinese culture who cannot become a legitimate king because of bad timing and his vices. The pirate king falls into this category. He was "a water demon holding sand in its mouth, bound to make people sick by shooting their shadows; a sea monster hidden in atmosphere to create deceptive mirage" 如蜮含沙，勢必射人，如蜃藏氛，勢必迷空.[31] Chinese dynastic legitimacy is predicated on benevolent and moral rulers.[32] However, Wang Zhi's outlawry in Yan Congjian's account manifests less his nature than the life that he had been living.

Yan's sympathetic interpretation of Wang Zhi correlates to Yan's acknowledgment of the importance of maritime trade. In his critique of the Zhejiang and Fujian Provincial Military Commander Zhu Wan's 朱紈 (1494–1549) short-sighted decision to close down the maritime trade bureau in Ningbo, Yan writes, "If trade stops, then the barbarians would be deficient of supply, not to mention folks like Wang Zhi. How could they but not feel constrained and impoverished" 由是貿易不通，夷人且將乏用，而況王直輩其有不窘困受縛者乎?[33] Regarding opening maritime trade, Yan Congjian's contemporary scholar-officials held different views. The Instructor of Linjiang 臨江 Prefecture Chen Jian 陳建 (1497–1567) posited that the weakness in the Ming's navy and army originated from the prohibition of maritime trade, which in term gave rise to the piracy that challenged Ming's military defense. Therefore, the Ming court must maintain maritime trade to protect the empire. Supervising Secretary Qian Wei 錢薇 (1502–1554), on the other hand, held that the sea ban affirmed the Ming empire's official tributary world order and could stop the pirate raids.[34]

---

29. Yan Congjian, *Shuyu zhouzi lu*, 84.

30. Yan Congjian, *Shuyu zhouzi lu*, 84.

31. Yan Congjian, *Shuyu zhouzi lu*, 75.

32. Shelley Hsueh-lun Chang, *History and Legend: Ideas and Images in the Ming Historical Novels* (Ann Arbor: University of Michigan Press, 1990), 35.

33. Yan Congjian, *Shuyu zhouzi lu*, 75.

34. For a survey about how Ming officials and Ming court responded to the maritime trade prohibition and pirate raids, see Kwan-wai So, *Japanese Piracy in Ming China dur-*

But Yan Congjian's political and moral vision of the Ming empire over-rules his sympathy toward the pirates and maritime trade. He envisions a susceptible Ming empire simultaneously facing such internal traitors as Wang Zhi and Xu Hai, corrupt officials at the imperial court, and external Japanese barbarians. Deeply rooted in an orthodox Confucian moral vision of the world, Yan Congjian genuinely distrusts free trade and free market. Traders are spies (*xijian* 细奸). Powerful merchants are "patrons of the pirates" (*wozhu* 窝主).

Yan's political view of the Ming empire parallels the orthodox Confucian moral imagination of the empire in the pseudohistorical narrative *Proclaiming Harmony* and the historical novels *Romance of the Yang Family Generals* (*Yangjiafu zhongyong yanyi* 楊家府忠勇演義) and *The Water Margin*. In *Proclaiming Harmony*, the emperor's "good and evil intention" (*xinshu zhi xiezheng* 心術之邪正) determines the *yin* and *yang* balance of the empire and the cosmos.[35] The simultaneous rising of rebellious bandits, treacherous ministers, and invading barbarians indicates the ruler's immoral rule. By contrast, the Ming historical novels mainly blame the empire's debacle on corrupt ministers. In the *Romance of Yang Family Generals*, the Yang family generals' unconditional loyalty to the Chinese emperors sets them on a journey to perilous frontiers. Wherever they go, they are overshadowed by gloom from two domains, tricky barbarians on the northern frontiers and the corrupt minister Pan Renmei 潘仁美 at the Song capital of Kaifeng. Also in *The Water Margin*, the corrupt minister Cai Jing manipulates the submitted bandit heroes to sacrifice their lives for the empire's military campaigns against the Khitans and the uprising peasant army led by Fang La 方臘 (1074–1121).

Yan avers that the empire's corruption will lead to the "people's rebellion" (*quncheng* 群逞). The pirates and the piracy raids already signal people's deepened resentments against the government. But if the government is unwilling to eliminate the Japanese pirates, then bandits and pirates would pillage everywhere, which would cause further resentments. Anger spreads like a disease. Disagreements and division rise among the ministers, generals, and soldiers. "They suspected that the government colluded with the pirates; rumors spread" 遂疑軍門通賊，流言四播.

Yan's ambivalent attitude toward pirates is tied to his conviction that

---

ing the 16th Century (East Lansing: Michigan State University Press, 1975).

35. William O. Hennessey, *Proclaiming Harmony* (Ann Arbor: Center for Chinese Studies, University of Michigan, 1981), 4; Anonymous, *Xuanhe yishi* 宣和遺事 (Shanghai: Zhonghua shuju, 1936), 9.

bribery is the root of the Ming empire's maritime piracy trouble. A double-edged sword, the strategy of bribery both defeats and captures Wang Zhi and Xu Hai and causes the Ming empire's downfall. Presuming that materialistic pirates turn profits by betraying their ally, Commander in Chief Hu Zongxian sent tens of thousands of taels of silver to Xu Hai to bribe him, presuming that pirates care only for profits:

> "What you need is no more than profits. The treasure you gain through pillage is no better than the goods you enjoy at leisure. Besides, although the bond between Your Honor and Wang Zhi are as intimate as lips and teeth, Wang Zhi has already sent his adopted son to submit to the court. If you do not abandon your weapons to submit, do you want Wang Zhi to enjoy the riches all by himself?"

> 足下所求不過欲多得利耳，與其鏖戰而取劫掠之財，孰若安閒而享所自制之貨？且直与足下固唇齿也，直已遣子入款，朝廷赦其罪，将官之矣。足下不于此时解甲归顺，他日使直独保富贵，孤立将安所为也！[36]

Hu also bribed Wang Zhi. Wang Zhi in *The Pirate Raids* is arrogant and adamant. By contrast, Wang Zhi in *Strange Realms* is easily bribed into joining Hu Zongxian's cohort. At Hu Zongxian's behest, the two envoys arrived on the Gotō Islands with a "huge bribe" to persuade Wang Zhi to submit: "Hu spent more than tens of thousands of silver on Wang Zhi, the same as he bribed Xu Hai. Wang Zhi was secretly delighted" 不吝巨萬，一如餉徐海時。直頗心喜。[37] Wang Zhi agreed to submit, although remaining suspicious of Hu.

Bribery is used in other strategic ways as well. It can transform into a tool to implement the strategy of *jian* 間—"division" or "betrayal"—to divide the pirates. This is how Hu Zongxian defeats Xu Hai. Having learned that Ye Ma and Xu Hai were rivaling for a courtesan, Hu Zongxian offered Xu Hai a bribe to persuade him to capture Ye Ma for the Ming. Meanwhile, he also gave Ye Ma a gift and convinced him that Xu Hai remained faithful to him. Following Hu's instruction, Xu Hai worked with Ye Ma to invite Ming officials for a banquet. After the banquet ended, Xu Hai dismissed Ye Ma's bodyguards and soldiers, and he then rowed a boat to carry the Ming officials home. They continued to drink on the trip back until Ye Ma became completely drunk; they then arrested him.

36. Yan Congjian, *Shuyu zhouzi lu*, 85.
37. Yan Congjian, *Shuyu zhouzi lu*, 88.

Further, Hu Zongxian forged fake letters to divide Xu Hai and Chen Dong 陳東. From time to time, Hu Zongxian bestowed luxury gifts such as hairpins, earrings, gold jewelry, and kingfisher feathers to Xu Hai's two courtesans to persuade them to ask Xu Hai to subjugate Chen Dong. Nonetheless, Hai hesitated to do so because Chen Dong was the secretary of the younger brother of the Japanese king on Satsuma Island. Hu Zongxian then forced Ye Ma, imprisoned because of Xu Hai's treachery, to write a letter to Chen Dong with a fake request: that Chen commanded a troop to execute Xu Hai. Then, Hu Zongxian schemed to have Xu Hai read the false letter, leading Xu Hai to think that Chen Dong betrayed him 宗憲出葉麻囚中，令其詐為書於東，乞兵賊殺海。其書故不以遺東，陰泄之於海。海得書，謂東等叛己.

Although Hu Zongxian successfully defeated the pirate kings and their ally, his collusion with the corrupt minister Yan Song 嚴嵩 (1480–1567) ultimately drove him to imprisonment and suicide. Yan Congjian laments that the same strategy of baiting (er 餌) brought forth Hu Zongxian's leadership role as the commander in chief and hence his downfall 宗憲之獲保首領，蓋能以餌王直者，餌世蕃耳，亦可悲夫. Yan Congjian concludes that "powerful ministers within the court prevent loyal generals from making military achievements at frontiers" 所謂權臣在內，而大將豈能立功與外者.[38]

Yan Congjian endorses the diplomatic strategy of baiting and bribery in the Ming empire's dealing with the pirates. Yan explains that the concept of baiting is derived from Jia Yi's 賈誼 (200–168 BCE) strategies for dealing with the Xiongnu: "Three Appearances and Five Baits" (sanbiao wu'er 三表五耳). The strategies entail the appearance of trustworthiness and brotherly friendship with barbarians, the appearance of loving barbarians, and the technique of favoring barbarians. The Five Baits are food, music, wealth, garments, and favor, which can effectively corrupt the nomadic barbarians' minds. In history, the Gao emperor of the Han once used 400,000 ounces of gold to bribe Chen Ping and ultimately take over the Chu kingdom.[39] The Ming similarly adopted the policy of jimi 羈縻 (loose reins) when dealing with the Latter Jin Duoyan's 朵顏 three tribes in the Liaodong region.

---

38. Yan Congjian, *Shuyu zhouzi lu*, 118.

39. Also see the discussion of five baits in the Han dynasty in Tamara Chin, *Savage Exchange: Han Imperialism, Chinese Literary Style, and the Economic Imagination,* Harvard-Yenching Institute Monographs 94, (Cambridge, MA: Harvard University Asia Center, 2014), 185.

Yan Congjian's opinion differs from the conservative views of the Grain Transport Commander Wan Biao 萬表 (1498–1556), Luo Yuejiong 羅日褧, and Gu Yingtai 谷應泰 (1620–1690). In *Haikou yi* 海寇議 (*Discourse on Maritime Bandits*), Wan Biao emphasizes legal enforcement of the sea-ban policy. Since legal inefficacy caused the piracy raids, the pirates must be executed to enforce the law. In *All Guests*, Luo Yuejiong also holds that "powerful ministers violated the imperial laws" 貴臣抵于法, which led to "Japanese slaves gradually achieving their aims" 倭奴益得志. Thus, Luo Yuejiong praises Hu Zongxian's execution of Wang Zhi to enforce the laws.[40] Similarly, in *Ming wokou shimo* 明倭寇始末 (*Survey of the Maritime Piracy in the Ming*, early Qing), Gu Yingtai opines that ineffective military laws (*junfa* 軍法) led to pirates rampantly assailing the three coastal provinces.[41]

Directing attention to the ambivalence of the diplomatic strategy of baiting, Yan Congjian wants to provide an adequate explanation of the complicacy of the piracy raids and to reveal the dilemma of the sea ban policy. He offers an allegorical narrative of the piracy raids, perceiving the historical reality from a moral perspective. Advocating that history writing should adopt the philosophy of the *Annals of Spring and Autumn,* he notes that historiography should "praise and blame" the history, in addition to recording historical events 春秋之法，功過當不相掩.

The Empire of Authenticity: Betrayed Pirates and the Moral Narratives in He Qiaoyuan's *Emperors' Tributes* and Xu Xueju's *Thorough Records*

In He Qiaoyuan's *Emperors' Tributes*, the envoys' encounter with Wang Zhi is cited almost verbatim from *Pictorial Compendium of Governing the Seas*. The difference lies in Wang Zhi's reaction to the envoys' words. He decided to submit immediately, following his favorite mistress Shao Hua's 少華 advice. So he kept Jiang Zhou as a hostage and sent his ally to kill pirates as demonstration of their willingness to submit to the Ming.

As in his narrative of Sino-Java relations, He Qiaoyuan highlights China's moral agency. He relates that Hu Zongxian delivered the message that the lenient Ming emperor will "tremendously reward" (*houyu* 厚遇) Wang Zhi's resignation. And in so doing, the Ming will display its moral power

---

40. Luo Yuejiong, *Xianbin lu*, 58.

41. Gu Yingtai 谷應泰, *Ming wokou shimo* 明倭寇始末 (Taibei: Yiwen, 1967), 26.

and authority (*weide* 威德) to various foreign countries: "Consequently, leaders of foreign countries will alienate Wang Zhi and his gang" 諸國酋種遍示之國家威德，則直黨自攜直勢自孤.[42] This moral power correlates to the authenticity of Han Chinese race and ethnicity, which legitimizes the Ming empire's sovereignty. He Qiaoyuan includes the Ming Hongwu emperor's edict, which was brought to Japan by the diplomat Yang Zai 楊載 to declare the first Ming emperor's ethnic and moral legitimacy:

> Heaven favors life and detests vice. Ever since the year of Xinmao, the central plain of China was in turmoil. At that time, Japanese bandits raided Shandong. They were taking advantage of the demise of the Yuan empire. I am from the ancient lineage of China. Ashamed of the Southern Song emperors' defeat, I led military troops to conquer the Mongol Yuan, and over twenty years, I recovered the authentic sovereignty (*zhengtong*). Spies then reported that Japanese soldiers raided coastal China. They abducted Chinese people's wives and children and brought harm to sentient beings. Therefore, I composed a letter to notify you: when the edict reaches you, if you consider yourself a subject of the Ming empire, then you carry the memorial to pay tribute to the imperial court. If not, then train your army to defend yourself. If you desire to be bandits, I will then summon an armada to arrest you islanders, reaching all the way to your capital, capturing you alive. I will represent the Heavenly Way to conquer the non-benevolent. Only you the king can decide what to do.

> 上帝好生而惡不仁，我中國自辛卯以來，中原擾擾，爾時來寇山東，乘元衰耳。朕本中國舊家，恥前王之辱，師旅掃蕩，垂二十年，遂膺正統。間者山東來奏；倭兵數寇海濱，生離人妻子，損害物命，故修書特報，兼諭越海之由。詔書到日，臣則奉表來庭，不則修兵自固。如必為寇，朕當命舟師揚帆捕絕島徒，直抵王都，生縛而還，用代天道，以伐不仁。惟王圖之。[43]

Predicated on the binary of Han Chinese superiority and barbarian inferiority, the imperial edict condemns the Yuan empire's illegitimacy and immorality and insinuates the Japanese regime's barbarian nature. The

---

42. He Qiaoyuan, *Wang xiang ji*, 6082.
43. He Qiaoyuan, *Wang xiang ji*, 6048–49.

Japanese king reciprocates this view and decides to submit tribute to the Ming empire, presuming that the Ming represents the authentic *Huaxia*:

Lianghuai said to Yi, "Although this small country is far, how can I not admire China? The Mongol Yuan and Japan are both barbarians, but they belittled us. Our previous king was not convinced. The Mongols dispatched an envoy surnamed Zhao to persuade us [to submit to them]. Before his words ended, the army has already lined up along Japan's coast. Now the envoy said that the new emperor is also surnamed Zhao. Is he a descendant of the Mongol?" Xu then said, "The Great Ming emperor is a sage. He was born Chinese and he rules China. He is not to be compared with the Mongols. What the Mongols did, the Great Ming Son of Heaven does not do. Besides, I am not the Mongol dynasty's envoy." The Japanese king was then silent. He treated the envoy with respect and proper etiquette. He dispatched his monastery diplomats to follow Yi to declare their submission to China.

良懷語秩曰：小國雖遠，曷不慕中夏，惟蒙古與我等夷。輒小國
我。我先王不服，蒙古使其使趙姓者誘我好語。語未既，兵列海
涯矣。以天之靈，雷霆波濤一時為盡。今使者雲中國有新天子顧
使者亦趙姓，其後邪？豈亦將誘我欲兵之秩？徐曰：今大明天子
神聖，生中夏而帝中夏。不比蒙古人。蒙古人所為，大明天子不
為。且吾非元使。後能兵兵我。王氣沮。禮秩有加。遣其臣僧祖來
隨秩奉表稱臣。[44]

The Ming emperor's racial and ethnic authenticity is tied to his Han Chinese bloodline, which becomes the main parameter for establishing the Ming regime as representing *Huaxia*. Race and ethnicity mark the legitimacy of Ming sovereignty.

Sovereign and ethnic authenticity intertwines with He Qiaoyuan's condemnation of the pirates as villainous and the piracy raids as detrimental to the Ming economy. Betrayal and division lead to the loss of wealth. Having heard that Xu Hai was defeated, Wang Zhi decides to submit to the Ming's military headquarters. Hu Zongxian's betrayal of Wang Zhi also brings disaster to coastal people. He first requests the emperor open the maritime market to manifest the Ming's moral authority. But Regional Inspector Wang Bengu 王本固 opposes him, claiming that "people in

---

44. He Qiaoyuan, *Wang xiang ji*, 6049–50.

Jiangnan spread rumor about Hu Zongxian receiving abundant gold as a bribe from barbarians" 江南人洶洶言憲大得夷金. To protect his reputation, Hu decided to execute Wang Zhi. Then, believing that they have been betrayed, the enraged pirates pillaged more often along the coast. They looted countless treasures and killed tens of thousands of people.[45]

For He Qiaoyuan, morality lays the foundation for commerce. In the chapter "Records on Commerce" (*Huozhi ji* 貨值記), He Qiaoyuan advocates for morality-based commerce:

> Sima Qian's "Commodity Producer" indicates that root wealth [agriculture] is better than branch wealth [commerce]. Does this not mean that we should be diligent and perseverant in farming and practice filial piety, brotherly love, benevolence, and righteousness to cultivate oneself? When the Wu emperor of the Han dynasty took over the empire and Jiangnan, he summoned people to him and admonished them on heaven and earth, *yin* and *yang*, benevolence and righteousness, history and presence. . . . He also commanded rich people to pay taxes. At that time, Shen Xiufu in the Wu kingdom was the richest person in Jiangnan. The emperor detested his vile influence. In order to extinguish the ridiculous and bizarre behaviors of extremely wealthy people, he sent people to destroy his treasure basin and abandon the debris at the city gate. Shen was exiled to frontiers. The emperor alerted the world in such way. This echoes those knights-errant in ancient times who robbed the rich for righteousness. The artist Ni Zan of Wujin and the literatus Gu Zhongying of Kunshan both belittled money and expended as much money worth of ancient tycoon Yi Dun's assets to wander around as the seven recluses of the Eastern Jin. We cannot work with these hermits to boost our economy. I read through history and recorded a few biographies of wealthy people. But the gist of this chapter differs from Sima Qian's "commodity producers."

> 太史公傳《貨殖》，謂本富為上，得非勤力治田畝，躬行孝弟，篤於仁義者耶！高帝初定天下，征江南諸郡民。稱大家者悉赴闕，既至造於廷，親訓諭之。凡天地陰陽，性命仁義，古今治亂紀綱，法度賦役供給，風俗政治得失之故，諄諄累數千言。恐其遺忘，刻書摹本分賜之。又召天下富人，以實京師立稅戶，人材之科付之。事位以寓，既富方穀之意維。時吳人沈秀，富為江南最。帝惡

---

45. He Qiaoyuan, *Wang xiang ji*, 6095–6103.

其力，俾人主眂其聚寶盆之城門之下，以絕怪詭譎之邊郡，風警天下。無得如古人閭巷布衣，豪俠義行，擬諸侯王者矣。若武進人倪瓚，昆山人顧仲英，皆以猗頓之資，游意東晉之習，並坐見法。此則惡輕浮逃虛之士，不足與共興教化者也。余覽傳記得富者數人，仿太史公作《貨殖傳》而為之，而指歸則異焉。[46]

He Qiaoyuan advocates commerce and ethics. Good ethics, in other words, will generate wealth. He illustrates this point with a story. A filial son's father loses his official title, causing the family to become impoverished. At first, they make their living by farming. But farming does not generate much income, and the family falls deeper into poverty. So that he can support his parents, the filial son begins to engage in business, and the family quickly becomes rich. With enough money, the filial son is not only able to provide for his parents but also to offer charity to poor people. Later, he is promoted as a high-ranking official and exercises his functions to help people in the religion. The mindset of orthodox Confucian moral supremacy thus leads He Qiaoyuan to believe that China should not trade with the corrupt Japanese barbarians. Yet he supports the official maritime tributary trade because a sea ban will only lead to piracy raids. Ming government officials should supervise the maintenance of the tributary system to manifest imperial authority.

In *Thorough Records*, the vice censor in chief and provincial governor in Fujian Province Xu Xueju (native of Lanxi 蘭溪 of Zhejiang, *jinshi* 1586) similarly considers the fundamental value of imperial authority and authenticity. He emphasizes that the piracy raids violate "the imperial body" (*guoti* 國體). In chapter 2, we have seen how late Ming literati tapped into the authority of the emperors' edicts and words to channel their narratives of the cross-border conflicts in the history of Sino-Javanese relations. However, in the case of piracy raids, many scholar-officials valued words less than military force. Guo Ren 郭仁 (*jinshi* 1547), secretary of the Ministry of Justice, for example, hoped to emulate the Hongwu emperor's diplomatic strategy who issued edicts to Sanfoqi to pacify the Chinese maritime merchants' revolts in Sanfoqi. Guo Ren advised the Jiajing emperor to similarly issue imperial edicts to Japan to solve the raiding conflict. The Ministry of War turned down Guo Ren's proposal, however. They contended that imperial edicts concern "the imperial body," which should be carefully protected with utmost precaution:

---

46. He Qiaoyuan, *Wang xiang ji*, 5879–80.

"Because the Japanese pirates have reached their aims, the piracy raids this year became even worse than those in the past. It is unlikely that words can acculturate and pacify the pirates. If their crime of violating China is not penalized, and a compromise is reached through comforting the enemy, then it will not strengthen imperial authority. If the Ming empire has not captured the criminals before remonstrating the pirates to put down their arms, then "the imperial body" is not respected. Besides, we have been systematically training soldiers and selecting generals. We need to fight till they fear the Ming's imperial authority and feel guilty. Only until then, the emperor will extend benevolence between Heaven and Earth and issue an edict to grant them their lives. Further, when the Hongwu emperor lived, Sanfoqi only obstructed China's trading and traveling routes. Its crime is not comparable to the arrogant aggression of those Japanese dwarf slaves. Recently, Korea has presented a memorial to return Chinese prisoners. Korea also has animosity against China. If we ask Korea to deliver our edict to Japan, Korea probably does not want to do so. Your subject personally thinks that it is inconvenient [to deliver imperial edicts to Japan]." The emperor followed the advice of the Ministry of War.

蓋倭寇方得誌，恣肆比之往者，益為猖獗，恐未可以言語化誨懷服也。若猾夏之罪未懲，而綏以撫諭，非所以蓄威；糾引之黨未得，而責以斂戢，非所以崇體。矧今簡將練兵，皆有次第，待其畏威悔罪，然後皇上擴天地之仁，頒恩諭以容更生，未為晚也。且祖宗時，三佛齊止因阻絕商旅，非有倭奴匪茹之罪，朝鮮近上表獻俘，心存敵愾，如復令其宣諭，恐亦非其心矣！臣竊以為不便。上從部議。[47]

In other words, China's diplomatic policy of "cherishing men from afar" works only when China's imperial authority and authenticity is not challenged.

Xu Xueju constructs his own moral narrative by rearranging the textual evidence from *Veritable Records of the Ming* and *Pictorial Compendium of Governing the Seas*. In the official account, Hu Zongxian differed from the Ming court in his views on maritime trade and the pirates. In *Thorough Records*, the envoys' visit to Japan (1556) resulted in the famous

---

47. Xu Xueju 徐學聚, *Jiajing dongnan pingwo tonglu* 嘉靖東南平倭通錄 (Shanghai: Shenzhou guoguang she, minguo), 13–14.

Ningbo incident (1523), which has been discussed in chapter 3. Instead of seeing Wang Zhi, the envoys visited the provincial governor of Suō (in present-day Yamaguchi Prefecture) who returned the Chinese prisoners together with a Japanese imperial seal. The prefect of Bungo Province (in present-day Ōita Prefecture) also sent Buddhist monks to present a memorial and tributes to China as an apology. But Hu Zongxian speculated that although Bungo presented tributes, there will be no accompanying seal as an official token of the tributary exchange. Although the provincial governor presented a gold seal and a memorial, he was not the Japanese king. Therefore, the Chinese envoy Jiang Zhou tarnished the "imperial image" by passing along misinformation and must be punished. Further, the Japanese showed their sincerity and confessed their guilt when they returned the Chinese prisoners. In return, Hu proposed to send the Japanese envoys back with gifts and ordered two Chinese envoys to deliver an imperial edict to the actual Japanese king. However, the Ministry of Rites turned down Hu's proposal, on the ground that issuing an edict concerns the "imperial body." The Ministry resolved the issue by ordering the Zhejiang provincial administration commissioner to request the two Japanese ambassadors send a message to their king. Xu Xueju's narrative thus reinforces the sanctity of imperial authority.

Xu Xueju further shows the moral authenticity and agency of trust. Hu Zongxian maintained a good friendship with Wang Zhi who then volunteered to submit to him, because Hu Zongxian advocated diplomacy and accepted the pirate king's proposal to open the maritime market. Hu also treated Wang and his ally in accordance with proper ritual and with genuine feeling. He provided the pirates salary, rice, meat, and wine for them to enjoy on the fleet, one hundred taels of gold expended per day. To reinforce their friendship, Hu and Wang exchanged their allies as tokens of their trust. But Hu Zongxian dared not to divulge any information to the emperor, who soon ordered Hu to execute Wang. Upon receiving the edict, Hu Zongxian became "profoundly guilty and depressed" 大愧，沮然不獲已. He secretively ordered the surveillance commissioner to put Wang Zhi into prison. But "remembering his promise to Zhi, Hu only hoped to release him" 然其實欲陰逸直，顧前盟. Nonetheless, Hu hurriedly executed the pirate in order to clear his name after the surveillance commissioner discovered his plan to free the captive. Despite his sense of guilt, Hu counted the pirate's death as a political achievement. However, Hu Zongxian's breaking his promise with Wang Zhi had catastrophic consequences. Wang Zhi's followers became increasingly resentful, spreading rumors about the Ming's untrustworthiness (*buzu xin* 不足信). The pirates announced that they will never concede again 撫之不復來. Disappointed, they plundered China more often, and "the calamities they made became even worse" 為禍更慘.[48]

In sum, both He Qiaoyuan and Xu Xueju show the importance of moral agency in maintaining imperial authority during the piracy raids. To He Qiaoyuan, Han Chinese ethnic authenticity legitimizes the Ming empire's sovereignty which is sustained through morality-based commerce and the officially supervised tributary trade system. To Xu Xueju, moral authenticity concerns performing Confucian ethics such as friendship and trust and the sanctity of imperial authority. His narrative conveys more his subjective interpretation and imagination, laying bare the irreconcilability and self-conflict between maintaining imperial authority and abiding to Confucian moral codes.

An Empire of Rustic Folks: Chivalric Pirates and the Narrative of Personal Response in Zhang Nai's *Wusong Records*

Zhang Nai, a native of Huating 華亭 in Gansu Province, obtained a *jinshi* degree in 1604. He was promoted to the director of studies in the Directorate of Education. Because he consistently submitted memorials to remonstrate with the emperor, the notoriously powerful court eunuch Wei Zhongxian 魏忠賢 (1568–1627) demoted him to the right vice minister in the Ministry of Personnel. In 1615, Zhang Nai published *Records of Pirate Raids in Wusong, 1554–1555* (hereafter *Wusong Records*), in which he notes his former profession as an imperial diarist of the "official history of the empire" (*guoshi* 國史) and as the rectification clerk in the Directorate of Education.

Writing sixty years after the piracy raids, Zhang Nai still asserts the importance of compiling this unofficial history on the raids, because composition about warfare is essential for historiography: "Victory and defeat in wars are perennial concerns, thus war writing is the theme of historiography."[49] Further, Zhang Nai sympathizes with individuals' experience of wartime suffering ("The Wusong people have never suffered from such atrocities before" 生民以來未有若斯之酷也) and further asserts that "one dares not to forget the peril" 安能忘危耶, explaining that trau-

---

48. Xu Xueju, *Jiajing dongnan*, 49–76.

49. Zhang Nai, *Wusong Jiayi wobian zhi* 吳淞甲乙倭變志, in *Huang Ming bao xun* 皇明寶訓 (Jinan: Qilu shushe, 1997), 667.

matic history must be recorded and remembered through history writing because "a chronology warns sage rulers" 日月以紀之以戒伏隍.[50] He focuses on the qualities and actions of various categories of people: "When rustic folks (*xiangqu* 鄉曲) strive, they are righteous and brave; when vendors and commoners make military achievements, they forget about themselves; when filial sons adhere to their nature, they can influence foreign peoples" 鄉曲之奮發義勇也販豎之依戰功而忘其身也；孝子之篤於性而能感異類也. In doing so, he underscores how an empire's warfare requires military subjects to fight on the battlefields and to sacrifice their lives. These "loyal souls and chivalric bones still reside among nine peaks and three rivers" 忠魂俠骨至今在九峰三流之間, he states.

Instead of praising or criticizing the actions of public authorities and the state, *Wusong Records* shifts the narrative focus to common people in the region and highlights how they reacted in the war. The account has two volumes. The first volume consists of five sections: the preface (*zongxu* 總序), "On War" (*jibing* 紀兵), "On Victory" (*jijie* 紀捷), "On Defeating Bandits" (*ji jianqu* 紀殲渠), and "On Defense" (*ji zhoufang* 紀周防). The second volume contains fifteen types of social groups who participated in the piracy war. Besides writing biographies of loyal, moral, and chaste martyrs, Zhang Nai also unconventionally adds the sections "Pedant Scholars" (*furu* 腐儒), "Furious Criticism" (*fengou* 忿詬), and "Drinkers" (*jiutu* 酒徒). He further eulogizes chaste women as moral examples, lamenting that women replaced men to embody the "lofty spirit between heaven and earth" 天地正氣.

Wusong Records represents Wang Zhi as a chivalric, intelligent, and trustworthy (*renxia duolüe* 任俠多略) pirate king who befriends various foreign pirates and traders.[51] In this account, Wang Zhi involuntarily turned into a renegade only because he wanted to help his Japanese friends from Satsuma Island. He became their guide to the Shuangyu 雙嶼 port where they marauded local villages. Zhang Nai underscores local people's agency to the extent that he argues that it was local monopoly of maritime trade that caused the piracy raids:

Ever since the two Japanese envoys fought against each other, the official maritime trade was suspended. Crooked merchants dominated foreign trade. Besides, they colluded with high officials' family clans to resist foreign traders. Foreign traders came sojourning

---

50. Zhang Nai, *Wusong Jiayi*, 666–93.
51. Zhang Nai, *Wusong Jiayi*, 673.

Figure 17. The Great Wall by the sea built in the Ming dynasty. Photo taken by Wang Yixian in Linhai 臨海.

in the region, and soon turned into pirates. Influential families ordered soldiers to expel them. Holding grudges, these barbarians colluded with such Chinese pirates as Wang Zhi and Xu Hai to hold sway on the seas.

自兩倭使爭做相攻殺，而市舶罷奸商得主番貨，而負其直又投貴官家，扼番人。番人盤踞不去，間為盜乃貴官家，又令官兵逐之番人，怨而並海不逞之徒如王直徐海者得借橫海上矣。[52]

Regional monopoly even causes the deaths of the anti-piracy officials Xia Yan and Zhu Wan. Unable to clear their names after the regional tycoons spread rumors about them, Xia Yan and Zhu Wan commited suicide. Thereafter, the Ming court no longer dared to intervene in the region.

Zhang Nai raises the voices of the region's common people. Under the rubric of "Drinkers," Zhang narrates that an alcoholic still wanted to drink his liquor even after the pirates had arrived. But after a pirate sliced him in

52. Zhang Nai, *Wusong Jiayi*, 672.

half with a sword, his head was still leaning toward his wine cup. The pirates laughed at the fact that his alcoholic addiction cost him his life. Zhang Nai then comments on such an idiosyncratic scene:

> The success a man desires will be his destruction; the high position the man craves will be his downfall; the faction one follows will be his death. In this world of crazy obsession, how could there be only one old drunkard?

夫嗜功者戮于功，嗜官者敗于官，嗜黨者死於黨，狂藥之中人寧獨一酒翁哉。

A commentator at the end of *Wusong Records* even questions the credibility of Zhang Nai's historiography. Pointing out its chronological errors in comparison with the more reliable accounts in *Pictorial Compendium of Governing the Seas* and *Haifang kao* 海防考 (*Research on Maritime Defense*), the commentator declares: "I would rather trust the people who have witnessed [and experienced] the events [than the people who have not]" 吾寧信其目擊者焉.[53]

In conclusion, this chapter shows that Cai Jiude, Yan Congjian, He Qiaoyuan, Xu Xueju, and Zhang Nai construct various versions of the pirate kings—Wang Zhi and Xu Hai—and the history of pirate raids. Cai Jiude's anecdotal narrative of bizarre events constructs a collective and abstracted "we" first-person narrative that presumes that pirates as a type are deceivers and tricksters flawed with lust, so they can be tricked and avenged in return through the strategy of "ensnaring the heart." Yan Congjian's political and moral vision of the Ming empire overrules his sympathy toward the pirates and maritime trade. Endorsing the diplomatic strategy of "baiting" and bribery in dealing with the pirates, Yan discerns that bribery also corrupts the administrative system, leading to his allegorical interpretation of the history. Both He Qiaoyuan and Xu Xueju show the importance of moral agency in maintaining imperial authenticity. To He Qiaoyuan, Han Chinese ethnic authenticity legitimizes the Ming empire's sovereignty which is sustained through morality-based commerce and the officially supervised tributary trade system. To Xu Xueju, moral authenticity concerns performing Confucian ethics such as friendship and trust and the sanctity of imperial authority. Finally, Zhang Nai displays commoners' personal response to the piracy raids. Collectively, the five his-

---

53. Zhang Nai, *Wusong Jiayi*, 667.

torical narratives demonstrate a paramount focus on public authorities and the state, and Zhang Nai's *Wusong Records* began to show a slight shift to common people and the non-state sphere. Chapter 6 continues to explore how different vernacular fiction writers and publishers in Jiang-nan channel their personal voices into the imaginative space of the romance between the pirate Xu Hai and the courtesan Wang Cuiqiao to negotiate aspects of the "ethic of authenticity."

CHAPTER SIX

Publishing the Pirate's Romance

Late Ming China witnessed a burgeoning commercial print culture. Prolific commercial publishing centers such as Nanjing, Hangzhou, Jianyang 建陽, and Sibao 四堡 rapidly emerged, decentering the state-controlled publishing business.[1] Kai-wing Chow notes that low-cost private commercial printing led to the expansion of a "literary public sphere." The wide dissemination of news and opinions through such channels as literary societies, fictional works and their paratexts, and the government gazette gave rise to public opinions, or *gonglun* 公論.[2]

Late Ming private publishing business, which comprised commercial and family publishers, contrasted with that of early modern Europe, where states still dominated printing.[3] As Adrian Johns has noted, piracy—of books and also of medicines, foods, and other commodities—during Europe's "first consumer age" in the eighteenth century helped to augment the importance of original works and to create "an ethic of authenticity and completeness."[4] By authenticity and completeness, Adrian Johns refers to the authenticity of books, medicines, machines, textiles, food,

---

1. Cynthia J. Brokaw, *Commerce in Culture: The Sibao Book Trade in the Qing and Republic China* (Cambridge, MA: Harvard University Asia Center, 2007); Cynthia J. Brokaw and Kai-wing Chow, eds., *Printing and Book Culture in Late Imperial China* (Berkeley: University of California Press, 2005); Lucille Chia, *Printing for Profit: The Commercial Publishers of Jianyang, Fujian (11th-19th Centuries)*, Harvard-Yenching Institute Monographs 56 (Cambridge, MA: Harvard University Asia Center, 2002).

2. Kai-wing Chow, *Publishing, Culture, and Power in Early Modern China* (Stanford: Stanford University Press, 2004), 16.

3. Haun Saussy, "In the Workshop of Equivalences: Translation, Institutions, and Media in the Jesuit-Reformation of China," in *Great Walls of Discourse and Other Adventures in Cultural China* (Cambridge, MA: Harvard University Asia Center, 2001), 15-34.

4. Adrian Johns, *Piracy* (Chicago: University of Chicago Press, 2009), 49.

and other "creative goods."[5] When plagiarized versions of these goods were labeled as "pirated" and when inventors called their rivals "pirates," such accounts of widespread imitation also fueled the war of print piracy.[6] In China, however, commercial print houses' reprinting of the texts from state publishers and other private publishers could not be technically considered "print piracy" because neither the state nor a specific publisher had control over printing. As we have seen in chapter 4's discussion of Feng Menglong's *huaben* story "Strange Encounter," one concern over falseness pertained to the notion of the "fake Japanese pirate" (*jiawo*). In late Ming China, the "ethic of authenticity" was more pertinent to cultural, moral, linguistic, and racial authenticity than to the authenticity of printed matter.

As with the English word "piracy," which signifies both theft by maritime marauders and theft of writing, the Chinese words *haidao* 海盜 (seafaring bandits) and *daoban* 盜版 (plagiarized publications) share the same character 盜 (theft). Although the word *daoban* did not exist in late imperial times, the pirating of printed texts sparked intellectual innovation in the book market and literary adaptation. And print piracy's expansion of print production and circulation ultimately gave rise to a public literary sphere separate from the sphere of political authorities. This chapter explores how fiction writers and publishers in Jiangnan constructed different political opinions and notions of "authenticity" by printing, pirating, and adapting the love story of the pirate Xu Hai and the courtesan Wang Cuiqiao.

The Chinese pirate Xu Hai's romance with Wang Cuiqiao rose to prominence in Ming-Qing Jiangnan and eighteenth-century Vietnam in spite of what was an obviously bad public image of pirates. Their speech was vulgar; they frequented brothels.[7] They were also prone to sexual violence: Japanese pirates' rape of Chinese women was a common literary topos in late imperial Chinese literature.[8] The generic storyline of the romance describes how Wang Cuiqiao, Xu Hai's favorite lover, manages to persuade Xu Hai to submit to China. But besieged and captured, Xu Hai dies after his submission. Realizing her true love for the pirate king, the courtesan commits suicide by jumping into the Qiantang River in Hang-

---

5. Adrian Johns, *Piracy*, 48.

6. Adrian Johns, *Piracy*, 43.

7. Robert Antony, *Like Froth*, 147.

8. Zhang Zhejun 張哲俊, *Zhongguo gudai wenxue zhong de Riben xingxiang yanjiu* 中國古代文學中的日本形象研究 (Beijing: Beijing daxue chuban she, 2004).

zhou. Wang Cuiqiao, thus, demonstrates her virtues of patriotic loyalism, female chastity, and romantic love, on all three fronts which are highly valued in late Ming culture.

The Xu Hai–Cuiqiao romance shows the contradiction between the military world of deception and betrayal and the culture of romance, which emphasizes sincerity and loyalty between lovers. Stephen Owen proposes the concept of the culture of romance as "a freely contracted romantic liaison" in the Tang romantic tales of Huo Xiaoyu 霍小玉 and Cui Yingying 崔鶯鶯.[9] In this culture of romance, the internal audience inclines toward the value of passion because it is based upon genuine feeling rather than social obligations. Courtesan Huo Xiaoyu allows herself to die pining for her treacherous lover, arousing the internal audience's rage at the celebrated poet Li Yi 李益 who breaks his marital promise by turning away to marry his cousin, as designated by his mother. The story of maiden Cui Yingying with student Zhang, on the other hand, problematically vacillates between the narratives of passion and moral duty. But the late Ming Xu Hai–Cuiqiao romance resolves the irreconcilable tension between the narrative of passion and the narrative of public duty through the courtesan's suicide and places tremendous emphasis on the terrain of public obligations.

The earliest legend of Wang Cuiqiao can be traced back to Xu Xuemo's 徐學謨 (1522–1593) *Biography of Wang Cuiqiao* (*Wang Cuiqiao zhuan* 王翠翹傳) collected in *Xu shi haiyu ji* 徐氏海隅集 published in 1577.[10] Although the story is mentioned in unofficial histories such as *The Pirate Raids, Strange Realms, Thorough Records*, and *An Appendix to the Record of the Extermination of Xu Hai* (*Ji Jiaochu Xu Hai benmo fuji* 紀剿除徐海本末附記), it was not fully developed until the 1620s, when the commercial printing of *huaben* short story anthologies became widespread in Jiangnan. Robert Hegel notes that the printing trend in the last two decades of the Ming dynasty and during the Ming–Qing transition was undisrupted by catastrophic societal and cultural breakdown and dramatic social change. He discerns the existence of a seventeenth-century market for expensive and large-format editions of fiction in commercial print centers.[11] It was this thriving commercial print culture that facili-

---

9. See Stephen Owen, "Conflicting Interpretations: 'Yingying's Story'" in *The End of the Chinese "Middle Ages": Essays in Mid-Tang Literary Culture* (Stanford: Stanford University Press, 1996), 149–73.

10. Chen Yiyuan 陳益源, *Wang Cuiqiao Gushi yanjiu* 王翠翹故事研究 (Beijing: Xiyuan chuban she, 2003), 27–28.

11. See Robert E. Hegel, *Reading Illustrated Fiction in Late Imperial China* (Stanford: Stanford University Press, 1998), 155.

tated the narrative development and circulation of the remarkable love story of Xu Hai and Wang Cuiqiao.

In these narratives, not only are Xu Hai and Wang Cuiqiao highly malleable characters, but the narrators have considerable leeway to freely design the plots and give agency to characters in order to channel their own political opinions and literary values. Particularly, Wang Cuiqiao's beauty, sexuality, and talent, combined with her loyalism, betrayal of Xu Hai, and suicide in addition to Xu Hai's rebellion and death inspire immense narrative imagination and impulse for revision. In such a highly moldable literary space, various authorial voices speak up to discuss their own views on aspects of "authenticity": fair judgment, Jiangnan's cultural authenticity, the legitimacy of loyalism and female fidelity, the truth of Confucian morality, and the appraisal of the authentic self.

The Syncretic Public Literary Sphere: The Juridical Fiction Writer and the Guilty Courtesan

Zhou Qingyuan was a scholar from Hangzhou, living in the first half of the seventeenth century. He published his short story anthology *Second Collection from the West Lake* (hereafter *The West Lake*) in 1623. The existing Ming edition was published by Yunlin Jujing tang 雲林聚錦堂 in Nanjing.[12] In the author's preface, Zhou complains that because his unparalleled talent has been unrecognized, he has experienced misfortune and poverty. Lamenting his ill fate, he confesses that he would rather become a courtesan who makes herself known to the world by playing the *pipa* lute or an illiterate man than become a scholar 懷才不遇，蹭蹬厄窮，而至願為優伶，手琵琶以求知於世，且願生生世世為一目不識丁之人.[13] A second prefacer, who names himself The Gentleman of Lakes and Seas from the Playful World Studio 湖海士題於玩世居, however, praises Zhou Qingyuan's accomplishment in publishing *The West Lake*. By doing so, he claims, Zhou has succeeded in introducing the culture of Hangzhou—Jiangnan's refined and authentic culture—to a popular audience:

---

12. *Zhongguo tongsu xiaoshuo zongmu tiyao* 中國通俗小說總目提要 (Beijing: Zhongguo wenlian chuban gongsi, 1990), 276.

13. Zhou Qingyuan 周清源, *Xihu erji* 西湖二集, in *Zhongguo gudai zhenxi ben xiaoshuo xu* 中國古代珍稀本小說續, eds. Hou Zhongyi 侯忠義 et al. (Shenyang: Chunfeng wenyi chuban she, 1997), vol. 12, 3.

The kings of Wu and Yue ruled for one hundred years. One hundred and fifty years after the Song royal family crossed the river to the South, numerous historical books have been written about the style and charm of the culture, the ancient ruins, and the marvelous stories [of Hangzhou]. But all these have not been translated into vernacular language in order to cultivate people. Su Shi says, "The West Lake of Hangzhou is like the beauty Xi Shi's eyebrows and eyes." If her eyebrows are not trimmed and painted by her loving husband as Zhang Chang [who painted his beloved wife's eyebrows] did, then it is like the West Lake is blocked by watercress. After Su Shi had dredged the lake, the West Lake's eyes and eyebrows began to show. Zhou Qingyuan's writing brings charm to the West Lake. For this reason, Zhou Qingyuan is a merited minister of West Lake. Even Bai Juyi and Su Shi cannot surpass him.

況重以吳越王之雄霸百年，宋朝之南渡百五十載，流風遺韻，古蹟奇聞，史不勝書，而獨未有譯為俚語，以勸化世人者。蘇長公云：「杭州之有西湖，如人之有眉目也。」而使眉目不修，張敞不畫，亦如葑草之湮塞矣。西湖經長公開濬，而眉目始備；經周子清原之畫，而眉目益斌。然則周清原其西湖之功臣也哉！即白、蘇賴之矣。[14]

The humorous prefacer compares *The West Lake*'s author to the celebrated governor of Hangzhou in the Southern Song dynasty, Su Shi, who dredged the West Lake and constructed the Su causeway across the lake. Zhou Qingyuan, too, brings renown to West Lake—by publishing stories on Hangzhou in vernacular language. For doing so, Zhou Qingyuan is applauded as "a merited minister of the West Lake."

The "merited minister" practices his judicial acts in "General Hu Made Military Achievements by Quelling Pirates" (*Hu Shaobao pingwo zhangong* 胡少保平倭戰功, hereafter "Quelling Pirates"), the last story of the anthology. Zhou Qingyuan describes the pirates as both righteous outlaws and dissolute gangsters. The recurring phrases *xiaoyao huanzai zhi weile ye he* 逍遙歡哉之為樂也呵 (carefree and merry) and *huanzai le* 歡哉樂 (merry) show the pirates as yearning for freedom and social justice and reveling in their lawless debauchery. Nonetheless, depicting the rivalry between the bustling maritime world and the sea-banning Ming state, the contention between the Zhejiang coastal region and the imperial court,

14. "Gentleman of Lakes and Seas" (pseud.), preface to Zhou, *Xihu erji*, 2.

the narrator ultimately reveals his sympathy with the Ming Commander and Censor Hu Zongxian. In "Quelling Pirates," the multiple expressions of indignation at the public's prejudice against Hu culminate in the form of political loyalty to the Ming.

The ballad that opens the story speaks to common people's concerns. Purportedly circulated in Hangzhou in the early years of the Jiajing reign, the folk song already shows a sympathetic view toward the pirate king Xu Hai and toward local people in Zhejiang. It reads:

東海小明王，	The minor king of the Ming on the East Sea,
溫台作戰場，	Uses Wenzhou and Taizhou as his battleground.
虎頭人最苦，	People with a tiger head suffer the most.
結局在錢塘。[15]	The ending will happen in Qiantang.

The lyrics elliptically tell of how Xu Hai, "the minor king of the Ming on the East Sea," led battles against the Ming army in Wenzhou and Taizhou (Taizhou is on the east coast of Zhejiang with Wenzhou to the southwest of Taizhou). The "tiger head" refers synecdochally to Chuzhou 處州 (to the west of Taizhou) (the "tiger head" radical constitutes the upper portion of the graph 處) in Zhejiang, where numerous people were drafted into the Ming army to fight in the battles against the pirates. The song's last line predicts that Xu Hai will be captured and executed in Hangzhou. The song establishes the work's overall sympathetic tone for the commoners and outlaws who suffer in war.

The narrator projects onto the pirates this sympathy for common people and the wish for social justice. The story depicts Wang Zhi, Xu Hai, and their ally as both rebellious and heroic, who are, in this respect, like the bandit heroes in *The Water Margin*: "the thirty-six heavenly soldiers and seventy-two earthly killers" 三十六天罡，七十二地煞之人. Detesting the Ming official administration's pervasive corruption, they flee to the sea. Wang Zhi frankly states his wish for social equality:

Wang Zhi said one day, "Now it is the world of officials and the rich. This is not our world. When we are wronged, where shall we go to

---

15. Zhou Qingyuan, *Xihu erji*, 565.

complain? Besides, muddle-headed and corrupt officials are numerous. Honest officials pitying commoners are few. They have obtained a *jinshi* degree. They have received countless favor from the court and enjoyed generous salary and benefits. They continuously receive bribes and are not good people. They harm people, preventing justice being served. Therefore, the bandit heroes from Mount Liang exclusively kill corrupt officials. Why don't we migrate overseas and be carefree and happy?

王直一日說道："如今都是紗帽財主的世界，沒有我們的世界，我們受了冤枉，那裏去叫屈？況且糊塗貪贓的官府多，清廉愛百姓的官府少，他中了一個進士，受了朝廷多少恩惠，大俸大祿享用了，還只是一味貪贓，不肯做好人，一味害民，不肯行公道，所以梁山泊那一班好漢，專一殺的是貪官汙吏。我們何如到海外去，逍遙歡哉之為樂也呵。"[16]

Wang thereafter achieves success as a maritime merchant and entrepreneur. Together with Ye Zongman, Wang builds maritime ships and smuggles gunpowder, silk, and cotton to Japan, Siam, and other Southeast Asian countries. After five to six years of trading, they become rich, and Wang Zhi "accumulated countless gold and silver" 積金銀無數. Yet he does not achieve this wealth by deceit: "If the goods were good, he would say they were good. If the goods were bad, he would say they were bad. He never cheated" 凡是貨物，好的說好，歹的說歹，並無欺騙之意.[17] Because of this honesty, Wang gains the confidence of those in his band: "Therefore, all the 'Japanese slaves' trusted him" 以此倭奴信服.

Wang Zhi's status as a king on the seas (*haiwai guowang* 海外國王) is stated matter-of-factly by his adopted son Wang Ao: "Why do you want to go see the Japanese king? There is a king here. He rules the thirty-six islands. You can let him pass around the edict. It is useless to meet the Japanese king!" 怎生要去見國王？這裡有一位徽王，是三十六島之尊。只要他去傳諭便是，見國王有何益哉！[18] Wang's kingly garments manifest his dominance on the seas, violating the land-based Ming's sartorial laws:

He wears a hair-tying flying-fish cap and a red dragon robe with narrow sleeves. Around his waist is a green jade beast-shaped hook.

16. Zhou Qingyuan, *Xihu erji*, 566.
17. Zhou Qingyuan, *Xihu erji*, 567.
18. Zhou Qingyuan, *Xihu erji*, 572.

On his feet he wears a pair of sea-horse-shaped black leather boots. The sun and the moon embellish his left shoe. Five stars appear on his right shoe. Patterns such as vases, flowers, and left-turning and right-turning wheels are embroidered on the robe. He is indeed a rogue king and a *raksha* of China.

頭上戴一頂束髮飛魚冠，身上穿一件窄袖絳龍袍，腰間係一條怪獸五絲碧玉鉤，腳下蹬一雙海馬四縫烏皮靴。左日月，右五星，或畫鈢瓶花勝之形，或書左輪右輪之字。寶刀如霜雪，羽扇似宮旗。果然海外草頭王，真是中國惡羅剎。[19]

However, the pirates' characterization is ambivalent. The idiom *huanzaileye* 歡哉樂也 (merrily) recurs to describe the pirates as debauched, simple-minded, and easily deceived and provoked. By contrast, the commander in chief Hu Zongxian is a visionary and a calm strategist. Hu treats the pirates courteously, showering them with gifts of gold, silver, and brocades and teaching them how to fight with Japanese swords. Appreciating Hu's help, Xu devotedly follows him, bringing him abundant seaborne treasures including armor made from the skins of sea creatures and, from his own possessions, a flying-fish-shaped crown. But even after Xu Hai's submission, Hu Zongxian remains suspicious, believing that "since Xu Hai came on an unscheduled date, fully armed, he harbors a wolf's ambition. If he is not exterminated, he will cause trouble later" 徐海不依日期而來，又甲冑而進，曉得他明是狼子野心，若不剿除，終為後患. Hu successfully defeats Wang Zhi and Xu Hai by using the strategy of *jian*. To divide the pirates, Hu first bribes Xu Hai's two courtesan lovers, Wang Cuiqiao and Lü Zhu 綠珠, to slander Xu's allies, Chen Dong and Ye Ma. After Xu captures Ye Ma, Hu forges a letter from Ye Ma asking Chen Dong to murder Xu Hai in revenge. After reading the letter, Xu Hai captures Chen Dong and turns him in to Hu Zongxian. Afterward, Hu cunningly convinces Chen Dong to send his pirates a false letter claiming that Wang Zhi has submitted and will help the Ming to capture the pirates. Suspicious, the pirates ambush Shen Village. At the same time, fearing for his life, Xu Hai flees his camp with his two courtesan lovers, only to be discovered by Chen Dong's pirates. In the ensuing battle, Xu Hai is cornered, and he jumps into the sea and drowns.

To defeat Wang Zhi, Hu Zongxian uses the *jian* strategy of betrayal and division. Hu Zongxian again falsifies a letter, informing Wang Zhi of the

---

19. Zhou Qingyuan, *Xihu erji*, 573.

emperor's declaration of war against him and offering protection if Wang submits. Hu arranges for the letter to be read "accidentally" by Wang's collaborators Wang Ao and Ye Zongman, whom Hu invited to enter into his bedroom. The two believe what Hu has falsely written in the letter—that Hu will protect them. Fearing a war, they send a message to Wang Zhi, requesting him to submit.

In "Quelling Pirates," the contending viewpoints—the narrative of love and the narrative of political loyalty—are reconciled through Wang Cuiqiao's guilt-induced suicide:

Wang Cuiqiao sighs several times: "I hate that I am ill-fated, fallen into the brothel world. I was abducted by Xu Hai. Although he is a pirate, he treated me as his best friend and never made any mistake. For the sake of China, I deceived him. It is I who betrayed him, not Xu Hai who betrayed me. Since I have betrayed him, how can I be the wife of this commander?" Finished speaking, she jumps into the water and drowns herself.

王翠翹再三嘆息道："自恨平生命薄，墮落煙花，又被徐海擄掠。徐海雖是賊人，他卻以心腹待我，未曾有失。我為國家，只得用計騙了他，是我負徐海，不是徐海有負於我也。我既負了徐海，今日豈能復做軍官之妻子乎?" 說罷，投入水中而死。

Wai-yee Li points out that late Ming courtesans like the talented and patriotic Liu Rushi 柳如是 (1618–1664) are famous for their dramatic gestures and heroic persona. They are credited with significant roles in the public realm during the catastrophic political turmoil of the mid-seventeenth century.[20] "Quelling Pirates," however, shows the dilemma a late Ming courtesan faces between the culture of romance and the public realm of politics. Wang Cuiqiao saves the country at the expense of her romantic love for Xu Hai. When the pirate king of free will is betrayed by the woman he genuinely loves, the narrative evinces an irreconcilable conflict that must be somehow resolved. Wang Cuiqiao's suicide thus releases such tension.

Downplaying the romantic love of the courtesan and the free will of the pirate, the narrator praises Wang Cuiqiao's loyalty to China. She is differentiated from the legendary femme fatale Xi Shi 西施 and the female warrior Madam Yang. Xi Shi (who appears in *The West Lake* pref-

---

20. Wai-yee Li, "The Late Ming Courtesan, 46–73.

ace) helped the King of Yue 越 (496 BC–464 BC) to conquer his enemy Fu Chai 夫差 (d. 473 BC) by seduction. Afterward, she sought seclusion at West Lake with her lover Fan Li 范蠡 (536 BC–448 BC). Madam Yang was the wife of Li Quan 李全, a leader of rebellious peasants in the Southern Song. In *The Peony Pavilion*, the "treacherous" Madam Yang would rather be a pirate than receive the title Queen of Quelling the Jurchen Jin 討金娘娘, bestowed by the Southern Song emperor. Zhou Qingyuan eulogizes Wang Cuiqiao as "loyal to our country" 忠於我國之人. In earlier dynasties, such as the Northern Song, the rhetoric of female fidelity is to reproach the conduct of men and ultimately to promote political loyalty for men.[21] Similarly, Zhou Qingyuan's advocacy for the loyal courtesan implies his moral criticism of the pirate and his gang. Ultimately, the narrator sympathizes with Hu Zongxian who, albeit bringing peace to people, unfortunately becomes the victim of the Ming court's political persecution:

> Later on, [as the idiom goes,] "When birds are extinguished, bows and arrows are abandoned." Hu Zongxian died from the imperial court's political persecution, charged for spending too much money. Dear audience, *The Art of War* states, "A military troops of 100,000 soldiers will spend one thousand gold per day." It also states, "Brave men will stand out for a big reward." How can one calculate money and food when it comes to warfare? The imperial court also persecuted Hu for being an ally of the corrupt administer Yan Song. It has often been the case that when powerful ministers dominate in the capital, great generals can hardly make achievements at frontiers. This is why Yue Fei eventually died at the hands of the evil minister Qin Gui. It is ultimately impossible to achieve great accomplishments. When heroes want to thoroughly accomplish a mission, they have no other way but to do indecent things, to be obsequious to the powerful. We need to know their bitter hearts. They tolerate wrongs to make their names and reach their goals. How could you only grumble and criticize? I hope that people in the world will open their eyes and broaden their minds. Be tolerant, so that people in the future can do things.

---

21. Beverly Bossler, *Courtesans, Concubines, and the Cult of Female Fidelity: Gender and Social Change in China, 1000–1400*. (Cambridge, MA: Harvard University Asia Center, 2012), 139.

後來鳥盡弓藏，蒙吏議而死，說他日費鬥金。看官，那《孫武子》
上道："興師十萬，日費千金。" 又說道："重賞之下，必有勇夫。"
征戰之事，怎生銖銖較量，論得錢糧？又說他是奸臣嚴嵩之黨。
從來道，未有權臣在內，而大將能立功於外者，所以岳飛終死於
秦檜之手，究竟成不得大功。英雄豪傑任一件大事在身上，要做
得完完全全，沒奈何做那嫂溺叔援之事，只得卑躬屈體於權臣
之門，正要諒他那一種不得已的苦心，隱忍以就功名，怎麼絮絮
叨叨，只管求全責備！願世上人大著眼睛，寬著肚腸，將就些兒
罷了，等後來人也好任事。[22]

This passage shows the anthology's syncretic vernacular language. The vernacular phrases (*houlai* 後來 [afterward], *youshuo dao* 又說道 [speak again], *zensheng* 怎生 [why], *meinaihe* 沒奈何 [no other way but], *zhide* 只得 [have to], *zhengyao* 正要 [need to], *zenme* 怎麼 [how could], *zhi-guan* 只管 [only], *jiangjiu xieba* 將就些吧 [be tolerant]) channel the narrator's indignation at the injustice the commander in chief endures. Classical language idioms, i.e., *Niaojin gongcang* 鳥盡弓藏 (when birds all perish, bows are put in storage), and citations from the classics suggest how "Quelling Pirates" incorporates vernacular fiction into the classical world of history writing. The narrative structure of "Quelling Pirates" emulates the historical narratives discussed in chapter 3. While those long historical narratives feature an endless series of linked events and numerous characters, "Quelling Pirates" revolves around a single character, Hu Zongxian, in a relatively independent event.[23] The preference for history writing is also reflected in Hu Zongxian's classical-language speech that manifests his strategic intelligence. For instance, the author/narrator copies Hu Zongxian's classical-language instruction to the two envoys to the Gotō Island verbatim from *Pictorial Compendium of Governing the Seas*: "Wang Zhi lives beyond the seas. It is hard to defeat him on ships. We must tempt him out, forcing him to lose his territorial strength" 王直越在海外，難與他角勝於舟楫之間，要須誘而出之，使虎失其負嵎之勢，乃可成擒耳.[24]

The riveting characters—the pirate king and the intelligent minister—show the syncretic and ambivalent nature of the public literary sphere in the vernacular story. Literati of the time already felt a deep sense of inse-

22. Zhou Qingyuan, *Xihu erji*, 566.

23. About the difference between novels and short stories, see Patrick Hanan's preliminary distinction in *The Chinese Vernacular Story*, 22–23.

24. Zhou Qingyuan, *Xihu erji*, 572.

curity about the Ming imperial identity that had been weakened internally by political corruption and externally by the piracy war and maritime merchants and emigrants. Nonetheless, the story compromises the rebellious position of the outlaws and advocates for the controversial politician who brought peace to the war-torn region. The short story's intended readers feel local people's suffering in the piracy raids and pervasive injustice in the society. The story speaks to a common need for fair judgment.

Praising Female Fidelity: The Loyal Male Author and the Chaste Female Knight-Errant

In 1632, Lu Renlong and his better-known brother, the publisher and writer Lu Yunlong 陸雲龍 (ca. 1587–1666), compiled and published the short story collection *Model Words to Shape the World* (*Xingshi yan* 型世言, hereafter *Model Words*) through the Zhengxiao Publishing House 崢霄館 (Lodge of Lofty Clouds), the brothers' commercial publishing house in Hangzhou. Like many of their contemporaries, the Lu brothers had failed the increasingly competitive civil examination. To make a living, Lu Yunlong worked as a private tutor, a ghostwriter, and a legal secretary (*muliao* 幕僚) for several local officials, such as Li Qing 李清, Wang Mianzhai 王勉齋, and Shen Chenquan 沈宸荃. Lu Renlong also worked as a tutor, a copier, and a ghostwriter for the local government.[25] Through Zhengxiao Publishing House, Lu Renlong also published a political novel on Mao Wenlong 毛文龍 (1576–1629) titled *Liaohai danzhong lu* 遼海丹忠錄 (*Records of Scarlet Loyalty on the Sea of Liao*) in 1630.[26] Two years before, the elder brother Lu Yunlong published a political novel on contemporary events titled *The Book that Condemns the Evil Minister Wei Zhongxian* (*Wei Zhongxian xiaoshuo chijian shu* 魏忠賢小說斥奸書).[27] The Lu brothers' publications show their keen interest in the politics of the Ming court and evince their loyalism to the Ming empire. The preface to *Model Words* articulates their sentiments:

> One has to be loyal to the person from whom one receives salary. Should one risk one's life for loyalty? Should not one risk one's life

---

25. Gu Keyong, 顧克勇, *Lu Yunlong xiongdi yanjiu* 陸雲龍兄弟研究 (Beijing: Zhongguo shehui kexue chuban she, 2010), 13–14.

26. For a thorough survey of the Lu brothers' biographies, see Gu Keyong, *Lu Yunlong*, 9–14.

27. Gu Keyong, *Lu Yunlong*, 42–43.

for loyalty? Should family be sacrificed for loyalty? Should not family be sacrificed for loyalty? With an unyielding mind, one can move heaven and earth, stimulate thought and spirit, and make sacrifice to emperors and forefathers. Alas! Enough! In death, one is alive! Today, I use the brush to represent heroes in the past. That [Li] Jinglong surrendered and died. His family was also eliminated. The difference [between him and the heroes] is as vast as the distance between the earth and heaven. "My patriotic heart will shine through history!" The patriotic heart of Minister Tie will illuminate more from now on!

食人之祿。忠人之事。忠何必殺身？亦何必不殺身？　忠何必覆家？亦何必不覆家？唯以不受磨滅之心。可以質天地，可以動思神。可以靖君父。嗚呼！已矣！死猶生矣！即今日之筆舌，尤足見當日之鬚眉。彼景隆之身亦死，家亦覆，不天壤哉！留取丹心照汗青！鐵尚書丹心從今當更耿耿哉！[28]

"My patriotic heart will shine through history" is a line from a poem by the Southern Song general Wen Tianxiang 文天祥 (1236–1283), who was executed by Kublai Khan for his loyalism to the Song when the Mongol Yuan conquered China. Minister Tie refers to Tie Xuan 鐵鉉 (1366–1402). Unwilling to succumb to Zhu Di 朱棣—the Yongle emperor (r.1402–1424)—who overthrew the throne of his cousin Jianwen 建文 emperor (r. 1392–1398), Tie Xuan was executed by the new ruler. The counterexample to this unwavering loyal subject is Li Jinglong 李景隆 (d. 1423). The nephew of the Ming emperor Zhu Yuanzhang 朱元璋 (r. 1368–1398), Li Jinglong was put to death by his uncle after he plotted to subvert Yuanzhang's throne. Referencing the two opposing examples of loyalty and treason, the Lu brothers declare absolute loyalty to the Ming empire.

Wang Cuiqiao and her love for the pirate Xu Hai become the metaphor for the Lu brothers' propagation of political loyalty in the seventh story of *Model Words*. "Commander in Chief Hu Cleverly Uses Hua Diqing; Wang Cuiqiao Dies to Repay Xu Mingshan's Love" 胡總制巧用華棣卿; 王翠翹死報徐明山 (hereafter "Death for Xu Hai") praises her fidelity (*lie* 烈) and chastity (*zhen* 貞). Her suicide, which she commits in mourning her dead lover and in defiance of Hu Zongxian's sexual transgression, is evidence of these virtues. The story opens with the cliché figure of the femme fatale: Xi Shi. She is reproached as a "cold-hearted woman" 薄情婦人 who betrayed

---

28. Lu Renlong 陸人龍, *Kuizhang ge cangben Xingshi yan* 奎章閣藏本型世言, ed. Li Wenhuan 李文煥 (Beijing: Zhongguo dabaike quanshu chuban she, 2002), 3.

the King of Yue's love by seducing the King of Wu, albeit on her lover's order. The narrator attests to the lovers' great love to underscore the gravity of her betrayal: "It is untrue that their love was not deep; it is undeniable that they knew each other's heart" 不可說恩不深，不可說不知心.[29] The narrator reasons that she deserved to be drowned by her second treacherous lover, Fan Li. By contrast, Wang Cuiqiao is described as a model woman—a "remarkable knight-errant among women" 女中奇俠. She is loyal to both the Ming empire and her pirate lover. Assessing the two women's characters, literatus Yu Huai 余懷 (1616–1696) declares that Wang Cuiqiao is superior to Xi Shi because she can fulfill both public and private obligations (公私兼盡 gongsi jianjin).[30]

Wai-yee Li notes that in late Ming literature a female knight-errant connotes "unconventional behavior, courage, generosity, resoluteness, and independent spirit" as well as interests in military affairs, commitment to loyalism, and an appreciation of an unconventional romantic relationship."[31] Wang Cuiqiao possesses precisely these unusual qualities. At a young age, she determines to sell herself to save her father, who is imprisoned after the granary he supervises accidentally burns down. She is first sold as a concubine to a petite official, Zhang Wangqiao 張望橋, in a small county near Ningbo. Unfortunately, Zhang turns out to be a henpecked husband, dominated by his wife in a topsy-turvy marriage. Soon after, Zhang dies in prison, and the wife sells Wang Cuiqiao to a brothel house. A wealthy man named Hua Diqing 華棣卿 redeems her with 180 taels of silver. Thereafter, she associates only with a cultured circle of literati and converses on the subjects of poetry, chess, and the zither. Wang Cuiqiao's fortunes change again when she travels back to Shandong to find her parents after the pirates raid coastal China. Abducted by the pirates, she is discovered by Xu Hai and becomes his favorite lover. As the pirates battle the Ming army, Hu Zongxian sends Hua Diqing as a military strategist to persuade Xu Hai to submit to the Ming. To repay her former benefactor's favor, she saves Hua Diqing's life from Xu Hai who captures him. She also proceeds resolutely to convince Xu Hai to submit.

Out of her love for the renegade, Wang Cuiqiao advises Xu Hai on how to strategically seek freedom by submission. "Since ancient times, no ban-

29. Lu Renlong, *Kuizhang ge*, 108.
30. Hua Wei 華瑋, *Mingqing xiqu zhong de nuxing shengyin he lishi jiyi* 明清戲曲中的女性聲音和歷史記憶 (Taibei: Guojia chuban she, 2013), 299.
31. Wai-yee Li, "The Late Ming Courtesan," 46–73.

dits have had a good ending" 自古沒有個做賊得了的,[32] she warns and reminds him that he is already in a dangerous situation because he has set foot on the land without any reinforcements from the sea. Cautioning, "once you fall, you cannot return" 若一蹉跌,便欲歸無路, she tells him to strategically surrender so that he might be able to obtain freedom once Hu no longer perceives him as a threat. She advises Xu to request the county of Zhoushan 舟山—a coastal port in Zhejiang where Asian pirates and Portuguese stationed in the late Ming—as his territory, to ask the Ming to open maritime trade, and to profit from trade with Japan. This way, she reasons, he will have opportunities to return to the ocean and be free. The shrewd courtesan even writes an eloquent submission letter in classical Chinese on the pirate's behalf.

In aiding her lover, Wang Cuiqiao is motivated by her own desire to spend her life with him. Once he is free, she tells Xu Hai, "Then we will dismiss all our soldiers and subordinates. We will become plain-clothed commoners at Linzi. Why shall we keep the army and suffer from fear every day?" 然後並散部曲,與妳為臨淄壹布衣,何苦擁兵,日受驚恐?[33] But the fiercely independent Xu Hai does not submit. He denounces Hu Zongxian's collusion with Yan Song and the corrupt Ming state, proclaiming his stateless sovereignty: "I, Xu Mingshan, am not subject to the Great Ming, nor subject to Japan. I am the son of Heaven beyond the seas. I kill freely. Why should I surrender and have to bear the bad temper of those damned officials?" 我徐明山不屬大明,不屬日本,是個海外天子,生殺自由。我來就招,受妳這幹鳥官氣麼?[34]

In the end, Xu Hai's struggle and the pirate war come to an end when he drowns himself rather impulsively in a fit of emotion (qingji 情急). The loyal courtesan is captured before she can die with him. Drunken Hu Zongxian molests the mournful courtesan, who soon takes her own life by jumping into the Qiantang River. Wang is compared to the filial daughter Cao E 曹娥 of Shangyu 上虞 (130–143) who threw herself into the river where her father was drowned. Wang's corpse is retrieved from the water and buried beside the Temple of Cao E. When Hua Diqing crosses the River of Cao E on a boat, Wang Cuiqiao appears in his dream. She is awarded the title Goddess of Loyalty and Chastity (zhonglie xianyuan 忠烈仙媛) by Heaven for her loyalty to Xu Hai and for her merits of saving the people of Zhejiang by bringing the war to an end. She assists Goddess

---

32. Lu Renlong, *Kuizhang ge*, 116.
33. Lu Renlong, *Kuizhang ge*, 118.
34. Lu Renlong, *Kuizhang ge*, 115.

Mazu in governing the ocean. She predicts that Hu Zongxian will be punished because he mercilessly executes the pirates after they have already surrendered (*zhuxiang* 誅降). The story ends with Hu Zongxian's death in prison.

Hu Zongxian expresses guilt about Wang Cuiqiao's death: "Her death is actually my death. How can I not be saddened" 爾之死，實予之死。予能無憮然歟? He even composes a eulogy for her.

> She is remarkable in her ability to use her resilience to make tigers and wolves sleep in her bed. Half of the sentient beings living in southeast China were saved. Her sacrifice in territorial protection is known nine heavens above. She stopped the war and saved people from suffering. Before her remarkable achievement was complete, she perished in the water. Unlike the femme fatale Xi Shi, she defeated the enemy with her one-inch tongue. Unlike Xi Shi who was submerged in a leathered bag, she died to repay the favor she received. She is much more remarkable for her loyalty and righteousness. Her virtue is as profound as the ocean.

> 奇莫奇於柔豺虎於衽席。蘇東南半壁之生靈，豎九重安攘之大烈，息郡國之轉輸，免羽檄之征擾。奇功未酬，竟逐逝波不返耶。以寸舌屈敵，不必如夷光之盅惑。以一死殉恩，不必如夷光之再逐鴟夷。爾更奇於忠，奇於義，爾之聲譽，即決海不能寫其芳也。[35]

The Ming official endorses Wang Cuiqiao's fidelity and chastity in the end.

The end-of-story commentary by Yu Hou 雨侯 (likely Lu Renlong himself) continues to foreground the significance of female fidelity and chastity while also offering a misogynistic view of those virtues:

> When reading the *History of Tang,* I found that when Shi Bo captured and sent the bandit Huang Chao's wife and concubines to the Tang emperor, the emperor reproached and interrogated them. The wife said, "You, the emperor, criticize us women for not being able to die for our husband. What place do you have for your subjects?" The emperor then ordered her be executed at the market. She did not look regretful at all. Overall, women are ill-fated. They resemble

---

35. Lu Renlong, *Kuizhang ge,* 122–23.

withered petals floating in the wind. How can they have autonomy? Death can manifest their loyalty. It is fitting for her name to shine in history.

予常讀唐書，見時溥送黃巢姬妾至，帝臨軒責問。其為首者對帝有雲，"帝以不能死節責婦女，置公卿于何地乎？" 帝命殺之市，臨刑無戚容。蓋薄命紅顏，如風飄殘萼，哪能自主？卒能以死酬恩，宜其光史冊也。[36]

Lu Renlong legitimizes his narrative of Wang Cuiqiao's suicide as an act of chastity and fidelity with an emperor's words. Katherine Carlitz has discussed that the late Ming "theater of virtue" that sought to foreground patriarchy, loyalty, and imperial ideology cruelly tapped into the self-inflicted female body in four types of stories of "filial piety, virginity, resistance to remarriage, and resistance to rape."[37] Siyen Fei further argues that the cult of chastity and female suicide that began in the highly commercialized late Ming society became a useful means for male literati to perform "political activism." Literati could claim themselves as a cultural authority when they spoke for underprivileged women who performed acts of chastity and fidelity.[38] In the narrative, Wang Cuiqiao dies for her lover, as rendered in Chinese, *xunqing* 殉情 (death for love). In aligning the courtesan's romantic love with loyalty to the Ming state, Lu Renlong asserts his own political agenda in publishing *Model Words*, establishing himself as an authorized publisher in Hangzhou and the Jiangnan region.

Pirating the Pirate's Romance: Advocating Moral Truth to Save the World

Model Words was pirated at least twice, first under the title *Huan ying* 幻影 (*Illusions*, ca. 1643) and then under the title *Sanke pai'an jingqi* 三刻拍案驚奇 (*Third Amazement*, early Qing dynasty). The publications were attributed to two pseudonyms—The Awakened Daoist 夢覺道人 and The

36. Lu Renlong, *Kuizhang ge*, 124.

37. Katherine Carlitz, "Desire, Danger, and the Body: Stories of Women's Virtue in Late Ming China," in *Engendering China: Women, Culture, and the State, eds.* Christina K. Gilmartin et al. (Cambridge, MA: Harvard University Press, 1994), 101–24.

38. Siyen Fei, "Writing for Justice: An Activist Beginning of the Cult of Female Chastity in Late Imperial China," *The Journal of Asian Studies* 71, no. 4: 991–1012.

Playboy of the West Lake 西湖浪子.[39] To hide that *Illusions* was a pirated edition of *Model Words*, the publisher of *Illusions* deleted all the paratextual material of *Model Words*, including the preface, inscriptions, prologues, marginal comments within chapters, and chapter-end comments. The publisher of *Third Amazement*, however, used *Model Words*'s original woodblocks when publishing it at the beginning of the Qing dynasty.[40] This is suggested by the fact that the printed works are identical except for the omission from *Third Amazement* of *Model Words*'s eighth, ninth, twelfth, seventeenth, and twenty-fourth stories, all of which involve Qing-dynasty taboo words related to Tartars or barbarians.[41] In both anthologies, "Death for Xu Hai" appears as the seventh story. In *Third Amazement*, the story has an abbreviated title, "In Life, She Pays Back Her Parents; In Death, She Repays Xu Hai's Love" 生抱花萼恩，死謝徐海義.

A new preface added to both works compares truth to fiction. Although unofficial histories, or yeshi 野史, transmit morality, the prefacer claims, "marvelous" (qi 奇) and "strange" (guai 怪) stories discovered in the neglected and wasted archives of the past are also regarded as worthy of transmission through "printing" (shouzi 授梓). For the prefacer, fiction as illusion is only the form by which to convey the work's actual content, truth. Having traveled to the beautiful Tiantai 天台 mountains and visited historical ruins, the author observes that "mountains and rivers are fantastically transformed" 山河變幻. By this, he probably means that the society at the end of the Ming is in wartime turmoil. When real world experience becomes surreal, the fictional then turns truthful. At the foot of the mountain, he discovers a few works of vernacular fiction. Referring to them as *yeshi*, he extols their moral worth:

> Loyalty, filial piety, marital love, brotherly love, and friendship should be recognized as truth. Alcohol, sex, money, and anger should be relegated as illusion. Prosperity can suddenly become illusion, only leaving shadows of goodness and badness. These are to be transmitted to posterity and elaborated upon by idlers. Then people will respect beauty and detest ugliness. Amazement and

---

39. Chen Yiyuan 陳益源, *Wang Cuiqiao gushi yanjiu* 王翠翹故事研究 (Taibei: Liren shuju, 2001), 3.

40. Chen Yiyuan, *Wang Cuiqiao*, 123. Chen Qinghao held another view that *Third Amazement*'s woodblocks were carved based upon the woodblocks of *Model Words*. See Chen Qinghao 陳慶浩, "Xingshiyan pingzhu jiaozhu ben xu," in *Xingshiyan pingzhu* 型世言評註 (Beijing: Xinhua chuban she, 1999).

41. Chen Yiyuan, *Wang Cuiqiao*, 120.

astonishment. Are these not marvelous? Today, I chose the most marvelous stories and put them in print. This is not worthless.

君臣、父子、夫婦、兄弟、朋友之理道，宜認得真；貴賤、窮達、酒、色、財、氣之情景，須看得幻。當場熱哄，瞬息成虛，止留一善善惡惡影子，為世人所喧傳，好事者之敷演。後世或因芳躅而敬之，或因醜戾而憤之，驚驚愕愕，奇乎不奇乎？今特撮其最奇者數條授梓，非無謂也。[42]

An imaginary reader speaks up, criticizing the author's unethical and escapist practice of publishing fiction in times of political turmoil and social change: "Why do you only collect gossips and unofficial histories, undertaking an unimportant task?" 而徒嘵嘵於稗官野史，作不急之務耶？ The author defends himself:

Before I realized, I sighed: "You know who I am. It is not that I do not know what is going on in the world. Worldly chaos all comes from material desire, betrayal, and immorality. These vices transform the world to such a degree that it is inevitable there is warfare inside and outside the empire. Who does not know that wars should be ceased and natural disasters need remedy? But no approach worked! How sad! Since nothing works, why do you bother to listen to me blathering on? My vision is to rescue the world here and to let the world see. It can correct thoughts, emotions, and bring forth truth. There is ethics behind the Five Relations. There is righteousness in wealth and prestige. Although this anthology talks about the past, it aims to talk about the present. This is indeed my thought. Who says this is useless for the world?"

予不覺嘆曰："子非特不知余，並不知天下事者也！天下之亂，皆從貪生好利，背君親，負德義；所至變幻如此，焉有兵不訌於內，而刃不橫於外者乎？ 今人孰不以為師旅當息，兇荒宜拯，究不得一濟焉。悲夫！既無所濟，又何煩余之饒舌也？ 余策在以此救之，使人睹之，可以理順，可以正情，可以悟真；覺君父師友自有定分，富貴利達自有大義。今者敘說古人，雖屬影響，以之喻俗，實獲我心；孰謂無補於世哉！"[43]

---

42. Mengjue daoren 夢覺道人, *Sanke pai'an jinqi* 三刻拍案驚奇 (Beijing: Huaxia chuban she, 2012), 1.

43. Mengjue daoren, *Sanke pai'an*, 2.

The truth of Confucian morality, the author asserts, is an essential ethical remedy for the disordered world.

In the preceding discussions, I have demonstrated that the various versions of the Wang Cuiqiao–Xu Hai romance published in the last two decades of the Ming constituted a "public literary sphere" in which the author-cum-narrator instills his political opinions and literary values. "Quelling Pirates" constructs a syncretic literary sphere in which the author speaks to a common concern for fair judgment. "Death for Xu Hai" shows Lu Renlong's political agenda of his publishing business. His loyalism to the Ming state and advocacy of female fidelity authorize his publication enterprise. The publishers of *Third Amazement* and *Illusions* advocate for the truth of Confucian morality to legitimize their publications of vernacular fiction in social turmoil and channel their views toward social and political disorder at the end of the Ming dynasty. Within such a public literary sphere, the female body of the courtesan becomes the site for mediating conflicting narratives. The suicide of Wang Cuiqiao in "Quelling Pirates" reconciles the conflict between the public realm of politics and the culture of romance. In "Death for Xu Hai," her suicide for love adjudicates the corrupt official and becomes a surrogate for the male literati's advocacy of fidelity and chastity to demonstrate their political loyalty to the Ming state. Whereas the narratives of the Xu Hai–Cuiqiao romance in *West Lake*, *Model Words*, *Illusions*, and *Third Amazement* share a consistent storyline with variations, *The Romance of Jin, Yun, and Qiao* to be discussed in the next section makes a big plot development. A new female character appears as the double of Wang Cuiqiao, both of whom are married to a scholar—an opposite role type of the pirate king. The integration of the Xu Hai–Cuiqiao romance into the literary genre of scholar-beauty romance marks an awakened notion of the authenticity of the self—an authentic man of feelings (*zhen you qing ren* 真有情人)—among literati during the Ming–Qing transition.

Appraising the Authentic Self:
The Pirate Scholar and the Virtuous Prostitute

An anonymous author who named himself Qingxin Cairen adapted the early versions of the Xu Hai–Wang Cuiqiao story into *The Romance of Jin, Yun, and Qiao* 金雲翹傳 (hereafter, *The Romance*). The author's name can be translated as The Blue-Hearted Talented Scholar. "The Blue Heart" is a pun on the Chinese script *qing* 情 (love), which consists of the heart radical and the script 青 (blue green) as its graphic component. The earliest edition of *The Romance* is the Guanhuatang 貫華堂 edition, subtitled *Shengtan waishu* 聖嘆外書 (Secondary Collection of Jin Shengtan). Most scholars believe *The Romance* was written after the Ming fell. A literary critic dates the Guanhuatang edition to the Chongzhen 崇禎 reign (1611–1644), based upon following commentary printed at the end of the novel:

> Some say that the world has already been tilted toward the northwest, and the author still ignores life and death, indulging in absurdity. The crime of the author exceeds that of Zhuangzi. I think, however, Heaven still fills the southeast. Every script is a five-colored stone. The author's merit is no less than that of Nüwa.

> 說者曰：地已傾西北矣，而齊死生一味荒唐，作者之罪，出莊子上；吾則以為，天滿東南，字字是五色石，作者之功不在女媧下。[44]

"Heaven still fills the southeast" suggests that Ming dynasty was still existent, although the war with the Manchus had begun. It might be that the work was written between 1643 and 1645, when the Ming dynasty's fate was still uncertain. It might also be that the Ming had already collapsed and that it was the Southern Ming. Comparing the author to Nüwa, the human creator who mends the broken heavens with five-colored stones, the prefacer, like those of *Third Amazement* and *Illusions*, authorizes the publication of *The Romance* as an essential way to rescue the world from chaos.

Published during the Ming–Qing transition, *The Romance* was influenced by the cult of *qing* (love) as manifested by Tang Xianzu's *The Peony Pavilion*, the lore of Feng Xiaoqing 馮小青 (c.a. late Ming), and Feng Menglong's *History of Love* (*Qingshi* 情史). *The Romance* continues the trope of an "ill-fated beauty" (*hongyan boming* 紅顏薄命) from "Quelling Pirates" and "Death for Xu Hai" by comparing Wang Cuiqiao to Feng Xiaoqing. The legendary talented and miserable female poet Feng Xiaoqing is introduced into *The Romance* as the literary model or precursor for Wang Cuiqiao. Feng Xiaoqing exemplifies the talented beauty—the female genius who makes her name by her literary talent and extraordinary beauty and who dies young. A fervent reader of *The Peony Pavilion*, in

---

44. Dong Wencheng 董文成, *Qingdai wenxue lungao* 清代文學論稿 (Shenyang: Chunfeng wenyi chuban she, 1994), 31–53.

which the heroine Du Liniang dies from dreaming of her lover and is sub-
sequently resurrected by him, Feng Xiaoqing is a miserable and beautiful
concubine abused by her husband's first wife. She burns Xiaoqing's poems
and isolates her in a villa by the West Lake. After painting a self-portrait—
emulating Du Liniang—she dies at the age of nineteen.[45] Feng Xiaoqing's
legend began to circulate in Hangzhou from 1612.[46] In the preface, the
author reiterates that her miserable life gives rise to her fame:

> For example, Xiaoqing of Yangzhou was ranked the first in terms of
> talent, sentiment, beauty, and nature. However, she was married to
> an idiot husband. How unfortunate! Then she encountered that evil
> jealous wife and suffered tremendously. How sad! How painful! It is
> precisely such pain and sadness that moved those literati to com-
> pose literary collections and romantic plays to immortalize her as a
> star of her generation. Had Xiaoqing not encountered that evil
> woman, had she simply roamed among the little stars and turned
> her sorrowful clouds and resenting rains into poetic words of snow,
> moon, wind, and flower, then how could she have been immortal-
> ized! In sum, only grinding can test the firmness of the jadestone.
> Only burning can bring out incense's fragrance.

> 即如揚州的小青，才情色性無不第一。嫁了恁般的呆丈夫，也折
> 得勾了。又遇著那般的惡妒婦，生生活活直逼立苦殺了，豈不可
> 傷，豈不可痛！正惟可傷可痛，故感動了這些文人墨士，替他刻
> 文集，編傳奇，留貽不朽，成了個一代佳人。誰人不頌美生憐，那
> 個不聞名歎息！若令小青不遇恁般狠毒的女平章，稍得優遊於
> 小星之列，將愁雲怨雨化為雪月風花，亦何能留傳不朽哉！大都
> 玉不磨不知其堅，檀不焚不知其香。[47]

Traditional Chinese culture prescribes that women's education will
bring forth only misfortune to women.[48] Thus, besides stories of Feng

---

45. On the topoi of Feng Xiaoqing and women's inscribed poems on their portraits
in late imperial China, see Yuanfei Wang, "The Emaciated Soul: Four Women's Self-
Inscriptions on Their Portraits in Late Imperial China," *Nan Nü: Men, Women, and Gender in Imperial China*, June 2020, 22:1 36–69.

46. Ellen Widmer, "Xiaoqing's Literary Legacy and the Place of the Woman Writer in
Late Imperial China," *Late Imperial China* 13, no. 1 (1992): 111–55, see 114.

47. Qingxin cairen 青心才人, Tianhuacang zhuren 天花藏主人 ed., *Jin Yun Qiao
zhuan* 金雲翹傳, 5.

48. Kang-i Sun Chang, "Ming Qing Women Poets and the Notions of 'Talent' and

Xiaoqing, there were many other stories on fragile, talented, and beautiful girls who died young in late imperial China: Wu Wushan's three wives and fervent readers of *The Peony Pavilion*—Chen Tong 陳同 (d. 1665), Tan Ze 談則 (d. 1674), Qian Yi 錢宜 (1671–?)—the talented girl poet Ye Xialuan 葉曉鸞 (1616–1632), and the fictional character Lin Daiyu 林黛玉 from the Qing novel *Dream of the Red Chamber* (*Honglou meng* 紅樓夢, 1791). Including Wang Cuiqiao in this genealogy of female geniuses, *The Romance*, thus resonates with this Ming–Qing cultural trend of promoting and lamenting female talent and female literary fame.

Talented literary women are so cherished in scholar-beauty romances that their "ill fates" are reversed and compensated with happy endings. Ellen Widmer notes that Xiaoqing's story collected in *The Book of Female Talent* (*nü caizi shu* 女才子書, 1658) compiled by Xu Zhen 徐震 anticipates the evolving genre of scholar-beauty romances. The southern drama named "The Garden of Romance" (*fengliu yuan* 風流院, 1629) for example, re-narrates Feng Xiaoqing's tragic story as a romantic comedy. In it, a male scholar seeks an ideal mate and accidentally discovers her poems and falls in love with them even before he meets her. In the end, the scholar brings Xiaoqing back to life. They marry and live happily together. Widmer argues that the "despair of the late Ming and early Qing intensified bohemian impulses among a number of intellectuals. Where they might earlier have appropriated the work of a suffering woman to express their own alienation, they could now accomplish the same purpose by supporting a woman's career."[49] Such intellectual shift during the Ming–Qing transition was, in part, due to the rise of female literacy and female education,[50] in addition to the increasingly competitive civil examination system and the disorienting and traumatic Ming–Qing transition which, we could imagine, repressed and destroyed numerous male literati's careers. Writing about female geniuses could somewhat sublimate the male literati's repressed wishes.

Further, a scholar named Jin Chong 金重 and a beautiful maiden named Wang Cuiyun 王翠雲—Wang Cuiqiao's double—are created to form a new narrative. Generically different from "Death for Xu Hai" and

'Morality,'" in Bin Wong, Ted Huters, and Pauline Yu, eds., *Culture and State in Chinese History: Conventions, Conflicts, and Accommodations* (Stanford: Stanford University Press, 1998), 236–58.

49. Ellen Widmer, "Xiaoqing," 120, 117–18.

50. For female education, see for example, Dorothy Ko, *Teachers of the Inner Chambers: Women and Culture in Seventeenth-Century China* (Stanford: Stanford University Press, 1994).

"Quelling Pirates," *The Romance* is a scholar-beauty romance with a happy ending. The scholar-beauty romances reverberate with the sense of alienation, self-identity, and intellectual tendencies among these male literati. Martin Huang argues that the authors seek to "reclaim the purity of *qing*" and "by redefining 'chastity.'"[51] A recent study notes that scholar-beauty novels' emphasis on talent (*cai* 才) creates collective identity among literati men who had profound anxieties over their cultural identity in the early Qing.[52] Continuing these lines of thought, I see that such cultural identity and intellectual stress on female chastity concern a renewed notion of the authentic self, or an "authentic person of feeling" (*zhen youqing ren* 真有情人).

Pivoting around the unresolved tensions between loyalty and self-love, between the body and the mind, between one's exteriority and interiority, *The Romance* tells a complicated story of a talented beauty who turns into a prostitute and endures excruciating suffering precisely because of her virtue and authentic feelings. When her family faces political persecution, she volunteers to sell herself as a concubine to save the family from trouble. So committed is she to her purpose that, seeing that her father is unwilling to sign the contract, she threatens to kill herself:

> This is not some good thing that I want to volunteer to do. But if I do not do this, everyone will die. The Wang family clan will then be exterminated. If I sacrifice myself, then everybody will be saved. If you sign, then it will be fine. But if you do not, I will commit suicide by knife or rope, or by jumping into water or fire. This is better than seeing you die in exile, suffer, or being punished, going through this living hell.

> 甚麼好事孩兒要搶著做，只是若不如此，必至大家同死，王家宗祠一旦斬矣。想上想下，舍我一身，便全了多少大事。你們著畫字，我自不消說；若不畫字，我不是刀上便是繩上，不是水中就是火中，尋個自盡便了。決不看你們死的好。流的流，苦的苦，刑的刑，受這些活地獄。[53]

---

51. Martin W. Huang, *Desire and Fictional Narrative*, 206, 235.

52. Ying Zou, "Talent, identity, and Sociality in Early Qing Scholar-Beauty Novels," *T'oung Pao* 102, nos. 1–3 (2016): 161–208.

53. Qingxin cairen 青心才人 (pseud.), *Jin Yun Qiao zhuan* 金雲翹傳, Liu Shide 劉世德 et al. eds, *Guben xiaoshuo congkan* 古本小說叢刊 (Beijing: Zhonghua shuju, 1991), vol. 23, 4, 1513.

Once she makes use of her body to materialize her moral ideals, she faces a series of catastrophic consequences. She is soon deflowered by her purchaser, a ruthless pimp. She is sold to a brothel house whose madam repeatedly whips her to force her to relent and become a prostitute. Although she is saved and rescued recurrently, each cycle only makes her "fall into more difficult and painful predicaments."[54]

The prostitute's authentic self has more to do with her mind than with her physical body. As the novelist and publisher Master of the Heavenly Flower Sutra (Tianhuazang zhuren 天花藏主人) summarizes in the preface, "From her father, she is given her body. She abandons her body for her father. Since this body has already been abandoned, it is then like soil and wood, destined to death. If she can live, it is her great fortune. How can she still hold on to female chastity" 父由此身而生也，此身已為父而棄也。此身既棄，則土也，木也，死分也；生幸也，何敢復作閨閣想?"[55] This extreme contrast between the painfully tortured body and the virtuous mind is unseen in earlier narratives. By staging the female body in pain, The Romance emphasizes the importance of the virtuous mind and the role qing plays in defining a person's authentic self. The Master of the Heavenly Flower Sutra writes: "Generally, when the body is protected and the heart-mind is sullied, it is chastity turning into desire. When the body is humiliated and the heart-mind is unsullied, it is desire turning into chastity" 大都身免矣，而心辱焉，貞而淫矣；身辱矣，而心免焉，淫而貞矣。[56] A pure heart-mind is authentic chastity. A chaste body with a polluted mind is only a fake self. The Master of the Heavenly Flower Sutra considers feelings as inherent to the true self: "The lotus plants uncontaminated by the mud from which they grow suggest that their spirit corresponds to their nature" 而污泥生不染之蓮，蓋持情以合性也。[57] In other words, continuing and revising the late Ming anxieties over the incongruity between interiority and exteriority, The Romance proposes to authenticate a person's internal self through Confucian moral codes.

Such perspective is paradoxically both radical and conservative. Female chastity is emphasized from the very beginning of The Romance. In early chapters, Wang refuses Jin Chong's sexual advances in the name

54. Paola Zamperini, "Eros and Suicide in Late Imperial Chinese Fiction," eds. Paul S. Ropp, Paola Zamperini, and Harriet T. Zurndorfer, Passionate Women: Female Suicide in Late Imperial China (Brill: Leiden, 2001), 84–85.

55. Qingxin cairen, Tianhuacang zhuren, ed., Jin Yun Qiao zhuan, 1.

56. Qingxin cairen, Tianhuacang zhuren, ed., Jin Yun Qiao zhuan, 2.

57. Qingxin cairen, Tianhuacang zhuren, ed., Jin Yun Qiao zhuan, 2.

of preserving her virginity before marriage and thus her reputation.[58] Her narrative of chastity and authentic love seeks to revise the narrative of passion in the Tang romance of Cui Yingying and her student lover Zhang:

> If a girl yields to her lover because of deep *qing,* she will not be a virgin on the wedding night. . . . A girl will regret it greatly if she does not cherish herself, because this will lead to contempt on the part of a man. . . . If Yingniang had refused Scholar Zhang's request, she would not have suffered the fate of being deserted by him later. . . . Unfortunately, Yingniang casually yielded her body (*qing-shen* 輕身) to please him. Although Zhang took her body (*shensui nizhi* 身雖暱之), he actually despised her in his mind. I hope your plan for us envisions a long life together. I must behave according to what is right.[59]

> 祇恨始因情重，誤順良人，及至聯姻，已非處子。. . . 此固女子不能自愛，一開男兒疑薄之門，雖悔何及！. . . 使其始鶯娘有投梭之拒，則其後張生斷無棄擲之悲。正其始，自能正其終。惜鶯娘輕身以媚張生，張生身雖暱之，心實薄之矣。

Although she sounds like a moralist, she elevates authentic love to the level of moral regulation. If premarital sex does not lead to marriage between two lovers who freely elect each other, then such love is not authentic. In order to authenticate their love, the lovers must postpone consummation until marriage. Such a narrative also seeks to revise the concept of love and passion in the Ming play *The Peony Pavilion*, in the sense that the immediacy of love and passion must be postponed until legal marriage. The reconstruction of Wang Cuiqiao's identity as a chaste and talented beauty marrying a scholar evinces the narrative's self-containment that discontinues earlier narratives of passion and patriotic loyalism.

The Romance channels tremendously male literati's frustrations during the Ming–Qing turmoil. The novel's emphasis on the tortured female body underlines the mental pain that the frustrated male scholar suffers when he feels alienated and underappreciated. Her virtuous mind mirrors his authentic talent and virtue. The tortured female body also evokes readers' sympathy toward suffering and rage at social justice. Robert Hegel indi-

---

58. Martin W. Huang, *Desire and Fictional Narrative*, 211–24.
59. Translation cited from Martin W. Huang, *Desire and Fictional Narrative*, 219.

cates that succinct depictions of violence in *The Water Margin* are to engage the readers' imagination that brings action to life, giving power to storytelling.[60] *The Romance* similarly shows the power of such storytelling. Although the appearance of scholar Jin Chong indicates the new narrative's return to the genre of scholar-beauty romance and its emphasis on literary talent and moral conventions, female chastity and literary talent in contrast with the tortured female body suggests the barbarousness of wartime and the profound anxieties of the male scholars concerning their cultural identity in Ming–Qing transition.

Through Xu Hai, the author-narrator again channels his own frustration at the world of disorder, much as Zhou Qingyuan compares himself to a courtesan in the preface to *The West Lake*. Pirate Xu Hai further projects the frustrated author/scholar's wish to be a social rebel. He is a "hero" (*haohan* 好漢), "generous, broad-minded, and ambitious" 開濟豁達，包含宏大. In his early years, he studies Confucian texts, but later he abandons scholarly study to engage in business. He is rich and loves making friends. Hearing that Cuiqiao is "chivalrous" (*xiagai* 俠概), he visits her. He tells her about his ambition that he would rather be a notorious bandit than being nameless in the world.[61] This recurrent topos of a frustrated scholar wishing to become a social outlaw (a courtesan or a bandit) to make a name for himself is again manifested in *The Master of the Heavenly Flower Sutra* edition of the novel. Xu Hai nobly justifies his rebellion: "If I cannot put my talent to use, then Heaven betrays me. If Heaven betrays me, then I can also betray Heaven" 設若皇天負我，我亦可以負皇天.[62]

The predicament of loyalism at the expense of self-interest is shown through the death of Xu Hai. Considering Wang Cuiqiao his soulmate, Xu Hai rescues and marries her. In return, Wang convinces Xu Hai to stop waging war in the region. But they disagree on the matter of submission to the Ming. Wang is a loyalist and moralist. She believes that "the imperial court is honorable. Life is important. It is a slight matter to betray one person. Besides, bandits are traitors who should be exterminated" 朝廷為

---

60. Robert Hegel, "Imagined Violence: Representing Homicide in Late Imperial Crime Reports and Fiction," *Bulletin of the Institute of Chinese Literature and Philosophy*, no. 25 (September 2004): 68.

61. Qingxin cairen, *Jin Yun Qiao zhuan*, 1654.

62. This sentence is from the Tianhuacang zhuren edition. The Guanhua tang version does not have this sentence. See Tianhuacang zhuren, ed., *Shuang Hehuan* 雙合歡, *Zhongguo gudian guben xiaoshuo baoku* 中國古典孤本小說寶庫, vol. 8, ed. Sun Zaimin 孫再民 (Beijing: Zhongyang minzu daxue chuban she, 2001), 364.

尊，生靈為重，報私恩為小，負一人為輕，且為賊不順，從逆當誅。[63] Xu
Hai is an individualist. He wants freedom and prefers rebellion to submission. If he remains a bandit, then he still has freedom to conquer, plunder, and hold sway on the seas. If he surrenders, then he will be subjected to the emperor, the state, and the bureaucratic system.[64] Xu eventually listens to Wang and submits to the Ming, which turns out to be a mistake. Besieged, he is slain by a few arrows from the Ming army. Before he dies, he bellows, "My wife has ruined me" 夫人誤我. Holding a grudge, he dies standing still. Realizing her mistake, Wang prays to confess her mistake and console his soul.[65] His corpse then sheds tears and falls to the ground. She attempts suicide to compensate for her mistake and pay back his love. This narrative of loyalism again shows its predicament: loyalty at the expense of self-love and true feelings is inadequate, limiting, and can lead to suffering. It is this tendency toward loyalty that leads to Wang's continuous constraints and predicaments in life.

At the end of the story, Wang Cuiqiao is rescued by a Buddhist nun and finally marries Jin Chong, but their sexless marriage reinforces the moralistic narrative that resulted in her pirate lover's death. Xu Hai, the embodiment of freedom and free will, is completely erased in the theoretical discussions of feelings, talent, and nature presented in the prefaces of both editions.[66] The ostensibly happy ending disguises the radical conflicts between free will and physical containment. In conclusion, *The Romance* marks a paradigmatic shift from the public to the private and the literary, not through resolving the contending viewpoints of the Xu Hai–Cuiqiao romance but through diverting attention to the scholar-beauty narrative and repressing the dilemma, keeping the old problems at bay.

Fantasy, Rebellion, and the Vietnamese Epic *The Tale of Kieu*

Model Words was later transmitted to other locales in the Sinosphere. The Chinese novel was translated into Korean vernacular language in the eighteenth century and was preserved and perused by the royal house of Korea.[67] The celebrated Vietnamese poet Nguyễn Du 阮攸 (1766–1820)

---

63. Qingxin cairen, *Jin Yun Qiao zhuan*, 1684.
64. Qingxin cairen, *Jin Yun Qiao zhuan*, 1684–85.
65. Qingxin cairen, *Jin Yun Qiao zhuan*, 1694.
66. Qingxin cairen, *Jin Yun Qiao zhuan*, 1–2.
67. The world's only copy of *Xingshiyan* is Korea's Kyujaggak manuscript. See "Formation of Commercial Standard Novel in the late Ming Dynasty and Novel Reading of

adapted it into the Vietnamese epic *The Tale of Kieu* (*Kim Van Kieu truyen*), using the Vietnamese national script *chunom* ("Southern script," as opposed to the script of the "Northerners"), created in the fourteenth century. Nguyễn Du traveled to China as an envoy in the eighteenth year of the Jiaqing 嘉慶 reign (1813), around 150 years after *The Romance* was published.[68] He adapted the prose fiction, written in classical Chinese, into a poem written in the vernacular and in "six-eight" verse, a prevalent meter of folk poetry. Nguyễn Du's *The Tale of Kieu* struck a chord among Vietnamese people, who found great solace in the novel. As the translator points out, one reason for this popularity was a word that recurs throughout the poem: *oan* (wronged).

Copious Vietnamese scholarship has explored the translation of the Wang Cuiqiao story into *The Tale of Kieu*. I thus briefly comment here on the differing portrayals of Xu Hai (Tu Hai in *The Tale of Kieu*) and Cuiqiao (Kieu) in *The Romance* and *The Tale of Kieu*. As in the Chinese source work, Xu Hai is portrayed as a hero in the Vietnamese poem, although the metaphors used to describe him have changed: The Chinese version depicts Xu Hai as an antagonist—a merchant, not a scholar, and a chivalric hero who is a bandit or an outlaw. He is a force of resistance to the established imperial bureaucratic and civil systems. In *The Tale of Kieu*, however, the metaphors make the pirate a grand minister or a military hero. Tu Hai is described as having "a tiger's beard, a swallow's jaw, and brows as thick as silkworms—he stood broad and tall."[69] This physiognomic description alludes to the Han commander Ban Chao 班超, who abandoned his scholarly profession as a copier to become a diplomat for the Han emperor, establishing relations with foreign kingdoms in the western regions. The historic hero was known for having "a chin as round as a swallow's, and a short neck as stout as a tiger's" 燕頷虎頸.[70] Although "tiger's beard" in a Chinese context often indicates the danger of offending an authority or a powerful man, in *The Tale of Kieu*, this image may suggest Tu Hai's kingly status. He lives "free" "between the earth and heaven." Further, in the Chinese version, when Xu Hai and Wang Cuiqiao first

the King of the Joseon Dynasty: Kyujaggak Manuscript (奎章閣本) of *XingShiYan* (型世言)," *Journal of Korean Classical Literature* 47 (2015): 35–64.

68. Liu Yongqiang 劉勇強, "Zhongguo gudai xiaoshuo yuwai chuanbo de jige wenti" 中國古代小說域外傳播的幾個問題, *Shanghai shifan daxue xue bao* 36, no. 5 (September 2007): 31–39.

69. Nguyễn Du, *The Tale of Kieu: A Bilingual Edition of Nguyễn Du's Truyen Kieu*, trans. Huynh Sanh Thong (New Haven: Yale University Press, 1987), 113.

70. Nguyễn Du, *The Tale of Kieu*, 198.

meet, they like each other only "slightly" 兩下俱有幾分契愛. Evaluating Xu Hai, Cuiqiao says, "Although you appear heroic, you lack some kingly aura" 雄則雄矣，可惜少了一些王氣. Xu then replies, "Your words are sensible. But in my heart, I dare not expect to be a king" 卿可謂知言，然余心中亦未敢以王期也. In the Vietnamese version, Tu Hai immediately declares his love for Kieu upon meeting: "Two kindred souls have joined," and "We're not those giddy fools who play at love." Kieu also predicts that Tu will be an emperor: "One of these days, Chin-yang shall see a dragon in the clouds."[71] This alludes to Li Yuan 李淵 (618–626), commandant at Jin-yang 晉陽 in Taiyuan, who later became the first emperor of the Tang dynasty. In response, Tu Hai is "well pleased" and "nodded," expressing that indeed he is destined to be a king and that he has found his soulmate: "Through life how many know what moves one's soul? Those eyes be praised that, keen and worldly-wise, can see the hero hid in common dust! Your words prove you discern me from the rest—we'll sit together when I sit on high."[72]

Whereas *The Romance* emphasizes loyalty and chastity—traditional Confucian values—*The Tale of Kieu* recurrently shows an individual's wish for a happy and successful worldly life. Both versions relate that three years after Xu Hai and Cuiqiao's meeting, Cuiqiao refuses to leave her home, even as pirates pillage the area, because of her promise that she would wait for her lover. Soon after, Xu Hai sends a troupe to retrieve her for their marriage ceremony. Coming out calmly as if she has known this day would come, she commands the pirates to restore peace to the region. In *The Tale of Kieu*, the scene is dreamy and fantastic:

> Perplexed, she was still wavering when, outside,
> she now saw flags and heard the clang of gongs.
> Armor-clad troops had come and ringed the house—
> in chorus they all asked, "Where is our queen?"
> Ten officers, in two rows, laid down their arms,
> took off their coats, and kowtowed on the ground.
> Ladies-in-waiting followed, telling her:
> "By order we'll escort you to our lord."
> The phoenix-coach held ready for a queen
> Her glittering diadem, her sparkling robe.

71. Nguyễn Du, *The Tale of Kieu*, 113.
72. Nguyễn Du, *The Tale of Kieu*, 115.

They hoisted flags, beat drums, and off they marched—
Musicians led the way, maids closed the rear.
A herald rushed ahead—the Southern Court
Called all to its headquarters with the drum.[73]

The elaborate ceremony of the lovers' reunion suggests a dream-come-true moment, a celebration, and also a fantasy. Similar depictions recur when Kieu becomes consumed by the thought that she will live a happy life after Tu Hai's submission. In *The Romance*, Cuiqiao hopes Xu Hai will surrender because she places country, loyalty, and people over her personal feelings: "The imperial court is the most honored. Sentient beings are the most important. It is trivial to repay personal favor. It is light to betray only one person. Besides, being a bandit is treacherous. I will be killed if I follow a traitor" 朝廷為尊，生靈為重，報私恩為小，負一人為輕，且為賊不順，從逆當誅. *The Tale of Kieu*, however, tells that Kieu has a "guileless heart." She is bribed by the "sweet words and lavish gifts offered by Lord Ho Ton Hien. Believing that the provincial governor will appoint Tu Hai as a lord, she muses that she will be 'a lord's own consort, head erect.' I'll walk and make my parents glow with pride and joy. Then both the state above, my home below, I'll have well served as liege and daughter both. Is that not better than to float and drift, a skiff the waves and waters hurl about?'"[74] Kieu's mundane fantasy may well resonate deeply with the reading public. Indeed, the scene where Tu Hai lets Kieu wage war to seek revenge against her former foes is a favorite scene with most Vietnamese.[75]

On the other hand, in the Vietnamese version rather than in the Chinese version, Tu Hai is much more assured in his rebellion:

My own two hands have built this realm—at will
I've roamed the sea of Ch'u, the streams of Wu.
If I turn up at court, bound hand and foot,
what will become of me, surrendered man?
Why let them swaddle me in robes and skirts?
Why play a duke so as to cringe and crawl?
Had I not better rule my march-domain?

73. Nguyễn Du, *The Tale of Kieu*, 117.
74. Nguyễn Du, *The Tale of Kieu*, 129.
75. Nguyễn Du, *The Tale of Kieu*, xxxviii.

For what can they all do against my might?
At pleasure I stir heaven and shake earth—
I come and go, I bow my head to none.

Tu Hai's indignation is strengthened by the rhetorical questions in his speech. The mention of the Chu region may be an allusion to Vietnam. The translator notes that besides Kieu, it is Xu Hai, rather than scholar Jin Chong, that "firmly fixes Nguyen Du's tale in the Vietnamese people's affections." It is, then, not surprising that during the first phase of French conquest in the 1860s, *chunom* became the major written language of resistance groups.[76] *The Tale of Kieu* was also allegorically interpreted by controversial leaders such as Ton Tho Turong. The poem addresses the Vietnamese experience as victims, refugees, and survivors.[77]

---

76. John DeFrancis, *Vietnamese Writing Reform in Asian Perspective*, unpublished manuscript, University of Washington Library, 1982.

77. Nguyễn Du, *The Tale of Kieu*, xl.

Conclusion

Stories of the Sea

In 1621, the Jacobean playwright Joseph Fletcher's *Island Princess* was performed at court by the King's Men. For the first time, an English play staged its story on the Molucca Islands of the Malay Archipelago. The story tells that the governor of the neighboring island Ternata kidnapped the king of Tidore Island. The king's sister Princess Quisara announces to her local and Portuguese suitors that she will marry the man who can successfully rescue her brother. She urges her lover, the captain of the Portuguese, Ruy Dias, to accomplish the rescue mission so that his achievement can legitimize him as a suitor to marry her. This trope of Renaissance tragicomedy, the rescue of non-European women by European men— reflecting and resulting from European overseas colonial expansion— bespeaks the very colonial impulse of European conquerors and settlers to possess fecund Eastern lands.[1] At the end of the play, another Portuguese man Armusia wins. Realizing her true love for Armusia, Quisara converts to Christianity. Ania Loomba notes that the danger of "religious and sexual contamination" associated with the thriving trade in Moluccas leads to the possibility of featuring Catholics and substituting English gentlemen-merchants as heroes overseas.[2]

Before the Portuguese's arrival in the region, Europeans, Ottomans, Indians, and Chinese had been journeying to the Malay Archipelago for the vibrant Indian Ocean trade. The territory's domination became more

---

1. For a detailed study of the play's racial and religious discourse, see Ania Loomba, "'Break Her Will, and Bruise No Bone Sir': Colonial and Sexual Mastery in Fletcher's *The Island Princess*," *Journal for Early Modern Cultural Studies* 2, no. 1 (Spring/Summer 2002): 68–109.
2. Ania Loomba, "Break Her Will," 99.

difficult as new colonizers were forced to compete with more established powers in the area. This complicated colonial and international history of the Malay Archipelago is observed in a paragraph in the *Ming History* (*Ming shi* 明史, 1723) on Moluccas within the category "Foreign Countries" (*waiguo* 外國):

Moluccas, also called Miheliu, is located in the East Sea. The island is quite resourceful and rich. When the chieftain comes out, his manners and demeanors are quite majestic. All his subjects join their hands and kneel along the roads. Men shave their hair. Women comb their hair. The island has fragrant mountains. After the rain, the fragrance flows all over the earth. Residents cannot exhaust this resource. The chieftains load exotic goods in his storehouse in order to trade with foreign boats. The East Ocean does not produce clove. Only this place has it. Cloves can shelter people from illness and bad omens. Therefore, Chinese people often trade here.

. . . At that time, although the Dutch occupied Moluccas, they led their people to return to their country and then came back every one or two years. After the son of the Portuguese king inherited the throne, he then hoped to realize his father's wish by attacking Moluccas when the Dutch were away. So they took over Moluccas, killed their chieftain, and appointed their own entrusted person to rule the islands. Before long, the Dutch came back and took over the city again, chasing the Portuguese away, and appointed the son of the deceased chieftain of Moluccas. Since then, they often engaged in battles. Common people suffered deeply. The Chinese sojourners on the islands went to persuade the Portuguese and the Dutch leaders to stop battling. The main island was divided by the Wanlao high mountain. North of the mountain belonged to the Dutch; south of the mountain belonged to the Portuguese. Moluccas were taken by the Portuguese and the Dutch.

美洛居，俗訛為米六合，居東海中，頗稱饒富。酋出，威儀甚備，所部合掌伏道旁。男子削發，女椎結。地有香山，雨後香墮，沿流滿地，居民拾取不竭。其酋委積充棟，以待商舶之售。東洋不產丁香，獨此地有之，可以辟邪，故華人多市易。...時紅毛番雖據美洛居，率壹二歲率眾返國，既返復來。佛郎機酋子既襲位，欲竟父誌，大舉兵來襲，值紅毛番已去，遂破美洛居，殺其酋，立己所親信主之。無何，紅毛番至，又破其城，逐佛郎機所立酋，而立美洛居故王之子。自是，歲構兵，人不堪命。華人流寓者，遊說兩

國，令各罷兵，分國中萬老高山為界，山以北屬紅毛番，南屬佛
郎機，始稍休息，而美洛居竟為兩國所分。[3]

Although Luo Maodeng's *Eunuch Sanbao's Voyages on the Western Ocean*
does not mention Moluccas, places in the Malay Archipelagos portrayed
in the novel include Ceylon, Sumatra, Java, as well as an imaginary country of women near Java. As discussed in chapter 2, the Chinese novel
regrettably evinces imperialistic and Han Chinese racist attitudes toward
the peoples and cultures in the region. For example, the female warrior of
the country of women, Yellow Balsam, shows her inferiority complex as a
barbarian woman when she proposes to marry the Chinese general Tang
Ying 唐英, although, with her superior magic, she contributes enormously
to the success of the Chinese army's conquest during the rest of the maritime journey.

Still, the Chinese "conquerors" and the "Chinese" culture that they pre-
sume they represent in the novel often face and have to compete with
established local powers and cultural resources. Buddhism and Islamism
are the two prominent cultures and religions that the Chinese "conquerors" frequently find themselves admiring and honoring. In Ceylon, the
body of Shakyamuni is enshrined in a Buddhist monastery. The Buddha's
body is perfectly preserved, immaculate and incorrupt. The Muslims in
Southeast Asia are highly respected, ranked lower only to the ruling class.
When the armada reaches Mecca, the Muslim king states that the government does not collect heavy taxes from people, and every household in the
country is wealthy. Because Zheng He is a Chinese Muslim, he goes to a
Masjid named "Paradise Monastery" (Tiantang libai si 天堂禮拜寺) to
pray. Apparently, Zheng He cannot conquer Mecca. Nor do the Chinese
consider whether the Chinese culture could substitute Buddhism or Islam.
But this does not mean that Chinese imperialism is not at work.

At the beginning of the book, I suggested that an early modern Chinese discourse of pirates came into being at the same time that the European Age of Discovery began. This Chinese discourse of pirates parallels
some early modern Western literature on colonial expansion and maritime expedition. But the categories of Chinese pirates of this period are
much more complicated and fluid than categories of pirates in early modern Western literature and history. The Chinese pirates were not only maritime explorers, conquerors, bandits, settlers, and collaborators, but also

3. Zhang Tingyu 張廷玉, *Ming shi* 明史 (Shanghai: Zhonghua shuju, 1936), vol. 223:
15.

renegades, captives, emigrants, and refugees. Many of them became Chinese diaspora. While the authors studied in this book are not themselves overseas Chinese, they are spies and travelogue compilers for local governments or dissidents, demoted officials, marginalized literati, commercial publishers and print piraters. Thus, their writings about pirates and the piracy raids contain their personal traits, values, and repressed wishes.

This book is my first and modest step into this comparative early modern seaborne literature, early modern literary production, and colonial and postcolonial studies. Examining these uncharted waters has revealed parallel themes and differences in Western and Chinese pirates. The book's purpose has been to define new concepts, practices, and materials for exploring the Chinese discourse of pirates. Pursuing a meaningful study of Chinese maritime literature and history, transnational encounters, diplomatic and cross-cultural exchange in early modern times requires a broader understanding of early modern Chinese literature and history through a comparative perspective. The early modern globality anticipated the unprecedented globalization today. The book has shown the inward and outward circulations of literary texts from Japan to China and from China to Vietnam (Chinese translation and transcription of Japanese *waka* poetry and Vietnamese adaptation of the Chinese pirate romance); the routes of migration, diplomacy, and wars in maritime Asia; the motions of early modern Chinese Orientalistic, imperialistic, and racist narratives of Japan, Siam, and Java; and the linguistic flows of Chinese fiction, travelogues, and histories. Rooted in the Chinese cultural tradition, the book has discussed the prototype of Chinese pirates as originating in the vernacular novel *The Water Margin* and explored how cultural memory of the Indian Ocean and the Silk Road shaped the discourse of pirates. It has also shown how Chinese tradition of philology, phonology, and translation were integral to the discourse of pirates. And the variable discourse of two Chinese pirate kings further shows how the concept of authenticity became crucial within a public literary sphere. I have thus grounded this study in the common images of pirates and oceans across cultures and literatures. The oceans of the sixteenth and seventeenth centuries were the arena for transnational encounters and cross-cultural exchange.

The future of the study of Chinese sea fiction in premodern times will continue to tell a new literary history of marginal people and un-canonical texts on the move. The discourse of pirates and of sea literature emphasizes the agency of Chinese pirates and seamen outside of China. These Chinese maritime merchants became rulers and influential figures in

Southeast Asia from the seventeenth century onward. Zheng Zhao 鄭昭, a merchant of Guangdong, for example, became the king of Thonburi after he helped Thai armies defeat a Burmese invasion. Simultaneously, Chinese stories were translated and adapted in Vietnam, Thailand, Indonesia, and beyond.[4] Claudine Salmon's edited volume *Literary Migrations: Traditional Chinese Fiction in Asia*, for instance, includes a few popular Chinese historical romances and fantastic novels in Java, such as *Yang Family Generals*, *Xue Rengui* 薛仁貴, and *Journey to the West*.

In these future studies, intercultural, interliterary, and interdisciplinary interaction no doubt receive greater emphasis. How does Chinese theatrical performance circulate in adapted forms in overseas Chinese communities? How do the Chinese plays performed in Southeast Asia and elsewhere overlap with and differ from Malaysian, Indian, and Indonesian treatments of similar themes and even those same plays? What is the relationship between rituals performed and stories told among the so-called ethnic minority peoples on China's borders? How were these rituals and stories transmitted from China's borders to Southeast Asia, India, the Middle East, Europe, and other places in the world? The exciting field of Sinophone studies has already covered the dialectic relationship between Sinitic communities both inside and outside of China. The interesting question for studies of premodern literature is how to trace the interaction of Han Chinese and non-Han Chinese languages, cultures and literatures to detect modes of literary circulation and adaptation. Writing a literary history of Chinese literature that contextualizes it within global history will be another challenge. The issues of periodization in European studies, East Asian studies, and other area studies, the focused deliberation of what constitutes "the middle ages" or the "early modern," should not distract us from this wider inquiry and perceiving the parallels and interactions among the cultures, histories, and literatures of the West and the East.

---

4. Claudine Salmon, ed., *Literary Migrations: Traditional Chinese Fiction in Asia (17th–20th Century)* (Singapore: Institute of Southeast Asia Studies, 2013).

.

Index

Note: Page numbers in italics refer to the illustrations and tables.

pay Xu Mingshan's Love" (Lu R. & Lu
Y.), 179, 184, 186
commerce, morality-based, 158–59, 165
"Commodity Producer" (Sima), 158
common people, 164–65, 172, 178
comparison, rhetoric of, 117–19
conch shells, 111, *111*
Confucian values, 28, 67–68, 82, 152, 165,
185–86, 191
corruption in Ming empire, 152, 172–73,
177–78
Crazy Su, 90
Crossley, Pamela, 11–12
Crying Phoenix (Mingfeng ji) (Wang
Shizhen), 111–12
Cui Yingying, 169, 192
cultural nostalgia of Chinese literati,
31–32
cultural primitivism, nakedness and, 65
Culture and Imperialism (Said), 3, 7
culture of land *vs.* maritime, 68

daoban (plagiarized publications), 168
David Der-wei Wang, 32, 49
"Death for Xu Hai" (Lu R. and Lu Y.). *See*
"Commander in Chief Hu Cleverly
Uses Hua Diqing; Wang Cuiqiao Dies
to Repay Xu Mingshan's Love" (Lu R.
and Lu Y.)
de' Conti, Niccolò, 48
Defoe, Daniel, 13
demonization, rhetoric of, 70–71
deng (group, class), 64
de Saussure, Ferdinand, 9
desire, notion of, 55
"The Diachronics of Early Qing Visual
and Material Culture" (Hay), 49–50
dialects (topolects): in folk songs, 103,
133–35; genuineness of, 102–3, 134–35;
and ideal accent of *Huaxia*, 87–88; influence on Chinese transcriptions, 96–
104; *vs.* national languages, 102; and
phonetic orthography, 103–4; presence
of in *huaben* fiction, 131–32; in vernacular fiction, 134. *See also* Wu topolect
diasporic communities, Chinese: creole
and Peranakan communities, 46; fear

of miscegenation among, 44–45; hybrid descent within, 46; in Japan, 125–
28; and Ming–Qing transition, 31; in
Siam, 37, 38; as spies, 126
dictionaries, bilingual, 89, 91–95, 96, 97,
101–2, 135
Dikötter, Frank, 114
diplomacy: bribery and baiting, 153–55,
165; "cherishing men from afar," 59–60,
64–65, 72, 82, 159–60; envoys, 41, 58,
60–63, 141, 150–51, 155–57, 160–61; and
Hongwu emperor, 58, 60–61, 65, 67,
156, 159; proclamations, 60; and relations with Japan, 59–60, 65, 80, 91–92,
155–57, 160–61; and relations with Java,
58–81; "Three Appearances and Five
Baits," 154; and Yongle emperor, 1, 58,
63, 67, 69, 73–74
discourse: concept of, 6–7; initiators of,
49; *vs.* narrative, 8, 60, 140
*Discourse on Maritime Bandits (Haikou
yi)* (Wan), 155
Dongyi tushuo (Cai R.), 118
*Dream of the Red Chamber (Honglou
meng)* (Cao Xueqin), 189
Drogön Chögyal Phagpa, 96
Du Liniang, 48, 188

edicts, 60–63, 87–88, 141, 143, 149, 156,
159–61
*The Edited Collection of Maps of Japan
(Riben tuzuan)* (Zheng R.), 91, 93
education and misfortune to women,
188–89
Elman, Benjamin, 95
Emperors' Tributes (He). *See Records of
Emperors' Tributes (Wang Xiangji)* (He)
*Emperor Taizu's Veritable Records (Taizu
shilu)*, 62–63
empiricism and study of Japanese language, 94–95
Encountering Sorrow, 52
encyclopedias, 87, 112–13
environmental determinism, 67–68
*Essentials in the History of Calligraphy
(Shushi huiyao)* (Tao), 90
ethnic authenticity, 11, 161, 165